Gender and Entrepreneurship

As well as being an economic phenomenon, entrepreneurship can also be read as a cultural one. Entrepreneurial action can be related to gender for a cross-reading of how gender and entrepreneurship are culturally produced and reproduced in social practices.

This groundbreaking new study considers both gender and entrepreneurship as symbolic forms, looking at their diverse patterns and social representation. Presenting an ethnographic study of the gender structuring of entrepreneurship, the work employs three strategies:

- a critical survey of gender studies, which argues that entrepreneurship is a cultural model of masculinity that obstructs the expression of other models
- ethnographic observations conducted in five small firms describe how business cultures are 'gendered' and how gender is the product of situated practices
- an analysis of how discursive and narrative practices in business cultures constitute gender and entrepreneurship

Gender and Entrepreneurship is essential reading for postgraduate students, researchers and academics with an interest in entrepreneurship, business and management, innovation economics and gender studies.

Attila Bruni is Lecturer of Sociology of Organization/Organizational Ethnography at Venice University, Italy. **Silvia Gherardi** is Professor of Sociology of Organization at the University of Trento, Italy. **Barbara Poggio** is Lecturer of Sociology of Organization at the University of Siena, Italy.

Management, Organization and Society
Edited by Professor Barbara Czarniawska, *Göteborg University, Sweden*
and Professor Martha Feldman, *University of Michigan, USA*

This series presents innovative work grounded in new realities, addressing issues crucial to an understanding of the contemporary world. This is the world of organized societies, where boundaries between formal and informal, public and private, local and global organizations have been displaced or have vanished, along with other nineteenth-century dichotomies and oppositions. Management, apart from becoming a specialized profession for a growing number of people, is an everyday activity for most members of modern societies.

Similarly, at the level of enquiry, culture and technology, and literature and economics can no longer be conceived as isolated intellectual fields; conventional canons and established mainstreams are contested. **Management, Organization and Society** will address these contemporary dynamics of transformation in a manner that transcends disciplinary boundaries, with work which will appeal to researchers, students and practitioners alike.

Gender and Entrepreneurship

An ethnographic approach

Attila Bruni, Silvia Gherardi
and Barbara Poggio

Routledge
Taylor & Francis Group

LONDON AND NEW YORK

First published 2005
by Routledge
2 Park Square, Milton Park, Abingdon, Oxon OX14 4RN

Simultaneously published in the USA and Canada
by Routledge
270 Madison Avenue, New York, NY 10016

Routledge is an imprint of the Taylor & Francis Group

© 2005 Attila Bruni, Silvia Gherardi and Barbara Poggio

Typeset in Sabon by
Keystroke, Jacaranda Lodge, Wolverhampton
Printed and bound in Great Britain by
Antony Rowe Ltd, Chippenham, Wiltshire

British Library Cataloguing in Publication Data
A catalogue record for this book is available from the British Library

Library of Congress Cataloging in Publication Data
A catalog record for this book has been requested

ISBN 0–415–35228–2

Contents

Tables

Acknowledgements

This book originates from a series of research projects undertaken by ISTUD (Istituto di Studi Direzionali) with funding from The European Community and the Italian Ministry of Labour and Social Security. We are grateful to all those whom we met in the course of our work, in particular Daniele Boldizzoni, Patrizia Di Pietro, Pasquale Gagliardi and Luigi Serio, who assisted us at every stage of our research.

We wish to thank Helene J. Ahl, Howard Becker, Barbara Czarniawska, Martha Feldman, Patricia Yancey Martin and Albert J. Mills for their accurate reading and commenting on previous versions of the book.

We are also indebted to the institution in which we work: the Department of Sociology and Social Research, of the University of Trento, and our colleagues of the Research Unit on Cognition, Organizational Learning and Aesthetics (RUCOLA).

Our research would not have been possible without the generosity of the male and female entrepreneurs who gave us their time and attention, allowing us to enter their enterprises and, in part, their lives. We especially wish to thank all those that we met during our fieldwork and who shared their thoughts and experiences of work with us. We are particularly indebted to Adrian Belton for his generous assistance in translating and to the reviewers for their careful reading and perceptive comments.

This book has been a collective undertaking by its three authors, whose names appear in alphabetical order. Scientifically responsible for the research was Silvia Gherardi, who also wrote the Introduction, Chapters 1 and 6. Attila Bruni authored Chapters 2 and 4 and the Appendix, and Barbara Poggio wrote Chapter 5. Chapter 3 was written jointly by Silvia Gherardi (section 1) and Attila Bruni (sections 2 and 3).

Introduction

Gender and entrepreneurship as entwined practices

This book considers the social practice of co-producing gender and entrepreneurship to be a material and a semantic space in which meaningful collective actions are carried out and contextually organized around a shared practical understanding. The field of entwined practices is the domain in which to study the nature and transformation of the activities called gender and entrepreneurship, as collective accomplishments sustained through interactions and mutual adjustments among the people involved in them.

As well as being an economic phenomenon, entrepreneurship can also be read as a cultural one. Entrepreneurial action is an archetype of social action, and as the institutionalization of values and symbols it can be related to gender for a cross-reading of how gender and entrepreneurship are culturally produced and reproduced in social practices. Doing business is a social practice, and so too is 'doing gender', but the latter is less evident than the former because common sense attributes gender to the corporeality of persons and therefore to their being rather than their doing and saying. Yet when men and women set up as entrepreneurs they do not separate the two practices; instead, they reproduce the normative meaning of what it is to be a male or female entrepreneur in a single cultural model framed by a cultural as well as an economic context.

The symbolic meaning of enterprise is encapsulated by the mythological figure of Mercury and by the mercurial personality: shrewd, pragmatic, creative, open-minded and adventurous. The features of entrepreneurship reside in the symbolic domain of initiative-taking, accomplishment and the relative risk. They therefore reside in the symbolic domain of the male. When these same features are transposed to the symbolic domain of the female, however, they become uncertain. It is necessary to justify female enterprise, because it is not an immediately shared and self-evident social value. The symbolic order of gender assigns the sphere of activity and proactivity to the male, while it associates passivity, adaptation and flexibility with the female.

In a culture, however, the symbolic gender order is not immutable: it is not static but dynamic and therefore varies across time and space. The meaning itself of gender, insofar as it is historically and culturally situated, lies in its deferral by gender relationships (Gherardi, 1995; Gherardi and

Poggio, 2001). Contextualized, situated and historicized gender relationships attribute a circumscribed meaning to male and female in a culture, and they always do so in relation to the archetypes of maleness and femaleness which define difference and found the order of language.

Therefore, the first problem – if indeed it is a problem – is that entrepreneurship is located in the symbolic universe of the male. Entrepreneurial action sustains and sets value on only one kind of masculinity, and entrepreneurship as a set of norms and values based on hegemonic masculinity raises a cultural barrier against femaleness and against alternative forms of masculinity.

The first argument of this study on gender and entrepreneurship is that the concept itself of entrepreneurship, while pretending to be gender neutral, comprises a gender sub-text which renders maleness invisible and thus sustains the a-critical reproduction of hegemonic masculinity. This contention translates into the methodological choice of studying gender at the level of interactions and discursive practices; that is, in what entrepreneurs do and say when they are practising gender and business at once. Indeed, to study women entrepreneurs without examining the gender structuring of entrepreneurship is to legitimate the 'gender blindness' which renders masculinity invisible and turns it into the universal parameter of entrepreneurial action, the model with which every entrepreneurial act must comply because it is the norm and the standard value. When masculinity is made invisible, the male entrepreneurial model is universalized and stripped of gender. Thus made universal, it is proposed or prescribed independently of a person's gender: women who wish to become entrepreneurs are required to comply with an apparently neutral set of values, while men are required to comply with those of 'entrepreneurial' masculinity.

Being a female and an entrepreneur may mean that the woman concerned has learnt to cross the boundaries between the two symbolic universes of male and female. We therefore assume that being a woman and an entrepreneur involves learning competent performance of both the practices connected with entrepreneurial activity and those connected with exhibiting the gender behaviour appropriate to it. Likewise, being a man and an entrepreneur may involve a positional rent yielded by gender membership. The two practices are not distinct. Indeed, they are intimately bound up with each other in the materiality of bodies, in discursive practices and in the artefacts that mediate the relation between body and activity. Therefore the book seeks to describe the gendering of the social practice called entrepreneurship, since there is renewed interest in social practices among contemporary social theorists.

Indeed, Schatzki, Knorr Cetina and von Savigny (2001) talk of a 'practice turn' in analogy to the 'linguistic turn' of some years ago. The heuristic power of studying practices is understood to be as follows: counteracting idealism, going beyond problematic dualism (as action/structure, human/non-human elements), questioning individual actions and their status as the building blocks of social phenomena; displacing the mind as the central phenomenon in human life; and viewing reason not as an innate mental faculty but as a practice phenomenon. Feminist studies have for some time criticized the taken-for-granted dualisms (mind/body, public/private, male/female) and instead studied both subjects and objects, structure and agency in their performativity (Butler, 1991; Bruni and Gherardi, 2002). Distinctive of feminist studies is their focus on human activity, on the grounds that it is embodied – that is, intertwined with the nature of the human body – and that all knowledge is situated knowledge (Gherardi, 2003a). The body is the meeting point for mind and activity, for individual activity and society. This, therefore, is the reason for studying how entrepreneurship embodied in different bodies constitutes different practices, since bodies and activities are constituted within situated practices.

Nevertheless, there is no unified practice approach (Schatzki, Knorr Cetina and von Savigny, 2001) and to study practices is not easy for several reasons[1] (Martin, 2003): practice unfolds in time; the tacit knowledge involved in competent behaviour is highly unlikely to be verbally expressed; in time practices become almost automatic and therefore are reproduced without much awareness of them. Scholars who choose to concentrate on practices lean towards a materialist approach which examines the human and non-human networks that form and orient activity. The intermediaries of human and non-human activities – artefacts, people, texts, symbols – not only mediate activities but propagate practices in time and space and shape individual and professional identity (Bruni and Gherardi, 2001).

Entrepreneurship as a cultural practice rests upon activities that are founded on embodied understanding, rooted directly in the gendered body and its symbolic representation. Consequently, a gender analysis of entrepreneurship differs from an analysis of women entrepreneurs because it examines the way in which gender is culturally constructed by those social practices that constitute the social phenomenon of entrepreneurship, without assuming a full correspondence between gender on the one hand, and men and women on the other.

Gender as a relational concept enables exploration of how women are attributed female characteristics and males masculine ones, and how 'doing' gender is a social practice which positions persons in contexts of asymmetrical power relations. In other words, it shows how inequalities in social opportunity are based on difference, the intention being to show that gendering is a practice that anchors other practices (Swidler, 2001).

In the subjunctive mode

We set out to examine patterns of entrepreneurship and gender on the assumption that both can be interpreted as symbolic forms which subtend interactive and discursive practices. We shall see the meanings of both in the interpretations given to them by entrepreneurs in what they say and what they do. This book is sustained by a rhetoric which seeks to convince its readers, not by using the canonical principles of science founded on objectivity and detachment, but by inviting them to draw on their imaginations to enter the world presupposed by the text. Perhaps not all our readers will be familiar with the world of entrepreneurship, but they will certainly be prisoners of the gender trap like us, and have personal experience and knowledge of it. The metaphor of the 'trap', in its ambiguity, denotes a symbolic place from which there is no escape (being trapped), but simultaneously the possibility of change (avoiding the trap). To look at gender from the gender trap – to use the words of the anthropologist Byron Good – is to 'subjunctivize' reality. In this regard Good cites Bruner, who partitions knowledge into paradigmatic, which is typical of analysis and science, and narrative, which is typical of accounts of the world in everyday situations. In our exploration of the indeterminacy of reality and in soliciting such exploration in our readers, we have relied on narrative knowledge. Good (1994: 153) writes that narrative is effective (and the reader may assess whether ours is) inasmuch as it turns reality in the subjunctive: 'the reader of a well told story grasps the situation from the points of view of the diverse actors of the drama, experiencing their actions and the story as indeterminate and open, even though the text or the story has a fixed structure and ending'.

The subjunctive is the mood relative to desire, wishfulness, possibility or likelihood. It denotes the world of 'as if' and therefore the possibility that things could be otherwise. By contrast, the indicative is the mood used to express factuality. As Bruner (1986: 26) writes 'To be in the subjunctive mode is [. . .] to be trafficking in human possibilities, rather than in settled certainties'.

Hence, our reason for conducting ethnographic analysis of gender in entrepreneurial contexts is to press the reader's empathic knowledge and imagination into the service of various scenarios. We authors have recounted the social representations of gender and entrepreneurship, the processes by which gender is erased to sustain a purported neutrality, and the resistance of gender to this erasure. And we have also set out the narratives which constitute manifold subjectivities in the roles of male or female entrepreneur and traced some of the many diverse patterns of entrepreneurship. It is now up to the reader to decide whether our book has stimulated her or him to enter a world where reality is thought in the subjunctive.

We shall now explicitly state the premises that delineate our departure point, so that the reader may assess their coherence.

- *Premises on entrepreneurship.* Entrepreneurial action is considered in terms of its cultural dimension, the processes by which value is attributed to its various components (for example, risk, money and innovativeness), and the ways in which entrepreneurship is socially represented in the discursive practices with which subjects describe, explain and legitimate to themselves and others what they do when they 'do entrepreneurship' and when they think of themselves as entrepreneurs and present themselves to others in that guise.

- *Premises on gender.* Our assumptions on gender pertain to what is known as 'social constructionism' (Gergen, 1982), and therefore gender is defined as 'the gender we think and the gender we do'[2] (Gherardi, 1994). This approach follows in the tradition of studying gender dynamics as an active accomplishment (West and Zimmerman, 1987), as performativity (Butler, 1993), as a two-sided dynamic of gendering practices and practising of gender (Martin, 2003). It considers reality to be a socio-material construction and gender to be a relational category which acquires meaning and structure through the social practices that constitute it: at the structural level, at the cultural level, at the level of social interaction among people ascribed gender memberships, and at the psychological level where persons assume a gender identity and present themselves through it as belonging to a gender category. We wanted to destabilize gender categories by showing that gender is the historico-material product of 'positioning' practices (Gherardi, 2003a).
- *Premises on change in gender relations.* All the social sciences are reflexive (Giddens, 1979) in that they change the phenomena that they analyse, but studies on gender – judging from the magnitude of the changes that have come about in the last thirty-odd years – have had an especial impact on society. The most pervasive of them, we believe, although it has been less thematized as such, is the crisis of hegemonic masculinity (Connell, 1995). The authority and the autoritativeness of a form of masculinity that has historically claimed to represent universality – because the category 'man' comprised persons of different gender and therefore erased gender as a dimension of power and difference – has been progressively delegitimated in numerous spheres of society. Within companies, the man/agerial model (Collinson and Hearn, 1994) based on the hierarchy, control, authority and rationalization that sustained one form alone of masculinity has been called into question by 'lean' organizational forms and supportive leadership styles. In the world of work, the gradual supplanting of manual labour (and its more 'male' connotations of fatigue, risk and general unpleasantness) by 'knowledge' work has undermined the social categories of male and female work. The destabilization of gender categories and gender relations is a pervasive social phenomenon that traverses the boundaries between spheres – public/private, family/work or inside/outside the firm – where they were previously kept separate.

On the basis of this set of premises, we chose three methodological strategies:

1   a critical reading of the discourse on women entrepreneurs intended to support the hypothesis that entrepreneurship is a cultural model of

masculinity – a rhetoric of masculinity – which obstructs the expression of alternative models;

2   reflexive ethnographic fieldwork in five small enterprises which sought to describe how enterprise cultures are gendered and how gender is produced by a social practice, that is, by a 'doing';

3   an analysis of discursive practices intended to show how the identity of the entrepreneur is constructed through entrepreneurial discourse; and thus that language, and its mobilization in practice, is the medium for a system of representations of the places of the enterprise, women and men in society.

Put in other terms, gender will be described as something that people 'do' – a social practice situated in interactive contexts – and not as something that people 'have', whether by socio-biological attribution or by socio-cultural ascription. It is in their relationships with others, in their interactions, that individuals create their individuality. And this process is mediated by language, which actively constructs the world and is expressed through discourse. Interactive and discursive practices produce representations which structure social reality and the activities within it.

To our knowledge, an ethnography of gender as an entrepreneurial practice and of entrepreneurship as a gender practice is an approach that has not been explored so far. An ethnographic approach to gender in entrepreneurship aims to what Geertz (1973) called 'a thick description' of the culture of entrepreneurship and within it the practice of gendering situated in interactions and discourses. Our purpose is to describe the features of an array of 'social worlds' (Becker, 1982) and their fabric of meaning and humanity through a close look at the social practices revealed in everyday interaction, and in texts produced in the field as examples of mundane discursive practices.

The field for observing the gendering of entrepreneurship was chosen by applying, not abstract criteria of representativeness of the firms, but rather criteria of expected diversity. That is to say, we decided not to investigate exemplary cases, given that the literature on women entrepreneurs already abounds with histories constructed around 'exceptional figures'. We preferred to study a non-individual entrepreneurial function and to look for situations in which the gender of the entrepreneurs mingled with the gender inscribed in the product, and with particular regard to firms belonging to the industrial cultures of both the north and the south of Italy. Finally, we wanted to include the variable 'sexual orientation' in our study of gendering practices within firms.

The ethnographic fieldwork was conducted in five businesses. One was a small company which publishes a monthly magazine of gay and lesbian culture. Two were owned by women: one recently started up in the centre of Italy using funds for the promotion of female entrepreneurship; the other located in northwestern Italy and run by two sisters who had inherited it from their grandfather. Of the other two businesses, which were located in the south of Italy, one was the realization of a business idea by a man who had capitalized on his crafts skills to found a family business; the other was a recent start-up, again using funds to promote entrepreneurship, headed by three brothers and a sister, who was the leading figure in the business.

Field observations in each of the five companies lasted for a working week, during which period the researcher 'shadowed' the entrepreneur. Every day of observation included an interview on the following topics: the history of the firm, business risk, innovation, the entrepreneur's relationship with money and future prospects.

The member of our group who conducted the fieldwork did not do so as a 'detached observer' of an objective reality but as a participant in an inter-subjectively meaningful reality which he helped to construct jointly with the other subjects involved in the action context. The purpose of the participant observation was therefore not to record an objective reality in order to provide a faithful description of objective events – as a realist ethnography would want – bur rather to participate intersubjectively in a reality shared with the other subjects in a situation which he helped bring about and to make visible, and where the 'small events' or incidents caused by his/her presence were collaboratively interpreted. The ethnographer, in a reflexive conception of his role, participated and observed just as much as he was observed and made a participant by the people whom he met.

We have expressly referred to the fieldworker as 'he' in order to emphasize that the choice of a male was intended to accomplish what the Chicago school (Hughes, 1958) calls a 'subversion' of the rules: because common sense identifies gender as a theme pertaining to women, the presence of a woman asking questions about gender might have given rise to connivance. For the sake of symmetry, it was decided that a woman should carry out the analysis of the texts collected during the fieldwork. In this case the intention was to exploit the distance between the person who interpreted the interviews and the person who had collected them and knew their contextual and rela-tional features. A text can be read by numerous readers, each of whom has a subjective understanding of it because a text is not objectively meaningful. Thus the social reality investigated – gender and entrepreneurship – is an open text amenable to plurisignification and a reiterated interpretation.

An overview

An overview of the contents of the book may give the reader a better grasp of how we organized our ethnographic material.

Chapter 1 seeks to familiarize the reader with the 'entrepreneur-mentality', a neologism which denotes the existence of a discourse on the art of being an entrepreneur and the nature of entrepreneurial practice (who can be an entrepreneur? what kind of activity does s/he undertake? who or what does s/he manage?). Entrepreneur-mentality is constructed through the discursive practices of entrepreneurs, the media that represent their achievements, and the scientific texts that expound theories of entrepreneurship; and in its turn it becomes the plot and constraint for entrepreneurial action and discourse. In particular it brings out the manner in which studies on women entrepreneurs have helped to make the masculinity of entrepreneurship invisible. We asked ourselves 'how are women's businesses represented by the most common research methods and interpretations of entrepreneurship studies?' The practices of social scientific research are involved in the process of mobilizing the ideas and behaviours that mark women entrepreneurs as 'the Other' or 'the Alter'. Focusing on women entrepreneurs from the implicit standpoint of the dominant culture is to contribute to the invisibility of hegemonic masculinity.

Chapter 2 examines the social construction of masculinity, of hegemonic masculinity and of the various masculinities embedded in particular social practices. Its intention is to put forward the thesis that entrepreneurship is a form of masculinity. This argument is further developed in Chapter 3, where we set out our interpretative framework of gender as cultural practice and describe the methodology that we believe is best suited to analysis of how gender and entrepreneurship interweave as situated practices.

Chapter 4 introduces the reader to the five field studies, offering at first an intricate description of the gender and entrepreneurial culture through selected 'episodes' in their reciprocal shaping. We shall interpret how in their 'doing' gender and entrepreneurship day by day, people constantly move back and forth between the two sets of practices, as it suits them and as it works best for them. We singled out five main processes in their performances: handling the dual presence (shuttling between differently gendered symbolic spaces); performing remedial work (to repair the cultural order in crosswise situations); boundary keeping (the defence of different symbolic spaces); 'footing' (which enables people to adjust their stances within a particular frame to disrupt its referents); and 'gender commodification' (the exploitation of the symbolic space of gender as terrain on which to (re)construct market relations).

Chapter 5 examines the relationship between gender and entrepreneurship as a discursive practice by analysing the texts collected in the form of interviews during the fieldwork. Attention shifts to how gender and entrepreneurship are told in the field trough narrative practices. We consequently illustrate how discursive practices are constitutive of the identity of the entrepreneur, as *loci* for the transmission and reproduction of power and gender. The main discourse *loci* here are risk, innovation and money. We analysed both the discourses and the narratives in order to unpick the rhetorics used to recount – and therefore narratively to construct – the subjectivity of an entrepreneur. Each narrative account comprises three overlapping and interweaving stories (that of the individual, that of the family and that of the company) that assume differing significances according to the type of positioning performed.

Chapter 6 principally discusses how in doing gender and gendering business a third practice – 'doing family' – is anchored in the previous two. Highlighted by the narrative analysis of the stories collected was the interweaving between the business and the family in its dimensions of gender and generation. This was particularly evident when we considered discourses on future plans for oneself and for the family (the couple or the parents): this, contrary to the standard literature on entrepreneurship, is not distinct from plans for the business. Nor did we find the existence of a sharp separation between public and private; rather, the narratives were laden with interpenetrations between the two domains.

Finally, for those readers who may be more interested in methodology we added one appendix devoted to a reflection on ethnography as a research practice. It is inspired by self-interrogation – now customary among qualitative analysts (Alvesson and Skoldberg, 2000) – on the research method adopted and its implications for future research. In our case, we organized our treatment on the basis of the three questions that Garfinkel (1996: 9) suggested that researchers should ask themselves on concluding their inquiry: a) 'What did we do?'; b) 'What did we learn, but only in and as lived doings that we can teach?'; and c) 'How can we teach it?'

1 How a gender approach to entrepreneurship differs from the study of women entrepreneurs

Reflection on the social construction of gender and economics (and business economics in particular) started late in comparison with other scientific disciplines. Its most obvious contentions were the following: men have always dominated the scientific community; gendered attitudes to entrepreneurs make women invisible (Reed, 1996; Mirchandani, 1999); analysis of women's experiences are inadequate, biased or distorted (Ferber and Nelson, 1993: 2). During the same period, management and organization studies took a 'gender-neutral' approach to entrepreneurship (Baker, Aldrich and Liou, 1997), but they did so by studying male entrepreneurs and considering their female counterparts to be only a tiny minority not worthy of particular attention. Moore and Buttner (1997: 13) maintain that until the beginning of the 1980s almost nothing was known about female entrepreneurs, and that entrepreneurship studies concerned themselves almost entirely with men. It was therefore during the 1980s that scientific discourse on female entrepreneurship and women-run organizations began to gain ground. Public attention was directed towards the matter by claiming that it was an emerging social phenomenon. We start from this discursive construct to take a deconstructionist gaze[1] on how it has been asserted as an objectively true point of departure for studies on women entrepreneurs. The discourse on entrepreneurship and the choice of words we use to define entrepreneurship (Gartner, 1993: 232) set the boundaries of how we think about and study it.

Foucault (1972: 49) defines discourses as 'practices which systematically form the object of which they speak' and discourses on women entrepreneurs are linguistic practices that create truth effects, i.e. they contribute to the practising of gender at the very same time that they contribute to the gendering of entrepreneurial practices. Therefore if we pay attention to how an 'entrepreneur-mentality' is gendered, we can see the gender sub-text beyond the practices of the scientific community studying women entrepreneurs and contrast them with the study of gender as a social practice.

Entrepreneur-mentality

We use the neologism 'entrepreneur-mentality' – paying implicit homage to Foucault's term 'governmentality' (1991)[2] – to highlight how an entrepreneurial discourse is mobilized as a system of thinking about the nature of the practice of entrepreneurship (who can be an entrepreneur, what entrepreneurship is, what or who is managed by that form of governance of economic relations) which is able to make some form of that activity thinkable and practicable, both to its practitioners and to those upon whom it is practised.

The term 'entrepreneur-mentality' signals the existence of a discourse on the art of being an entrepreneur and the nature of entrepreneurial practice. Entrepreneur-mentality is constructed through the discursive practices of entrepreneurs, the media that represent their achievements, and the scientific texts that expound theories of entrepreneurship, and in its turn becomes the plot and constraint for entrepreneurial action and discourse.

We now focus on how social studies of women entrepreneurs tend to reproduce an androcentric entrepreneur-mentality which makes masculinity invisible. Our thesis is reflected in a study (Ogbor, 2000) which deconstructs the discourse on entrepreneurship to show that 'the concept of entrepreneurship seems to be discriminatory, gender-biased, ethnocentrically determined and ideologically controlled' (p. 629). Social studies have played a part in the discursive construction of entrepreneurship as a male construct which normatively sustains a model of economic rationality allegedly universal and universally applicable regardless of differences in context, class, gender and race (Ahl, 2002). They do so through a single generic process: the 'othering' of the non-male. The term 'othering' (Fine, 1994; Schwalbe *et al.*, 2000) encapsulates the process by which a dominant group defines into existence an inferior group, mobilizing categories, ideas and behaviours about what marks people out as belonging to these categories. The practices of social scientific research are involved in the process of othering like any other mundane practice, as the above authors note. To focus attention on women entrepreneurs from the implicit standpoint of the dominant culture, or even from a social movement standpoint, contributes to their continual othering.

We argue in particular that even so-called 'women's studies' on female entrepreneurs, or feminist studies on feminist organizations, render masculinity invisible: both – albeit in different ways – portray women's organizations as 'the other', or 'the alter', and sustain social expectations of their difference, thereby implicitly reproducing the normative value of male experience.

We shall develop this argument to stress the difference (and the consequences of a failure to differentiate) between studying women entrepreneurs and studying gender as a social practice enacted by women and men within a discursive domain (entrepreneur-mentality) that shapes their actions and their discourse.

We begin with a 'social fact' – the increase in female entrepreneurship – and explore the rhetorical strategies deployed for its construction as worthy of attention and therefore as a possible subject for social research. Economic studies – by means of the instruments of quantitative analysis most congenial to them – tell us that the 1990s saw an increase in female entrepreneurship in most of the developed countries (NFWBO, 1995; Duchéneaut, 1997). Socio-economic studies – by means of analysis of statistics on labour-market participation – tell us that the phenomenon differed qualitatively from a simple expansionary trend (Barbieri, 1999). For example, in Italy during the 1990s, self-employment by women was no longer a 'fall-back solution' except in a very small number of cases (Barbieri, 1999; Zanfrini, 1999). The majority of self-employed women were now adult, committed to their work on a full-time basis, mindful of the employment choice that they had made, and unwilling to change it. The majority of the dissatisfied women were younger in age and not yet socialized to a career in self-employment, or else they were former dependent employees who had tried to set up on their own and regretted their decision to leave the tranquillity of a steady job. Only a few had entered self-employment or entrepreneurship from unemployment. Barbieri (1999) also points out that a distinctive feature of the 1990s was the specialization and differentiation of occupations and sectors of activity. Those years saw increased numbers of women working in the professions, as partners in cooperatives, in business services and social services; but their numbers declined or were stationary in traditional activities and services like retail and small-scale commerce, or in the traditional manufacturing sectors in which women work as 'helpers' for other members of the family. Consequently, female entrepreneurship is now growing in sectors where there is space for professional growth and demand for specialist skills, and it is declining in the traditional and low-skilled sectors. These features are not exclusive to Italy but seem to be shared by the European countries and also by the United States (Barbieri, 1999).

In its turn, the social fact denominated 'independent female work' is rhetorically represented as part of the quantitatively broader social phenomenon labelled 'women's work', characterized by the anomaly of the 'glass ceiling', that is, by vertical segregation. The close attention paid by social studies since the 1980s to the relationship between women and the economy in the so-called 'developed' countries sheds important light on how it has been explained and how it has been institutionalized.

An articulate explanation (Adler and Izraeli, 1988, 1994), has used the following arguments:

- The dramatic increase in female employment since the Second World War. The greater visibility of female work has led to realization that women as human capital are under-utilized.
- The interest that institutional actors (political, economic and in research) now show in demographic changes. Declining birth rates in the more developed countries will give rise to a shortage of skilled male labour.
- The globalization of the economy is driving a search for 'excellence' and

for new competitive advantages. There is a consequent need to maximize the potential of the human resource in all its forms.

- The demand – ever more explicit and insistent – advanced by women for access to higher managerial positions as a consequence of their greater investment in education and training. Companies find it increasingly difficult to ignore female potential when recruiting or promoting employees.

Evidently, these four explanatory factors – the quantitative importance of an 'objective' phenomenon, its subjective salience on a scale of importance, the global economic dimension, and the formation of a social demand – are also the criteria for legitimation of a 'scientific fact' among the producers of knowledge. Thus, in the entrepreneur-mentality, the increase in women entrepreneurs during the 1990s was an unquestioned, objective fact and a scientific topic (Gutek and Larwood, 1987; Powell, 1993; Fisher, Reuber and Dyke, 1993).

We may therefore say that the institutionalization of a line of inquiry situated in the assumption that enterprise is a rational economic activity, and in a conception of gender citizenship (Gherardi, 2003b) as cultural integration through equal opportunity policies, has encouraged research on women entrepreneurs, while also promoting economic and labour policies targeted specifically on that category of women. Moreover, in a Europe marked by the considerable importance and homogeneity of Community policies transposed into national ones and the widespread presence of SMEs, the issue of women entrepreneurs centres on their importance as actual or potential actors in new models of local development, either because they own or run small firms or because – thanks to public intervention – they can be given opportunities to start new ones.

Whereas the figure of the woman entrepreneur has entered the discourse of the scientific community, its representation by the media still clings to the old gender stereotypes. We briefly review the findings of a study of the Italian economic press conducted at the same time as our research (Bourlot, 1999; Magatti, Monaci and Ruggerone, 2000: xxiv–xxvi):

- Female protagonists are frequently described as mavericks, more ruthless and determined than their male counterparts.
- The conservatism is apparent in stereotypes of the iron lady, the boss's girlfriend who becomes his wife, the heiress. Besides being dismissed as a factor for change, female entrepreneurship is generally viewed as marginal to the dynamism of the firm.
- Female entrepreneurs are described mainly in relation to the family business and in terms of their family role. A woman entrepreneur is such inasmuch as she belongs to a family of entrepreneurs; she is the designated heir flanked by a male spouse or relative. A constant theme is the difficulties of these women in balancing work and domestic duties.

The assumption is therefore that their natural place – and their primary social responsibility – is the family.

The role of the media in the social construction of entrepreneurial discourse is all the more important because they replicate themes and notions in the specialist literature, which they merely popularize. Hence both scientific texts and the specialized press render the 'naturally' male gender of the entrepreneur invisible and uncontroversial. Not only is an entrepreneur usually a man but also the rhetorical figure of the 'family business' is constructed more on the business than on the family, which is treated as a non-cultural, non-historical, apolitical and even non-emotional entity (Katila, 2002). The understanding that also the family is constantly created by ongoing societal discourses and practices prompted Sajia Katila to investigate the moral order (what is valuable in a family and worth striving for, and what are the basic principles according to which one of its members is expected to behave) in Finnish agricultural family businesses. The family as stereotype removes from critical scrutiny the fact that both women and the family have changed. While the family plays a role for women entrepreneurs – as most studies state – male entrepreneurs are not asked questions about work–home conflict (Ahl, 2002).

Having delineated the cultural context in which entrepreneur-mentality is grounded, and the most widespread reasons in the scientific community for legitimating the study of women entrepreneurs, we may now inquire as to the consequences of such research. We shall investigate two bodies of literature in particular – business economics literature and studies of feminist organizations – and the consequences of their implicit assumptions on gender in terms of a 'gendered' politics of knowledge. We shall explore their gender sub-text: that is, how gender is (re)produced through power-based processes underlying relations presented as abstract, neutral and objectified (Smith, 1990; Benschop and Doorewaard, 1998). Our argument will be that their gender sub-texts discursively operate – albeit in different ways – toward a common process of 'othering' women entrepreneurs and rendering masculinity invisible. A gender approach – which considers gender as a material and discursive practice – is therefore more suited to revealing the reciprocal construction of masculinity and entrepreneurship.

Women entrepreneurs: the victims of gendered research practices

Our purpose in this section is not to conduct an exhaustive survey of the literature on female entrepreneurship but to bring out the gender sub-text implicit in it, and the consequences. In discussing the literature, we shall refer mainly – though not exclusively – to an internal working document (Monaci, 1998)[3] which describes the state of the art mainly with reference to Europe. Since a similar state of the art is presented by other literature overviews (Franchi, 1992, 1994; Brush, 1992; Magatti, Monaci and Ruggerone, 2000; Ahl, 2002), we take it as representative of the discourse on women entrepreneurs.

Studies on female entrepreneurship[4] are broadly divided among five thematic areas (Monaci, 1998):

1 the 'breeding grounds' of female entrepreneurship;
2 patterns of female entrepreneurship;
3 the barriers against female entrepreneurship;
4 the motivations of women entrepreneurs;
5 the organizational and managerial methods – the 'enterprise culture' – of women entrepreneurs.

We shall now investigate how implicit assumptions on gender relations have steered research and the production of scientific knowledge. In examining each of the above five areas, we shall first set out the arguments adduced in support of the diversity of female entrepreneurship. We shall then deconstruct these arguments to show that the rhetorics used to explain diversities support a process of othering. A table (Table 1.1) will summarize the elements making up the gender sub-text of the business studies literature.

The 'breeding grounds' of women's entrepreneurship

The business economics literature reports that the great majority of women entrepreneurs are not only concentrated in the tertiary sector (commerce and especially services) but also began work in that sector, the traditional area of dependent female employment. At least three arguments have been mobilized in explanation of the tendency for women to create new businesses mainly in services:

1 It is the sector of which they have most knowledge and experience.
2 The fact that women frequently lack specific technical skills tends to dissuade them from starting businesses in the manufacturing and high-tech sectors, and also reduces their likelihood of surviving in those sectors.
3 The greater difficulty encountered by women in obtaining financial resources induces them to choose low capital-intensive activities, like those in the services sector.

Besides the patterns of female entrepreneurship just outlined (concentration in the tertiary sector, relative discontinuity with previous work experience), at least two further features have been identified in the business literature (Monaci, 1998): (i) the small size of businesses created and run by women;[5] (ii) the lower profitability in terms of turnover or sales of female businesses compared to male ones.[6]

This description reflects a state of affairs evinced by the statistics and by quantitative research (Franchi, 1992; Rosa *et al.*, 1994). It is therefore socially regarded as reasonable and plausible. But to what extent does the researcher's understanding of gender relationships shape the way research is done and explanations are offered (i.e. how the knowledge produced contributes to the reproduction of gendered policies)? And with what consequences? Let us take a deconstructive look at the above explanations.

In the first instance women entrepreneurs are represented as constructing ghettos within entrepreneurship, notably in more backward sectors where skills are an extension of what has been naturally learnt through gender socialization; sectors that are easier to enter and which therefore have little value. Women entrepreneurs are 'the others' with respect to the humus on which the entrepreneurial character is rooted and with respect to the grounds – the sectors – in which it develops.

In the second instance female entrepreneurship is connoted with the devaluation implicitly associated with the 'female' gender, and this devaluation is perpetuated in the prescriptive literature, which urges women entrepreneurs to assume the values of rational action: orientation to results, efficiency, control, competition. Thus the values of entrepreneurship are institutionalized as male and 'superior', while female entrepreneurship is represented as the result of gender properties: its 'weakness' is the 'natural' expression of the weak sex as reflected in society and the economy. But what are the consequences of such a gender representation in academic knowledge? The disciplines that study organizations, management, or business economics have institutionalized as 'objective and universal knowledge' the experiences of the 'strong' entrepreneurship manifested by male entrepreneurs operating in market conditions different from those faced by female entrepreneurs. Thus, female entrepreneurs are 'the other' in terms of which the male entrepreneur is defined, so that the academic disciplines represent experiences and points of view of only one part of the entrepreneurial phenomenon. Masculinity constructs the definition of entrepreneurship, and male entrepreneurship is used as the benchmark for entrepreneurship as a whole.

The feminist critique has for some time attacked the tendency of researchers who study women to use men as their standards of comparison (Calvert and Ramsey, 1992), to construct the experience of women as 'other than' (Irigaray, 1974) and to ask 'why aren't they like us, or how can they become like us?' (Nkomo, 1992: 496). Because the production of knowledge is based on gendered ideas, it maintains and reproduces a system of gender relations which renders masculinity invisible while giving corresponding visibility to 'other' experiences – whether these are firms owned by women or by non-white, non-heterosexual entrepreneurs who do not compete in the market as the canons of the for-profit enterprise dictate. For mainstream researchers, 'other' entrepreneurship becomes visible when it is viewed using the anthropological categories of diversity and with a desire to assimilate minorities. A knowledge constructed on implicit gender assumptions thus becomes in its turn an instrument of dominance because it is used to draw boundaries among categories of persons, to exercise control over resources and to devise support policies for a category of persons labelled as second-sex entrepreneurs.

Patterns of female entrepreneurship

Against the background of the trends just described, attempts have been made to draw up typologies of women entrepreneurs. If the best-known classifications are combined (Goffee and Scase, 1985; Cromie and Hayes, 1988; Franchi, 1992; Monaci, 1998), it is possible to identify the following 'ideal-typical' profiles of women entrepreneurs:

- the 'aimless' young women who set up a business essentially as an alternative to unemployment, or because they have scant career prospects or opportunities for self-fulfilment in dependent employment;
- the 'success-oriented' young women for whom entrepreneurship is not a more or less random or obligatory choice but a long-term career strategy in which – given that they usually do not start with specific skills – they invest heavily by taking up opportunities for training (which usually combines with a high level of schooling) and developing a solid network of business relations;
- the 'strongly success-oriented' women with the same features as the previous category but who are older and have more previous work experience (often in senior positions), usually without children, and who view entrepreneurial activity as an opportunity for greater professional fulfilment or as a means to overcome the obstacles against career advancement encountered in the organizations for which they previously worked;
- the 'dualists', often with substantial work experience (frequently in senior management), who must reconcile work and family responsibilities (especially childcare) and are therefore looking for a solution which gives them flexibility in their dual role;
- the 'return workers', or women (usually low-skilled) who have quit their previous jobs to look after their families and are motivated by mainly economic considerations (for example, supplementing the income of a husband in precarious or low-income employment) or by a desire to create space for self-fulfilment outside the family sphere;
- the 'traditionalists', or women with family backgrounds in which the owning and running of a business is a longstanding tradition, and who can therefore rely on both good knowledge of entrepreneurial methods and, more concretely, a network of relations functional to running the business;
- the 'radicals', or women motivated by a culture antagonist to conventional entrepreneurial values who set up initiatives (typically in

the form of cooperatives and collective enterprises) intended to promote the interests of women in society.

When we take a critical stance on these explanations and look for the gender sub-text inscribed in them, we find that the patterns of female entrepreneurship are depicted as reflecting women's private life-courses: interruptions, discontinuities in business, ways to plan their futures which do not distinguish between business plans and personal plans. This representation highlights implicit gendering processes in two ways: by drawing a boundary between the public and private (assuming different logics of action in each domain and splitting the woman's life in two non-communicating domains), and by naturalizing women through their representation only in relation to the reproductive life-cycle.

In fact, if entrepreneurial activity belongs to the symbolic universe of the public, any signs of the private must be expunged therefrom because they represent anomalies, paradoxes and phenomena which demand explanation. Male entrepreneurs are located in a space of representation in which business is rational action in a public arena, and their 'private' features are made invisible so that they do not interfere with the entrepreneurial project. The only exception in this ideal iconography is the intergenerational transmission of enterprises – a predominant theme in the European literature on SMEs – which symbolizes that reproduction interferes with business and that a business is a legacy both material and ideal.

On the other side, patterns of female entrepreneurship are represented in a social space lying at the intersection between the reproductive life-cycle (childlessness, child-bearing, the empty nest, extended motherhood) and the entrepreneurial project. Can aimless, dualist, 'return', traditional female entrepreneurs inspire confidence in the business world? The implicit sub-text at work in this representation states that family duties take priority in women's lives, and therefore that women are not trustworthy entrepreneurs. At work in this representation are the implicit assumptions that reproduction is a mainly female responsibility, that it should predominate over other responsibilities and that reproduction is a natural fact which does not distinguish giving birth from child raising. The rhetorical figure of the working mother is anchored in nature, and it is a discourse figure that has no male counterpart. Fathers and working fathers are absent from the representation.

The social profiles of female entrepreneurship are cultural artefacts which reflect the power relations based on what Michel Rosen (1984: 317) calls 'hierarchical segmentation and value appropriation'. The divide between public and private establishes a hierarchy, not just a difference between the two terms, and the values associated with them reproduce gendering processes at work in the production of identities, cultures and artefacts.

The barriers against female entrepreneurship

Studies conducted in the majority of the Western countries (mainly North America and the countries of the European Union) identify three main types of barrier against female entrepreneurship:

1   The socio-cultural status of women. To identify the primary role of women with family and domestic responsibilities reduces the credibility of women intent on setting up businesses in various ways.
2   Access to networks of information and assistance. It may happen, for example, that women in greatest need of technical support and training are treated dismissively by consultants and interlocutors with little confidence in their abilities A factor that may prevent women from developing their own businesses is the difficulty of joining informal networks, which are often the main source of information and contacts, but which equally often comprise more or less overt mechanisms of gender exclusion (Aldrich, Reese and Dubini, 1989) even if the difference in density of the networks is not relevant.
3   Access to capital. Women entrepreneurs who decide to supplement their capital with outside funding usually meet more resistance than men. Whether they are applying to an institutional financier (a bank, a finance agency), a friend, a relative or even a spouse, they are likely to come up against the assumption that 'women can't handle money'.

Deconstructing the gender assumptions implicit in the mainstream entrepreneurial literature finds an ally in research on minority-owned firms. The literature on these firms has shown that the presumption is that their failure is due to psychological or racial non-conformity, not to discriminatory behaviour consequent on prejudices and stereotypes (Chotigeat, Balsmeier and Stanley, 1991; Butler, 1991; Feagin, 1987; Ogbor, 2000). These studies describe a 'discrimination-in-lending' due to prejudices and stereotypes (and the myth of the inability of women to handle money is certainly one of these), although the argument usually adduced in defence of this explanation is that such businesses are economically less viable. Of interest is Thompson's (1989) explanation for the persistence of the prejudice: namely that it springs from acceptance of the neoclassical view of a capitalist economy and its individualistic assumption. People who fail are individually responsible for their choices, or they do not possess the appropriate character traits.

The arguments concerning the barriers against female entrepreneurship have contributed to the social reproduction of a gender sub-text which represents women as 'lacking in' status, networks and credibility. In its turn this representation structures social perceptions of institutional actors and shapes their discriminatory, often unintentional, behaviour. The difficulties encountered by women entrepreneurs not only in gaining access to credit (Fay and Williams, 1993; Riding and Swift, 1990) testify and construct a difficulty in gaining access to resources made available by society. The social construction of the female as the second sex generates 'second-sexing' processes (Gherardi, 1995) which subtract legitimacy resources from women by devaluing the female.

Neo-institutional organizational studies (Powell and Di Maggio, 1991) have emphasized that organizations compete for symbolic resources and institutional legitimation. Institutional isomorphism is the social process that makes organizations increasingly resemble each other as they incorporate social myths. And institutional actors in the state apparatus and the professions take decisions on the allocation of resources, or make other policy choices, on the basis of myths institutionalized in the context in which they operate. As a consequence, the institutionalization of entrepreneurial knowledge from the point of view of the dominant social group shapes a discourse on entrepreneurship which reproduces the same barriers that it helps to define. In fact, analysis of the cognitive maps of all the institutional actors involved in the implementation of local policies in support of female entrepreneurship in an Italian region highlights the isomorphism between the beliefs of actors and the perception of the barriers that their action should seek to eliminate (Codara, 1999).

The motivations of women entrepreneurs

The dominant discourse regarding the reasons why women may decide to start up a business distinguish between 'compulsion' factors which constrain women more out of necessity than choice, and positive or 'attraction' factors which induce women to see entrepreneurship as an opportunity.

Attraction is represented by motives such as (Monaci, 1998):

- a way to supplement an inadequate household income;
- a solution for entering in an activity in which formal selection criteria (qualifications, experience and gender) seem absent or less stringent;
- a strategy to obtain greater margins of flexibility and discretion in the management of work and family and an outlet for women deciding to leave dependent employment in organizations where they have experienced frustration in their work and a lack of opportunities for advancement.

Compulsion is depicted as:

- a search for independence and autonomy in work;
- a search for professional self-fulfilment;
- a search for income (in order to achieve financial independence or higher socio-economic status);
- the pursuit of a social mission (e.g. the social integration of the more vulnerable members of society).

In general, the entry of women into entrepreneurship seems to be a complex mix of constraints and opportunities, of external coercions and subjective aspirations. Yet, seen in deconstructive light, the interweaving of availability for the market and for the family which places adult women with family responsibilities in two systems which are in fact interdependent though symbolically separate is a normative model that produces drudgery, coercion, restrictions of time and cleavages of identity. At the same time those women able to cope with these constraints are represented as skilled in the management of flexibility and relational resources. The discontinuity between the two spheres of everyday existence – with the proliferation of *loci* of identity, and the endeavour to combine so many elements (times, relational styles, etc.) – is depicted as an identity resource for female entrepreneurs because it gives rise to opportunities and the ability to develop specific organizational, relational and institutional skills.

The mainstream entrepreneurial literature, though seeking to understand how women are able to cope with conflicting demands, represents the female as a resource for the market economy, given the ability of women to survive in a (social) hostile environment and female skills becoming valued. It first depicts ghettos for female entrepreneurship and then cites women's personality traits or economic inefficiency in explanation of why they remain in those ghettos. The joint effects of the institutional, historical and cultural factors that have confined women's choices to a narrow range of spaces are silenced. And finally, in explaining the phenomenon, the mainstream discourse 'discovers' the female abilities which make other economic strategies possible within those spaces and which justify the existence of niches. This discourse has constructed the female as a resource, but it has not discarded the categories of the gender hierarchy. As a result, the success of women entrepreneurs may be used to discipline less efficient forms of entrepreneurship, and the international division of labour reflects the gender structuring whereby men dominate the global scenario, leaving the domestic economy for women to deal with (Calàs and Smircich, 1993).

Thus, the claim made by a body of knowledge – entrepreneurship studies – that it is 'gender-neutral' is constructed in a context of instability and change in masculinity today ill suited to the model of economic rationality theorized when studies on entrepreneurship became institutionalized. In other words, the programme of research which examines the gendering of studies on entrepreneurship has produced a system of representations in which the female is presented as a resource and an advantage for the economy. The consequence of this shift is that Schumpeterian masculinity hampers the globalization of the economy, and the new resource of the female is used to discipline an obsolete model of masculinity.

The enterprise culture of women entrepreneurs

The mainstream business economics literature tells us that firms set up and run by women tend to display a set of distinctive features (Brush, 1992; Chaganti, 1986):

- The entrepreneurial logic of strategic planning and performance assessment. During the start-up and development phases of their businesses, it seems (Franchi, 1992; Monaci, 1998) that women tend not to use a *deliberate* approach, that is, a management model characterized by a distinct and rational sequence of actions (the identification of opportunities, the setting of objectives for corporate growth, the obtaining of resources, the production and marketing of goods/services, the articulation of a formally defined organizational structure). A significant proportion of female entrepreneurs instead use an *evolutionary* approach which moves through the following stages: identification of a gap in the market, the consequent development of a business plan, the investment of personal capital, an attempt to enter market niches with a single type of product/service, customer development and 'care', maintenance of the business on a small scale. The entire process is largely informal in character and the business may arise as an extension of a hobby or a domestic activity (e.g. catering). Initially, besides self-financing, frequent use is made of human resources present in the family circle (for instance, a husband or partner may keep the accounts or attend to marketing and logistics). Results are evaluated, not by economic parameters but rather in terms of qualitative criteria like the achievement of self-respect, self-fulfilment and customer satisfaction. Yet recent research has suggested that women entrepreneurs use criteria to measure success which differ from those of their male counterparts (Bigoness, 1988; Buttner and Moore, 1997). According to these findings, women tend to assess their performance in terms of intrinsic criteria like personal and professional growth (achieved by implementing their skills and self-valorization), rather than extrinsic criteria of an economic nature (sales volume, increase in the number of employees and of market share, etc.), which are still the benchmarks most widely used by men to assess their entrepreneurial performance.
- Informal structures of work organization and coordination styles based largely on direct relations and the affective involvement of employees (Rosener, 1990). Whereas men are mainly characterized by a 'transactional' style of leadership (involving the exchange of results for rewards and command through control), women display distinct abilities in 'transformational' leadership: a management style which seeks to foster positive interactions and trust relations with/among subordinates, to share power and information and to encourage employees to subordinate their personal aims and interests to collective ends. In short, these studies relate female managerial styles to a specific (natural or socialized) orien-

tation of women towards communication, cooperation, affiliation and attachment, and to a conception of power as control not *over* the group but *by* the group. Some authors explain this distinctive style of female leadership as resulting from the influence of primary socialization (Chodorow, 1978), which develops women's affective and relational resources and a propensity to communicate with others, to listen to them and to concern themselves with their needs. Accordingly, the argument runs, the activities that society has traditionally assigned to women have developed a culture of responsibility and an ethic of care whereby women constantly endeavour to satisfy the needs of all.

A more critical interpretation (Kanter, 1977; Beccalli, 1991; David and Vicarelli, 1994) suggests that, because women have not usually been able to wield formal authority in the organizations for which they work, they have been forced to develop other strategies to that end, most notably an ability (typical of those in positions of inferiority) to 'feel' and anticipate the reactions of others.

Social research on gendered entrepreneurship has sought explanations for the male–female difference, and as critical studies on leadership have convincingly shown (Calàs and Smircich, 1996) there is no better predictor of the existence of a difference than the presumption that it exists. In the great majority of cases, the research methods devised to measure differences find those differences that they are looking for, because they operationalize social myths. As a consequence, research practices reproduce labels which become quasi-objects through which ideas are conveyed and acquire material form (Czarniaska and Joerges, 1995).

For women entrepreneurs, therefore, their concern for relational aspects and the flexibility matured in so many supporting roles (clerical and secretarial jobs, staff positions in personnel offices and in public relations), as well as their everyday coordination of family and work responsibilities, is represented in business literature as a valuable organizational resource exploitable both for direct productive purposes and for symbolic use as admonition to the male workforce regarding the values of cooperation rather than status claims.

The rhetoric of a female business culture – based on the romancing of docile femaleness – has produced a specific discourse figure in Italy – the *impresa-donna* (the female-run enterprise) – which various institutional actors (interest associations, women's movements, progressive press) use to extol the female experience and to explain the fact that female businesses are 'different'. Female entrepreneurship is different because female entrepreneurs are women, and their socialization into gender models has produced values and behaviours which, though different, can nonetheless be evaluated. This discourse creates a social expectation of behaviour differences which bases itself on essentialist or culturalist assumptions and shapes a new normative model of female experiences.

While the view of entrepreneurship as 'gender-neutral' gave rise to a prescriptive literature which urged women to 'masculinize' themselves, the discovery of a 'good female' experience has produced a gendering programme which prescribes 'femalization' at all costs. Equal opportunities legislation which standardizes behaviour and envisages only one type of female experience has been widely debated in Europe and lies at the core of the concept of mainstreaming the gender agenda (Muraro, 2000).

Table 1.1 summarizes the main elements of the gender sub-text underlying studies on women entrepreneurs in the business literature.

However, since the theme of the distinctive enterprise culture brings us to the core question of female difference, we shall briefly examine another strand of studies which has yielded knowledge on the relationship between organization and women, but starting from a different epistemological position. We refer to the literature on feminist organizations. While the business literature assumes a 'neutral' standpoint in order to make women visible (and masculinity invisible), the feminist organizations literature theorizes a distinctive women's standpoint as a privileged knowing positioning. Our rationale for confronting the two epistemological positions resides in our desire to distance ourselves from both.

Feminist organizations and the women's standpoint

A discursive strategy in business literature depicts women entrepreneurs as unusual women, different from ordinary women, and they represent the result of a strategy of self-selection (Ahl, 2002). In looking for an explanation of the difference, the women's movement has been called on (Masters and Meier, 1988; Bellu, 1993; Anna *et al.*, 2000). These studies assert that the women's movement has created a new breed of women, has had an impact on women's risk-taking propensity and that more women entrepreneurs choose to start non-traditional businesses. Some women therefore are more entrepreneurial than others and in any case there are 'regular' women and women entrepreneurs who differ from the former. The idea that women perceive and approach business differently from men is well represented by Brush (1992) and her integrated perspective. Relying on Gilligan (1982) she suggests that women perceive their business as a cooperative network of relationships and as integrated into their life. This discursive strategy differs from 'the male norm' typical in the traditional business literature which cancels the gendering of entrepreneurship studies, and it has been called the discursive strategy of the 'good mother' (Ahl, 2002). The good mother rhetoric cherishes the small differences found in comparing men's and women's firms and leaning on 'feminine resources' (Carter, Williams and Reynolds, 1997; Buttner, 2001) models an alternative female entrepreneurial model. We wish to analyse the discursive strategies that assert women's difference starting from the women's standpoint.

Table 1.1 A deconstructive gaze at business economics literature on women entrepreneurs

Thematic areas	Explanations offered	Gender sub-text
Breeding grounds: services	i) It is the sector of which they have most knowledge and experience.	i) Female entrepreneurs as constructing ghettos within entrepreneurship.
	ii) Women frequently lack specific technical skills.	ii) Skills are an extension of what has been naturally learnt through gender socialization.
	iii) The greater difficulty encountered in obtaining financial resources induces them to choose low capital-intensive activities.	iii) Sectors easier to enter and which therefore have little value.
Patterns of female entrepreneurship	i) The 'aimless' young woman. ii) The 'success-oriented' young woman. iii) The 'strongly success-oriented' woman. iv) The 'dualist'. v) The 'return worker'. vi) The 'traditionalist'. vii) The 'radical'.	Patterns of female entrepreneurship are depicted as reflecting the reproductive life-cycle: interruptions, discontinuities in the business field, ways to plan the future which do not distinguish between business plans and personal plans. The 'radicals' are the only exception.
The barriers against female entrepreneurship	i) The socio-cultural status of women. ii) Access to information and assistance. iii) Access to capital.	Women as 'lacking' in: i) status; ii) networks; iii) credibility.
The motivations of women entrepreneurs	The entry of women into entrepreneurship seems to be a complex mix of constraints and opportunities, of external coercions and subjective aspirations.	This discourse has constructed the female as a resource, and 'discovers' the female abilities which make other economic strategies possible within those spaces, and which justify the existence of niches.

continued

Table 1.1 (cont.)

Thematic areas	Explanations offered	Gender sub-text
The enterprise culture of women entrepreneurs	Firms set up and run by women tend: i) to display distinctive features of the entrepreneurial logic of strategic planning and performance assessment; ii) to have informal structures of work organization and coordination styles based largely on direct relations and the affective involvement of employees.	While the view of entrepreneurship as 'gender-neutral' gave rise to a prescriptive literature which urged women to 'masculinize' themselves, the discovery of 'good female' experience has produced a gendering programme which prescribes 'femalization' at all costs.

When discussing the existence or otherwise of a feminist methodology, Harding (1987) distinguishes among three methodological positions: gender as a variable (based on positivist assumptions about reality and methodology, i.e. a feminist empiricism); a feminist standpoint perspective (theories for women which start from the experience and point of view of the dominated and point to their capacities, abilities and strengths); and poststructuralist feminism (critical reflection on how gender is 'done', order created and fragmentation suppressed).

The first methodology is characteristic of the majority of business lietrature and aims to make women visible, adding their experiences into mainstream research, while the second – the feminist standpoint approach – validates the knowledge or modes of knowing associated with femaleness and seeks to gain legitimacy for female knowledge which has been suppressed or marginalized. The first methodology characterizes the mainstream study of women entrepreneurs, while the third is present in our theoretical and methodological framework. The feature that radically distinguishes the feminist standpoint from poststructuralist feminism is the conception of 'action', change or political project. Whilst a modernist project views action as factual change, a postmodernist one sees the 'political' as residing in the destabilization of the categories used to construct gender, scientificity, objectivity and neutrality. The feminist standpoint will be addressed now, because it has made a major contribution to study of women's way of organizing within a political project and in face of efficiency (Acker, 1995).

Feminist organizations are an amalgam, a blend of institutionalized and social movement practices. They are organizations in tension, according to Myra Ferree and Patricia Martin (1995: 13), who define 'feminist organizations as the place in which and the means through which the work of the women's movement is done'.

It might be objected that feminist organizations and women's businesses are not the same empirical entities. On the one hand, feminist organizations are closely similar to other movement organizations (see the tension between internal participatory democracy and hierarchy); on the other, many women's businesses are cooperatives, or they have been established with an explicit commitment to feminist values or to values alternative to the mainstream. Nevertheless, inasmuch as they partly overlap, we can learn something, and above all we can reflect on the differences and similarities between them.

We have seen from the literature on women entrepreneurs that a social expectation has been created which fuels scientific research and the knowledge, both theoretical and practical, consequent upon it. The expectation is that women who run businesses do so in a manner different from men, either because they are women or because they have been socialized as women. And yet feminist organizations are enterprises (or institutions) born with the express intent of pursuing a political ideal and its practical accomplishment in their internal organizational practices. They are supposed to be run differently because they constitute a value statement. Our intention in discussing this literature is to argue that differences in organizing spring from the deliberate practice of alternative values, not from a natural difference, or from one due to socialization.

The feature shared by all feminist organizations is that, besides being made up of women, they are inspired by feminist and collectivist principles, with the consequent negation of leadership and formal structure. A further shared feature is the desire to create space for the expression of values alternative to those of dominant masculinity. Separatism is often the value that engenders organizations responding to the needs of women (from battered women's shelters to cultural organizations like bookstores). However, in countries where cooperative organizations are common and express a widespread culture, democratic organizations founded and run by women only also operate in manufacturing and services. From an organizational point of view, they are inspired by the same leaderless and structureless ideals embraced by the social movements contemporary to them in the 1970s and 1980s (Melucci, 1989).

When women attempt to invent feminist business and organizational practices, they are faced by the practical dilemma of trying to actualize democracy in concrete activities (Calàs and Smircich, 1996). Those who analyse organizational practices may refer to Table 1.2, in which Calàs and Smircich compare four classics in the literature: Koen (1984); Iannello (1992); Rothschild (1992) and P.Y. Martin (1993).

The principles that inspire these practices are very similar: participatory decision-making, flexibility, empowerment, care. And they are not so very different from the practices that we just reviewed under the label of women entrepreneurial culture. We believe that the literature on 'feminist organizing'

Table 1.2 A comparison of four 'feminist organizational practices'

Key features and design principles of feminist workplaces (Koen, 1984)	Modified consensus organization (Iannello, 1992)	Six characteristics of the feminine model of organization (Rothschild, 1992)	Feminist management (P.Y. Martin, 1993)
System of rotating leadership.	A distinction between critical and routine decisions: critical reserved for the many, routine delegated horizontally to the few.	Value members as individual human beings.	Asking the woman question.
Flexible interactive jobs designs.			Using feminist practical reasoning.
		Non-opportunistic relationships are valued.	Doing consciousness raising.
Equitable system of income distribution.		Careers are defined in terms of service to others.	
	Recognition of ability or expertise rather than rank or position.		Promoting community and cooperation.
Interpersonal and political accountability.		Commitment to employee growth.	
			Promoting democracy and participation.
	Empowerment as a basis of consensual process.	Creation of a caring community.	
			Promoting subordinate empowerment, power as obligation.
	Clear goals arrived at through consensual process.	Power sharing.	
			Promoting nurturing and caring.
			Striving for transformational outcomes.

Source: Calàs and Smircich, 1996: 228.

has often be taken as a model by research on 'gender as a variable', with its endeavour to verify differences among women's businesses empirically by examining leadership and managerial styles and attributing their presence or absence to nature or to culture. However, ambiguity as to the origins of differences is shared (as we shall see) by both strands of research.

A point with which we shall deal only briefly is whether it is sufficient to create a women-only organization for a new mode of organizing to be born. We cite such statements as: 'women's socialization makes them better equipped than men to perform the skills necessary for the creation of democratic and non-hierarchical organizations' (Brown, 1993), although the author warns against transforming this assertion into a new (alternative) determinism. *Women Organizing* is the title of the book by Helen Brown which deals with the organizing experiences of Women's Centres and by extension a non-hierarchical, participative organizational modality with diffused leadership. Unlike formal and hierarchical ones – those 'normal' in the sense that they constitute the model of organizational theory – these women's organizations stand at the opposite extreme of a hypothetical continuum where, according to Rothschild (1990), one finds

> a tendency in negotiating to seek equitable agreements rather than self-advantage, a preference for involving others rather than a unilateral style, a habit of cultivating others' talents and crediting them, a sense of responsibility for others' well-being and a desire for relationships at work that are valued in themselves.

Research on cooperatives of various sizes and voluntary organizations (so-called 'proximity services') – conducted from a European perspective and therefore in comparison with studies by other colleagues (Paton *et al.*, 1989; Laville, 1992; Macfarlane and Laville, 1992) – have shown that the constitutive values of democratic organizations give rise to an organizational culture which expresses rules of behaviour and patterns of organizing that are also evident in feminist organizations or in organizations formed by women alone.

In our view, the socialization of women to extra-domestic work, to organizational life, to organizing, does not come about in a context 'separate' from that of men; and we also contend that socialization to the private, to care, to nurturing does not create a protective carapace around the values that constitute the 'dowry' that women bring with them when they enter the public sphere. Otherwise, how can we account for those numerous men who prefer to work in or to found democratic organizations, so many of which are to be found in the tertiary sector? The traps of either/or logic, of oppositionism in thought, induce us to deny of the Other what we affirm of the One. The comparison can be drawn between democratic/hierarchical organizations but not between women's/men's organizations.

Another reason for focusing on Brown's statement is to reveal that behind the feminist standpoint – which in principle makes a knowledge claim (theories for women) – there lies a conceptualization of gender difference based on differential socialization.

The literature on feminist organizations, together with standard business studies on women entrepreneurs, reveals a process by which the woman's identity is always socially constructed as 'Other' with respect to the male entrepreneur, but it is thus constructed through a different mode of identity attribution and a different form of identity work. The business literature contributes to the othering of women entrepreneurs by subtly suggesting that difference is a deficit (difference as deficit), while the literature on feminist organizations suggests that difference is a plus (difference as pluses), although the identity founded on this resource is still 'other' with respect to the normative standard.

Because the literature on feminist organizations springs from a political project and propounds a mode of being and of doing business entirely at odds with the dominant culture, it is in danger of confusing a 'would-be' of and for women with 'womanhood' *tout court*, attributing them alternative abilities and values merely because they are women. This is the danger inherent in generalizations that end up by unintentionally creating a further normative model of femaleness.

The literature on feminist organizations, in implicit polemic with the dominant culture on organizations, appropriates a stigmatized identity and then re-proposes it to valorize and legitimate a collective identity. We call this process 'appropriative othering' in order to emphasize both the identity work required to create a 'moral identity' and the reaction to an oppressive identity code already imposed by a dominant group. The identity work done by the movement that surrounds feminist organizations, in order to assert 'alternative' values in management and in women managers, can be read as an attempt to deflect the stigma on women's experience as members of a powerless group by turning it into a moral identity, an 'alter'.

Consequently, both these strands in the literature contribute to the representation of women as 'other' or 'alter'. Whether they construe the difference as a deficit or a plus, they both put forward a normative model of doing business for women (or for feminist women), and they both reinforce hegemonic masculinity, either by rendering it invisible (by assuming a neutral point of view) or by absolutizing it (by assuming the women's point of view).

Both strands of literature, in sustaining the idea that men and women are different, sustain the current social order through the discursive practices that mould the entrepreneur-mentality. Ahl's (2002: 178) analysis of the discursive practices of eighty-one articles on women entrepreneurs reaches conclusions very similar to ours. She points to the following discursive strategies:

- Entrepreneurship is male-gendered, but thought of as neutral.
- It is based on four basic assumptions: economic growth is good and entrepreneurship is good since it furthers economic growth; men and women are different; a gendered division of a private and a public sphere of life; individualism.

She depicts three strategies which are used for reinforcing the assumption on men/women diversity:

1   making a mountain out of a molehill, i.e. stressing small differences between men and women while ignoring similarities and large overlaps;

2   the self-selected woman, i.e. when finding that men and women entre-
    preneurs seem more similar than different, one proclaims women
    entrepreneurs to be exceptions from regular women;
3   constructing the good mother, i.e. moulding an alternative, feminine
    entrepreneurship model.

For these reasons, we decided to set out in search of an interpretative frame
that did not presume the existence of a difference but instead examined
the social processes that produce, categorize and reproduce difference, or, in
other words, those cultural practices which produce gender in everyday social
and economic activities.

Can we do differently?

The purpose of this long journey through the literature on women entrepreneurs has been to highlight the difference between studying women and
studying gender. In the former case, the focus is on the differences between
women entrepreneurs and the scientific standard of entrepreneurship represented as 'gender-neutral' in that masculinity has been made invisible. In the
latter case, the difference is framed within a system of relations. Studying
gender means studying the social practices which categorize persons within
a binary system, attributing them features of masculinity or femininity, and
constructing symbolic systems which are defined by difference but which are
only meaningful within the reciprocal relation. One of the principal social
processes of gender construction consists in the discursive practices which
create everyday interactions and shape what is deemed to be knowledge and
transmitted as expertise and science.

A gender approach can therefore be defined as a heuristic strategy intended
to investigate how the categories that affirm or conceal gender relations are
created, and the social consequences of these categorizations. A gender
approach always expresses a politics of knowledge because it always starts
by investigating the point of view from which what is defined as knowledge
is produced, and for whose benefit. This is a conception of gender that
belongs within a postmodern sensibility and a programme of research that
seeks to destabilize the interpretative categories used to construct the black
boxes of science and scientific discourses in order to reveal their knowledge-
producing practices. It is for this reason that such close attention has been
paid to the systems of representation which language constructs and which
found disciplinary discourses as expert knowledge. While the discourse
of women entrepreneurs maintains the existence of an 'other' and grounds
otherness either on biological difference as 'naturally' accounting for social
destinies, or on the differential socialization which expresses and reproduces the sexual division of labour, a gender approach to entrepreneurship
maintains that it has been historically and culturally produced as a form
of masculinity which celebrates certain of its distinctive traits. As a discursive

practice, entrepreneurship produces its own subject: *entrepreneur* and not *entrepreneuse*.

A gender approach to entrepreneurship means to conceive entrepreneurship and gender as a conflated practice which sustains gendered relationships and in turn reconstitutes entrepreneurship and gender as social institutions. Our thesis is that entrepreneurship, as a form of masculinity, is a cultural barrier raised (and a technique of power used by a certain group in society) against other forms of masculinity and against entrepreneurial activity by women.

2 Gender as a social practice, entrepreneurship as a form of masculinity
A theoretical framework

The purpose of this chapter is to outline our theoretical framework for a gender approach to entrepreneurship.

Reviewing the debate, gender will be defined as a linguistic artefact, a theoretical concept, a feminist invention, an effect or a consequence of a system of difference, as well as a quasi-object whose meaning is enacted in appropriate situations. Our interest will focus on the 'doing of gender' (as a social and discursive practice) and on the formation of en-gendered subjectivities, thus questioning the rigidity of categories which create two and only two types of human character. From this point of view, rather than seeking to define what gender is, we are interested in showing what gender does and how gender is done in practice.

Both gender and entrepreneurship will be analysed as social practices, starting from the assumption that women cannot be studied in isolation from men, and bearing in mind that not only women are gendered. The equations 'sex = gender' and 'gender = women' are not only misconceptions due to inexperience, or to a linguistic operation which attenuates the social embarrassment caused by the word 'sex' by replacing it with a more genteel one. Rather, they are an ideological operation which allows gender studies to avoid calling the gender relation into question. In this manner, masculinity is made invisible, removed from critical reflection; it continues to be the prime term, the one in relation to which the other is defined by default.

Since it is one of the assumptions of this book that there can be no representation of female identity or difference unless it is set in dialectic relation to a male identity or difference – and therefore that the specificity of a gender approach consists in examination of the reciprocal relations and representations that people activate in their everyday lives – we think it is important to highlight the various rhetorics and practices of maleness that contribute to the construction of entrepreneurship as a form of masculinity.

We begin by describing the principal theoretical approaches to masculinity, showing that in recent years the literature has altered its view of masculinity from an intrinsic property to a 'critical issue' (Martin, 2001). Then, by means of a 'symbolist reading' of the literature on men and masculinities, we shall extrapolate various practices, rhetorics and images of masculinity which combine to constitute 'entrepreneurial masculinity'. Owing to its especial relevance to organization studies, we shall dwell in particular on the approach known as 'naming men as men': an approach which has prompted analysis of the contents and forms of man/agerialism (Collinson and Hearn, 1994, 1996), as well as a critique of hegemonic masculinity (Carrigan, Connell and Lee, 1985). By interweaving men, masculinities and management, these authors have sought to 'break the silence' (Harlow, Hearn and Parkin, 1995) that renders masculinity invisible and removes it from discourse. Doing gender and enterprise will therefore be interpreted as practical accomplishments, the effects of a mode of ordering bodies, texts, artefacts and situated knowledges.

Gender: a situated performance in the intersections between bodies, discourses and practices

Gender is a category that was invented by feminists in the mid-1970s to give form, substance and visibility to women's experiences. The use of the category has given rise to a political subject able to conduct autonomous reflection on the conditions of its own existence, and to a critique of what counts as 'knowledge'. The category of gender has given visibility to, and thereby enabled the investigation of, a social reality that was previously 'non-existent' because it lay beyond theoretical awareness. Moreover, by generating new knowledge, it has also modified gender relationships. The meaning of the term 'gender' is a social product which changes through the use made of it by society and the knowledge that it produces.

When the term 'gender' made its first official appearance in scientific discourse (Rubin, 1975), the expression 'sex-gender system' denoted the set of processes, adaptations, patterns of behaviour and relationships by which every society transforms biological sexuality into products of human activity. The term 'gender' first arose in the academic studies of American feminism (Nicholson, 1994), to be then imported into Europe with different outcomes but a shared endeavour in social studies. In fact, the evocative connotation implicit in the grammatical use of the term 'gender' arises from the act of classification and the social act of seeing human beings as two, and only two, types of individual. Gender is therefore a binary concept (men and women constitute gender) and it is the way in which human beings present themselves, self-represent themselves and are perceived in society. In this sense, gender is a relational concept subsumed by a dyadic code which entails constant relation and tension. As a consequence, the theoretical and analytical project in social studies is to determine – by exploring the relationships between men and women – how the concept of gender modifies the habitual schemas of social scientists.

A telling example in this regard is provided by Chiara Saraceno (1993) when she points out that, if the extension of economic analysis to women's work has uncovered a presence that was previously neglected, this should lead, not to sectional analysis 'of women', but rather to a redefinition of the term 'labour force', and to critical reflection on the measurement of market value. The same example can be set within organizational studies: what is required is not study of participation by women in organizational processes, but rather redefinition of 'organizational categories' so that they accommodate the experiences of men and women and reveal the ideological consequences of representing an abstract 'labour force' and a de-sexualized and dis-embodied worker in language.

French and Italian feminism view the body as the symbolic rather than physical origin of the subject 'woman' (Irigaray, 1974; Cavarero, 1990; Muraro, 1991). This subject is unable to 'auto-signify herself' because Western philosophical thought has imposed itself as male thought, devising a universal and neutral subject which defines and represents the world in its own terms. As a consequence, a woman is a paradox, a social construction, a representational effect. The questions of who is the female subject and what is a subject revolve around the centrality of language. The use of language by definition involves separation and differentiation, but also power. Male and female stand in a dichotomous and hierarchical relation: the first term is defined in positive as the One; the second is defined by difference, by default, as the non-One, that is, the Other. This was the lesson taught by Simone de Beauvoir (1949), from whom we have inherited the concept of second sex. When, immediately after the Second World War, de Beauvoir described the woman as the Other, the problem of language was not yet paramount, although the ontological problem was.

Teresa De Lauretis (1999) finds three junctures in a genealogy of the subject in feminist thinking: (a) a first phase when the subject Woman was signified as 'the Other' (de Beauvoir, 1949; Irigaray, 1974); (b) a second phase when there was a split subject, intersected by a plurality of differences by class, race and sexuality; c) and a third phase when there arose an eccentric subject, capable of multiple identifications and belongings, but also of dis-identification and displacements. The eccentric subject is not immune or external to gender; rather it is distant, critical, ironic, excessive.

Other images have been used to capture the idea of a subject which is at once internal to the language that produces it and resistant to it: the semiotic and the abject (Kristeva, 1977), the divine (Irigaray, 1982), the post-colonial (Spivak, 1987), the cyborg (Haraway, 1991), the lesbian (Wittig, 1992), the nomadic subject (Braidotti, 1994), the vampire (Stone, 1995). In this manner, feminist thought produced the cultural effect of de-legitimizing the unity and stability of the Cartesian subject.

The passage from the first phase to the second involved the shift during the 1980s from difference (in the singular and mainly as Female/Male differ-ence) to differences, while the passage from the first and the second phases to the third involved transition from a modernist project to a postmodern one. Within a modernist project the need for a political subject gives voice to a women's standpoint (or a feminist standpoint) which articulates the interests of a unified subject. As this women's standpoint searched for a common denominator, it extolled the condition of sameness. Equality of condition was varyingly founded on sexuality, reproduction, child-rearing, the sexual division of labour: the body, the mind or production relations were the foundation of communality. This desire to discover a common male/female bedrock led to undervaluation of the plurality of differences: class, gender and race modulated women's voices in different ways (Lugones and Spelman, 1986) and gender may not be the principal difference, or it may not be only gender that gives origin to differences. The overvaluation of sameness had a further consequence. Gender relations were based on a normative order which reproduced femaleness and maleness through socialization. For example, the project that gave rise to equal opportunity programmes in organizations was inscribed in modernity's conception of equality as assimilation and similarity. Quite different was the endeavour to deconstruct subjectivity into a plurality of variously positioned selves.

The postmodern assault on 'metanarratives', transcendental reason and the possibility of objective knowledge also interrogates the constitution of the 'feminine' within modernity. French (Cixous and Clément, 1986) and Anglo-American feminism (Weedon, 1987) have questioned the claims of many feminist theories that they articulate a privileged knowing subject, an essential feminine and a universal representation of woman. This approach contains the basis for a broader critique of how 'knowledge' is constructed, in so far as it depends on the possibility of representing a reality that does not exist outside its representation in language. It is through language that researchers constitute the subject of their knowing, their subjectivities as knowers, and what counts as knowledge as the difference from what is 'not knowledge', i.e. the 'other' in the discourse, the silenced term.

Poststructuralist analyses focused on language, subjectivity and discourse highlight three major issues:

- The notion of linguistic differencing, which is central to deconstruction, situates knowledge as conditional upon language. Language, rather than reflecting an independent reality, constitutes meanings, and every claim to knowledge is inseparable from the language that expresses it.
- Since language constitutes meanings, it is the medium through which our sense of ourselves and of situations – our subjectivity – is constructed. In Foucault's terms (1982), 'subjectification' is the process by which individuals objectify themselves so that they may recognize and commit themselves to a particular sense of their subjectivity.
- Every claim to knowledge is a discourse. Discourse concerns the particular historical, social and political situatedness of language and of subjectivity. Particular discourses support particular assumptions and processes embodied in institutions (government, family, enterprise), and discursive fields constitute arenas for the struggle over meanings and power. The assumptions and practices that prevail within a discursive field depend on which discourses are dominant.

On the one hand, modernist viewpoints pursue a project to identify the ways in which knowledge is gendered and to give visibility to feminine knowledge that has been marginalized or suppressed. They seek to legitimize a political subject – women – and conduct research from the women's standpoint. On the other hand, gender studies informed by a postmodern sensibility question subjectivity and awareness of its discursive 'positioning'. The subject position (Foucault, 1986) becomes a 'positioning' enacted and performed within an institutionalized use of language and other similar sign systems. It is within a particular discourse that a subject (the position of a subject) is constructed as a compound of knowledge and power into a more or less coercive structure which ties it to a gendered identity. A subject position incorporates both a conceptual repertoire and a location for persons within the structure of the rights pertaining to those who use the repertoire (Davies and Harré, 1990). A position is what is created in and through conversations as speakers and hearers construct themselves as persons: it creates a location in which social relations and actions are mediated by symbolic forms and modes of being. The decentring of subjectivity paves the way for analysis of how gender is enacted in and through practices, techniques and procedures.

The present work endorses deconstructionist and poststructuralist episte-mology but does not follow its methodology, although the latter's attentiveness to discourse has heightened our understanding of the relations between power and knowledge and of the means by which constellations of power/knowledge constitute gendered subjects in a determinate order of things. We are not interested in treating the world as a text, however, but rather in understanding how gender practices inscribe the world and impose form upon it. Our point of departure is an interest in the 'doing of gender' in situated encounters where language is the medium for enactment of gender relations and the discursive formation of en-gendered subjectivities, and the endless deferral of the meanings of gender.

Doing gender, deferring its meaning

The concept of 'doing gender' has roots in symbolic interactionism. Under the definition provided by West and Zimmerman (1987: 126), gender 'is the activity of managing situated conduct, in the light of normative conceptions of attitudes and activities appropriate for one's sex category', and 'doing gender involves a complex of socially guided perceptual, interactional and micropolitical activities that cast particular pursuits as expressions of masculine and feminine "natures"' (ibid.: 125).

Similarly, anthropologist Dorrine Kondo (1990) frames gender as a 'strategic narrative assertion'. Kondo says any behaviour is capable of being gendered as masculine or feminine based on a person's talk and action, within the constraints of the societal system of gender relations. And following the line of 'doing gender', Patricia Martin explores the implications of a two-sided dynamic – gendering practices and the practising of gender – for understanding gendering processes in formal organizations. She defines practising gender as 'a moving phenomenon that is done quickly, directionally (in time), (often) non-reflexively, informed (often) by liminal awareness, and in concert with others' (Martin, 2003: 342). 'Gender practices', 'gendered practices' and 'gendering practices' stand for a class of activities that are available – culturally, socially, narratively, discursively, physically – to be done, asserted, performed in social contexts. Practices per se are conceptually distinct from people who practise them. They are potential actions that people know about and have the capacity or agency to do, assert, perform or mobilize.

How we do gender is still a question central to micropolitics between the sexes, in the social construction of the everyday reality of our society and culture. This assertion presupposes that gender is a routine, methodical and recurrent accomplishment. Yet gender is one of the most powerful of symbols; indeed, the very word 'gender' encapsulates all the symbols that a culture elaborates to account for biological difference.

In order to stress the processual nature of difference, Derrida (1971) invented the term *différance*, which in French is pronounced the same as *différence* and incorporates the two meanings of the verb *différer*: defer in time, and differ in space. In expounding his conception of *différance*, Derrida (1971) began with the understanding of a sign as that which is put in place of the absent thing we wish to make present. In binary oppositions the second term is regarded as the perverted, corrupt and therefore undesirable version of the first. One of the best-known examples provided by Derrida (1971: 61) is the ancient Greek word *pharmakon*, which means both remedy and poison, good and bad at once. The word is intrinsically undecidable. When it is applied to those who are criticized it is used with the meaning of poison; when it is used for those whom the speaking subject favours, it means remedy. The word *pharmakon* is 'the medium in which opposites are opposed' and in which one side crosses over into the other – good/bad, inside/outside – in an endless game (Derrida, quoted in Cooper, 1989). The purity of the inside, says Derrida, can only be attained if the outside is branded as a supplement, something extra – an excess – which nevertheless plays a necessary central role in the formation of the inside.

Like *pharmakon*, gender is an ambiguous concept which includes both male and female. Not only are male and female different from each other (static difference), but they constantly defer each other (processual difference) in the sense that the latter, the momentarily deferred term, is waiting to return because, at a profound level, it is united with the former. The difference separates, but it also unites because it represents the unity of the process of division. Therefore, there are two ways of conceiving gender difference: as two separate terms – male and female – and as a process of reciprocal deferral where the presence of one term depends on the absence of the other. Derrida (quoted in Cooper, 1989) terms these two modes of thought 'logic of identity' and 'logic of the supplement' respectively. Because of their multi-individual dimension and supra-individual duration, male and female as symbolic systems possess a static aspect which creates a social perception of immutability, of social structure and institution. But male and female is also a social relation dynamic whereby meaning is processually enucleated within society and individual and collective phenomena. The symbolic order of gender is static difference and processual difference (Gherardi, 1995). Put better, it is the product of their interdependence: the impossibility of fixing meaning once and for all sanctions the transitoriness of every interpretation and exposes the political nature of every discourse on gender.

On the symbolist interpretation of 'doing gender', Gherardi (1995: 131) writes:

> Doing gender involves symbols, using them, playing with them and transforming them; it entails managing the dual presence: shuttling between a symbolic universe coherent with one gender identity and the symbolic realm of the 'other' gender. We do gender through ceremonial work and through remedial work. In the former kind of behaviour we stress the difference between the symbolic universes of gender; in the latter we defer the meanings of gender to situated interactions.

For cultural theorists to refer to gender as a situated practice they must conceive of language as discursive activity, in opposition to the structuralist, semiotic and poststructuralist conceptions of it as structure, system or abstract discourse.

We take from feminist postmodernism its emphasis on the problematic nature of language, subjectivity and discourse, and bearing it in mind we recast a category of the Italian feminist debate – the dual presence – in order to focus on the 'how' of performing gender in interactive activities and in discursive practices.

En-gendering the dual presence and mobilizing gender

The 'dual presence' (Balbo, 1979; Zanuso, 1987) is a category invented by Italian feminists in the 1970s to indicate cross-gender experiences and the simultaneous presence (in the imagination, consciousness and experience of women) of public and private, of home and work, of the personal and the political. The expression 'dual presence' denotes a frame of mind which, midway through the 1970s, came to typify a growing number of adult women who thought of themselves in a 'crosswise' manner with respect to different worlds – material and symbolic – conceived as different and in opposition to each other and, not coincidentally, pertaining to one or the other of the symbolic universes of gender: public/private, the family/the labour market, the personal/the political, the places of production/the places of reproduction (Zanuso, 1987: 43).

In short, the dual presence may be seen as the symbolic presence in a liminal territory of signification and re-signification where the boundaries between the symbolic universes of male and female became fluid and negotiable, where they intersect and merge. It is, that is to say, an activity which relates to the metaphor of the 'threshold' (*limen* in Latin): the invisible line (the slash) that separates and unites the inner and the outer, a symbol of transition and transcendence. Just as the threshold between waking and sleeping represents what no longer is and what is not yet, so liminality is the state of difference, of the 'original unifying unity of what tends apart' (Heidegger, 1927). This dialectical tension origins in structural ambivalence. The structuring of the symbolic world of gender differences is expressed in institutions, processes and dynamics which erect a symbolic order of gender based on static difference, but at the same time the collective and global meaning of gender differences is historicized into radically different symbolic and social structures, where the threshold between male and female is crossed innumerable times. Female experiences in the male symbolic universe – and vice versa – give dynamic redefinition to the concrete meaning of en-gendering subjectivities.

On this view, the body, as Teresa De Lauretis (1999) puts it with an apt expression, becomes only a 'symptom', and the passage from sex to gender is mediated, translated, enacted. De Lauretis inserts a hyphen in the verb 'to engender', thus producing an ironic neologism: to 'en-gender' (De Lauretis, 1999). While to engender signifies 'to produce', but has no gender con-notation, to en-gender represents the process of gender attribution, and of self attribution, as the effect of technologies of gender (De Lauretis, 1987) and more broadly as the effect of the technology of the self (Foucault, 1984). The act of representing and of self-representing is a symbolic action which incorporates both the product (gender) and its process of representation (the 'en-gendering') (De Lauretis, 1987). Thus, gender is interpreted as a social construct, as well as a representation, which confers significance (identity, status, prestige) on individuals in a given society and founds a historical system of domination. En-gendering (De Lauretis, 1999) is a neologism which adopts (and allows) the same logic as similar concepts – like racializing or sexualization – which point to the production of subjectivities as a socio-political process and communicate the idea that race, sexuality, gender are not natural properties of bodies, but Western cultural representations and practices. Insofar as sex, sexuality, race and gender are cultural artefacts enacted in and through social practices of signification which result in reality effects, it is socially important for a political subject to understand how knowledge production works, because it can be done differently. By thinking, being and doing in particular ways, human agents create 'truths' about the world, and the objects and people within it; but, as Foucault (1986: 46) argues, there are other, possibly limitless, ways of being, thinking and doing, which are no more or less 'true' than those which we currently practise. To study how gender is 'done' entails envisioning how it can be done differently. Destabilizing the categories of gender has a political effect, since it means that the boundaries between the signification domain of the one and the other may be crossed and that transgression is possible. And transgressing is what we already do even when we represent gender as an ordered accomplishment.

Handling the dual presence entails competence in transgressing the boundaries and shaping the boundaries of the liminal territory where the symbolic order of gender is redefined through suspension of pre-existing gender significations, then to re-emerge with its contents changed to redefine successive meanings. But en-gendering subjectivities is not only the effect of discursive practices, as some poststructuralist and deconstructive scholars assume or the so-called transgender approach argues (Butler, 1993), viewing gender as signified merely through performative practices. The materiality of en-gendering the individual is inscribed in the technologies of gender and in the institution of compulsory heterosexuality that sustain the gender ideology.

Gender becomes apparent when it is exercised and represented in institutional discourses and interactive practices. Therefore 'doing gender' while 'doing business' is the focus of our theoretical framework.

The centrality of discursive practices shifts the concept of doing gender from activity toward 'performativity', a concept introduced by Judith Butler (1990, 1994, 1999) and subsequently taken up by actor-network theory (Law, 1999), and by other analyses which question organizational identities (Dent and Whitehead, 2001; Bruni and Gherardi, 2001). Butler (1990: xii) proposes 'parodic practices based on a performative theory of gender acts that disrupt the categories of the body, sex, gender and sexuality and occasion their subversive resignification and proliferation beyond the binary frame'. Thus gender (and also organization, as we shall see) is a performatively enacted signification that 'released from its naturalized interiority and surface can occasion the parodic proliferation and subversive play of gendered meanings' (ibid.: 33).

The 'doing gender' approach tells us that gender achieves its form as a consequence of the relations in which it is situated, and it also tells us that gender is performed in, by and through those relations. Therefore, the performativity of gender relations constitutes the border between mutually exclusive categories: it resides in the slash that divides and unites the opposite symbolic universes of female/male, private/public, nature/culture, science/technology.

Gender relations may thus be analysed as the product – unstable and only partly under the individual's control – of what Law calls the 'heterogeneous engineering' that arranges human and non-human elements into a stable artefact. Following John Law, we may assume that:

> Each one of us is an *arrangement*. That arrangement is more or less fragile. There are ordering processes which keep (or fail to keep) that arrangement on the road. And some of those processes, though precious few, are partially under our control some of the time.
>
> (Law, 1994: 33, emphasis in original)

In focusing on the modes of ordering heterogeneous materials (people, texts, artefacts) into a social practice, we assume that gender is mobilized and situationally enacted (Bruni and Gherardi, 2001).

Patricia Martin (2001) proposes the concept of 'mobilizing masculinities' in interpretation of 'the practices wherein two or more men jointly bring to bear, or bring into play, masculinity/ies'. In mobilizing masculinity/ies at work, men may mobilize the material and discursive codes of practice of the profession. The ritualistic repetition of these normalized codes gives materiality to belonging to the community and may explain the persistence of masculinist discourses, jokes, behaviours and styles even in mixed gender practices.[1] The counterpart of mobilizing masculinity becomes competence in handling the dual presence.

Martin's analysis can be considered part of the research on 'doing gender' that originates from symbolic interactionism, but the concept of mobilizing is also part of the actor-network literature (Callon, 1986a; 1986b). The notion of mobilization is used in the actor-network literature in its dual political *and* physical sense: by means of mobilization (in its political sense), a role and a recognizable identity are conferred on an actor. The theory extends the meaning of the term as applied to social phenomena (a demonstration, an organized movement) to socio-technical and material systems (a technical drawing, an estimate, a cheque, a scientific report). We borrow both meanings of mobilization to describe the mobilization of gender as a social and material practice, since, in interpreting something as gendered 'masculine', the silent term is also present in a relation of supplementarity.

Now we can move on to outline the various images of masculinity in order to construct a text that does not a-critically assume the existence of a 'male subject' and then address the dynamics underlying the construction of the female. Both construct each other, and showing the plurality of forms that masculinity may assume is a further strategy for the deconstruction and critique of the homogeneous and homogenizing view of gender.

Making masculinity (in)visible

The distinctive feature of the literature on masculinity is its extreme diversity. Those authors that have dealt with the theme have done so from a variety of disciplinary points of view (anthropological, sociological, psychological), and according to the specific objectives of their inquiry. If we look at the origin of the debate, we find that analysis of masculinity was already being conducted at the beginning of the last century by psychoanalysts, especially Freudian, who saw in the concepts of 'libido' and 'sex drive' the idea of a masculinity that is 'natural' and directly dependent on biological sex – although this was mediated by specific social and cultural forms (Laqueur, 1990). Very often, however, the purpose of these studies was to construct a 'mythobiography' (Bernhardt, 1985) able to account for the history and (presumed) destiny of a generic 'man', whose subjectivity was created within a cultural tradition that gave an essentialist, rather than relational, interpretation to gender.

Making masculinity invisible: the essentialist approaches

The first wave of men's studies, the so-called (Illich, 1982; Carrigan, Connell and Lee, 1985; Connell, 1987; Collinson and Hearn, 1996) 'sociobiological approach', shared the assumptions of a biology that determines gender and considers the body to be akin to a natural machine which produces gender differences a-problematically reflected in society (Morris, 1969; Tiger, 1969; Tiger and Fox, 1971; Wilson, 1978). Darwinian evolutionism provided an explanation for the process: men's bodies incorporate a 'natural' masculinity which arises from evolutionary pressures upon the human race. Thus, besides male genes, men inherit a propensity for aggressiveness, familialism, hierarchy and territoriality. The more extremist studies maintained that the social organization is a product of the endocrine system, and that the patriarchate springs from the 'advantage of aggressiveness' that men possess over women (Goldberg, 1993). These studies were normative in their purpose: starting from a pre-established idea of maleness, they looked for the particular 'shortcomings' or 'disorders' that may be present in some men (of which homosexuality is one of the most striking examples).

Thus effected was a radical dichotomy between Male and Female. The discriminant in these studies was the physical characteristics of individuals, and they emphasized differences rather than similarities. Moreover, because they regarded male bodies to be 'one alone', their idea itself of masculinity was univocal. Burrell and Hearn (1989) noted that, in the realm of sexuality, for example, the biological approach presumed that masculinity is 'naturally' oriented towards heterosexuality and procreation. Metaphorically, the body is a 'machine' which 'works' and 'functions', the brain is 'wired' to produce masculinity, and men are 'programmed' to dominate. The theory treated humans on a par with animals, and it borrowed its vocabulary from evolutionist theories: men were 'predators' who 'fought' to 'conquer' and fulfil their 'destinies'. As Ivan Illich (1982) aptly (and ironically) pointed out, sociobiology thus acted as a sort of 'science fiction in reverse': whereas science fiction attributed meaningful behaviour to fantastic creatures, sociobiology attributed a social organization to sub-humans, elevating stereotypes and social prejudices to the status of scientific facts. Moreover, the approach was by its nature unable to explain change (historically, masculinity changes in concomitance with other social constructs) and multiplicity (there is not just one example of masculinity, but many of them) (Connell, 1995).

In parallel with the sociobiological paradigm there arose an alternative approach (in the wake of Malinowski's and Margaret Mead's anthropological studies of sexual behaviour) based on the conviction that human behaviour follows socially determined roles, and that gender membership is one such role. The idea was put forward by Ralph Linton (1936), who was the first to use the term 'role' to emphasize the contrast between male and female behaviour and to describe the almost infinite malleability of the sexual roles that a culture attributes to its members. It was thought that persons oriented their action by complying with the expectations of others in their regard, and that in so doing they performed a role (in our case, being 'Male' rather than 'Female'). In keeping with functionalist theories, a concordance was assumed among social institutions, the norms relative to sexual roles, and the 'physical' personalities of people. Typically, the argument ran, a social role is constructed through the various processes of role-learning, socialization and internalization performed by the socializing agencies: the family, the school and the peer group (Parsons and Bales, 1956).

For the social sciences, the body thus became a largely neutral surface on which a social symbolism was imprinted. Whereas for sociobiology all the social orders were equally the effects of human biology, the body became an unconstrained field for social action. This approach too had its metaphors, but they tended to be ones taken from art rather than engineering: the body was a 'canvas' to be painted upon, or a 'surface' to be imprinted, or a 'landscape' to be drawn (Carrigan, Connell and Lee, 1985). Because the purpose of these studies was to single out and describe the most widely performed roles, the literature on the male sexual role concerned itself mainly with aggregating and mixing psychological findings on mental attitudes, (quantitative) data on the differences between sexual roles, and images of masculinity collected from the media and autobiographical anecdotes (Connell, 1987). These theories had repercussions outside the world of academic research, with the creation (in the United States) of the 'Men's Consciousness Raising Group'. Authors like Bly (1990), Goldberg (1976, 1988) and Farrell (1974, 1986) proposed that men should rethink (and also reappropriate) their roles, especially in consequence of feminist thought. And also proposed was a 'masculinity therapy' designed to rediscover male archetypes and to integrate them into contemporary society (Clatterbaugh, 1990).

Although reliance on society and socialization to explain gender differentiation might strike one as a culturalist position radically different from sociobiology, the point is that 'Culture' was invoked as a new essence and 'pure thing' by which people became part of a 'Society', which therefore had to be analysed (like all sets) in neutral terms. The use of role as a category of social inquiry took it for granted that the incumbent of a sexual role was a malleable individual whose neutral existence was shaped by 'sex' (Illich, 1982). It was uncertain how role expectations were created, whether they could be changed and what processes they subsumed (Kimmel, 1987). More generally, the role approach was normative in its intent: a 'role' was defined a priori, and those who did not fit with it were deemed to be 'deviant'. It neglected the dimensions to which masculinity is related (power, autonomy, hegemony), and action (i.e. the personification of a role) was still tied to a structure defined by the (biological) dichotomy between Male and Female.

Yet if gender was conceived as an ascribed characteristic, there was a risk that the tautology would arise whereby men were vested with a male role merely because they were 'males', and women were vested with a female role merely because they were 'females'.

Making masculinity visible: naming the hegemonic masculinity

In the mid-1980s an article by Carrigan, Connell and Lee (1985) set the scene for the onset of a new wave in the debate on men and masculinity. In their introduction, the authors called 'for a realist sociology of masculinity, built on actual social practices' (Carrigan, Connell and Lee, 1985: 553), and, after marshalling Gayle Rubin's definition of 'the sex/gender system' (Rubin, 1975), insights from the gay liberation movement (Mieli, 1980; Fernbach, 1981; Bray, 1982), anarcho-Marxist publications (Red Collective, 1978) and other early critical studies on gender and masculinity (Tolson, 1977; Kessler and McKenna, 1978; Plummer, 1981; Herdt, 1981; Cockburn, 1983), they assailed the sex role approach as follows:

> Sex role theory cannot grasp change as a dialectic arising within gender relations themselves. [. . .] The result of using the role framework is an abstract view of the *differences* between the sexes and their situations, not a concrete one of the *relations* between them.
>
> (Carrigan, Connell and Lee, 1985: 580, emphasis in original)

As an 'object of practice', the authors declared, masculinity displays its distinctive feature – namely its claim to be 'hegemonic' – along three main dimensions (Carrigan, Connell and Lee, 1985):

1 *Power relations*, principal among which is the subordination of women to men and the supremacy of particular groups of men over others. In this respect, masculinity is 'hegemonic' in that it re-constitutes gender relations as a scenario within which that dominance is generated.
2 *Production relations*, constituted by the gender division of labour with its economic consequences and its definition of some forms of work as 'more masculine' than others. The 'hegemony' of masculinity acts here as a direct link between the gender order and the class order, creating economic incentives for acceptance of the patriarchal organization of family and labour.
3 *Cathexis*, or discourse based on the dominant model of sexual practices and desire. In this case, masculinity achieves its 'hegemonic' position through the organization and institutionalization of heterosexual relations between people.

Various forms of masculinity can be generated along these three dimensions, depending on the social relations in which they are embedded. The central idea was that these various masculinities rotate around a core consisting of 'hegemonic masculinity', with which they stand in a relationship of dependence (in the sense that they derive from it and are subordinated to it) and of complicity (in the sense that they benefit from its existence).

Thus a new concept appeared, that of hegemonic masculinity, and it soon became 'the standard', as Patricia Martin (2001) notes, for a new critical debate on men and masculinities[2] (Reskin, 1988; Messner, 1992; Collinson and Hearn, 1994, 1996; Horrocks, 1994; Harlow, Hearn and Parkin, 1995; Barrett, 1996; Kimmel, 1996; Jacques, 1997; McKay, 1997; Kerfoot and Whitehead, 1998). Areas of research comprised the *loci* of masculinity and gender practices in social relations, and in particular (Hearn, 1992):

- *The state*, as a patriarchal institution founded on the public(male)/ private(female) dichotomy, and as the source of a dichotomous vision of social life.
- *The labour market/the workplace*, as aspects of a 'male' system of thought which allocates different personal aptitudes to pre-established roles and institutionalizes relational practices according to the position occupied by persons within the reference structure. The productive(male)/ reproductive(female) dichotomy expresses their salient features.
- *The family*, as a patriarchal institution based on a division of roles and a marked emphasis of sexual difference. Its constitutive dichotomy is that between autonomy (male) and dependence (female).

The areas of inquiry proliferated and the very idea of a Masculinity turned into multiple masculinities which developed differently according to the times, places, relations and other dimensions of a person's social life, like ethnicity and/or social class (Aaltio-Marjosola and Mills, 2002). Attention focused on the processes that drive the formation of masculinity within institutional, productive and quotidian reality. Maleness (like femaleness, for that matter) thus became a social quality which could be assumed with greater or lesser 'intensity' (La Cecla, 2000), a complex of practices whereby identity was not an 'I am' but an 'I want, I move, I do' (Ricoeur, 1990). The male (and the female) became what Mauss (1936) called 'body technique', and Foucault (1984) after him the 'technology of the self', with regard to certain human abilities which, although they must be learnt (talking or walking, for example), instead seem to come 'naturally'. Midway between a condition and a faculty, these abilities are learnt and performed to the extent that they seem automatic: they are 'knowing how' (La Cecla, 1999), the being at such ease with one's body that the entire process of learning them (under duress or voluntarily) is forgotten.

The symbolics of masculinities: entrepreneurship as a form of masculinity

This section offers a 'symbolist reading' of the critical literature on men and masculinities. More specifically, it reviews the different dimensions in which masculinity has been thought to reside, and it extrapolates various practices, rhetorics and metaphors of masculinity which converge to constitute 'entrepreneurial masculinity'. We shall bear in mind the heuristic value of metaphors from a symbolic perspective (Eco, 1981): metaphors suggest analogies between apparently different phenomena, and by so doing they provide guidance and yield further interpretations within a fluid reality both observable and evocative, material and non-material, objective and subjective.

Using what Bolen (1989) has called a 'spiral method of inquiry', we shall begin with the theoretical analyses of masculinity loosely coupled to the theme of entrepreneurship (those that examine the ethnic or sexual aspects of masculinity, for example). We shall then discuss those analyses that deal with economic-organizational matters in particular. Each different form of masculinity will enable us to focus on the characteristics of the masculinity to be found in the construction of 'entrepreneurial masculinity', but which requires separate treatment if its nature is to be evinced (as well as to give due merit to the various studies examined). The exploration of other dimensions will enable us to show the multiple images of masculinities mobilized in the form of the 'entrepreneurial masculinity', according to specific cultural and historical practices. From a symbolic point of view, in fact, 'hegemonic masculinity' is a concept and also a metaphor which directs attention to an important aspect of masculinity (its 'hegemony') but at the same time obscures other of its features. Emphasising the 'hegemonic' character of masculinity is consequently an important conceptual and metaphorical operation which reveals the pervasiveness of gender processes and exposes and questions the 'competitive advantage' enjoyed by males (at least in Western societies), but it fails to account for all the forms and relational practices that it may assume. Accordingly, we concur with Patricia Martin (2001) when she argues that Connell's concept of hegemonic masculinity should not be taken to be a typology, even less applied to the practices culturally dominant in a particular place or historical period, lest other 'types' and practices of masculinity be overlooked – those that are not necessarily hegemonic, for example.

The order in which the different masculinities are discussed in what follows moves along a spiral which reflects the central interest of this chapter (the mutual production of masculinity and entrepreneurship) and proceeds as follows:

- masculinity and ethnicity (black masculinity);
- masculinity and sexuality (homosexual masculinity);

- masculinity and the family (patriarchal masculinity);
- masculinity and class (working-class and bourgeois masculinity);
- masculinity and myth (archetypal and heroic masculinity);
- masculinity and aesthetics (athletic masculinity);
- masculinity and organizations (managerial masculinity);
- masculinity and the market (entrepreneurial masculinity).

Masculinity and ethnicity: black masculinity

Following revival of interest in the thought of Frantz Fanon (1961), and prompted by third world/post-colonial feminist theory (Bhabba, 1994; Nkomo, 1992; Prasad and Prasad, 2002), one of the new directions explored by research is the interweaving between (male) gender and ethnicity (Westwood, 1990; Hearn, 1992; Segal, 1993).

This approach is mainly socio-historical in its perspective. It traces relationships between 'whites' and 'blacks' to the colonial period, seeking to show that the idea of an 'inferior black race' has often been accompanied by that of a 'black masculinity' marginalized with respect to that of white males (Mac an Gahill, 1994). The subjugation of other ethnic masculinities by white masculinity is a process that began with the 'civilizing' work of (white) missionaries and pioneers in the New World. Black masculinity has also been associated with a male strength and violence made too explicit to be socially acceptable. It has thus functioned as the negative of the physical character-istics associated with masculinity, taking them to their extremes and being represented as an excess of 'good' masculinity (Hoch, 1979).

These scholars consider ethnicity to be a relational category (like gender), and they view relations among 'races' (like gender relations) as frequently founded on power axes (Sinha, 1987). It is intuitively likely that the two categories share certain features and that they influence each other. In a research study on the interconnections between gender and ethnicity in the formation of organizational identity by hotel staff (for example), Yvonne Guerrier and Amel Adib (2003) have highlighted two particularly important processes in terms of racialization and en-gendering. The first is the pro-gressive redefinition of gender on the basis of ethnic membership, and vice versa. Male and female, that is to say, exchange their symbolic meanings with variation in the ethnicity of the subjects involved, giving rise to an identity and otherness that can be constantly renegotiated. The second process is, as a consequence, the construction of gender identity as a never-ending, often contradictory, process that must confront a hegemonic as well as white masculinity.

Masculinity and sexuality: homosexual masculinity

Some of the most significant contributions to the study of the dynamics responsible for the formation of masculinity were made by the awareness-raising campaigns of the gay movement during the 1970s and 1980s (Levine, 1979; Mieli, 1980; Campaign for Homosexual Equality, 1981; Beer and Munyard, 1983). The feature shared by these studies was their assault on the assumption that heterosexuality is the natural order of things. 'Patriarchal culture has a simple interpretation of gay men: they lack masculinity. [. . .] If someone is attracted to the masculine, then that person must be feminine – if not in the body, then somehow in the mind' (Connell, 1995: 143). Foucault, drawing on Hocquenghem (1972), identified medical science's assertions with regard to homosexuality as the matrix of a society which both produces and represses 'deviant' identities. When homosexuality was medically and scientifically categorized, it ceased to be a sexual practice (sodomy) and instead assumed a sexual/social identity (Illich, 1982; Brewis and Linstead, 2000). As Foucault (1978: 154) writes:

> [T]he notion of 'sex' made it possible to group together, in an artificial unity, anatomical elements, ideological functions, conducts, sensations, and pleasures, and it enabled one to make use of this fictitious unity as a causal principle, as omnipresent meaning: sex was thus able to function as a unique signifier and as a universal signified.

In fact, when a distinction is drawn between homosexual behaviour and homosexual identity, the operation highlights how homosexuality is historically situated and socially organized through the collective production of a subordinate masculinity associated with a social group with recognizable personal features (Plummer, 1981). Some authors (Fein and Nuehring, 1981; Shallenberger, 1994) read homosexuality as a 'stigma' (Goffman, 1963), and thus as something which changes a person's status from discreditable to discredited. However, the more recent studies conducted by the proponents of 'queer' and 'transgender' theory (Gonsoriek and Weinrich, 1991; Sedgwick, 1990; Stone, 1995; Jagose, 1997; Weed and Schor, 1997) prefer to regard gender as 'more than a "tag" that one wears, but [. . .], rather, a normative institution which seeks to regulate those expressions of sexuality that contest the normative boundaries of gender, [. . .] one of the normative means by which the regulation of sexuality takes place' (Butler, 1997: 27–8).

Analysis of homosexuality requires clarification of the significance of the body for a symbolic approach. The body is not a neutral medium; rather, its fundamental feature is materiality (Butler, 1990), so that discussion of masculinity as a symbolic process cannot ignore corporeal experience. What is corporeal, however, is not static and immutable, as demonstrated by transvestism and modern biotechnology (Haraway, 1991; Franklyn, Lury and Stacey, 2000). In social contexts, bodies (in the plural, because they all differ) acquire a historical dimension in which they actively participate. Some bodies, moreover, are more undisciplined than others, to the extent that they upset the assumptions of the reality in which they are situated. Homosexual desire does not depend on a 'diverse' type of body (Hocquenghem, 1978); yet it certainly belongs among bodily activities and upsets the order imposed by hegemonic masculinity. In this sense, it emphasizes the irreducibility of sexuality to gender or vice versa, but still insists on their reciprocal influences (Butler, 1997).

Homosexuality thus lays bare another presupposition behind social interactions in a patriarchal society: heterosexuality. The concept of heterosexuality has important consequences for the gender order in that it establishes some sort of connection among social and sexual roles and lays the basis for a definition of a strong form of masculinity to which weaker ones are subordinate (Ward and Winstanley, 2003). The studies by the proponents of queer theory are therefore not simply pleadings for an oppressed minority; they are a more general critique (and contradiction) of hegemonic, white and heterosexual masculinity.

Masculinity and the family: patriarchal masculinity

Horrocks (1994) traces the formation of masculinity by virtue of economic and political processes; yet he identifies the family as the specific *locus* of the formation of maleness. Apart from psychoanalytic analysis of the mother–son–father relationship, the family is interpreted as a patriarchal institution, with its division of roles and a marked emphasis on sexual difference. Horrocks identifies the main cultural stereotype sustaining the patriarchal family as the 'machismo' widespread in Western societies. However, this model often fails to account for real situations, because of greater female freedom, and also because of the increasingly frequent cases in which men do not fit the model. The portrait of masculinity that thus emerges is fragmented, constantly poised between introjected patterns of behaviour and the impossibility of performing them (Horrocks, 1994).

The idea itself of 'patriarchy', in fact, is a matter of controversy in critical studies on masculinities (see e.g. Walby, 1989 and 1990). The literature abounds with studies of patriarchy conducted from both a 'family' point of view (Eisenstein, 1981) and a 'public' one (Hernes, 1987), and numerous types of patriarchy emerge from cross-referencing the two approaches: Stacey and Davies (1983), for example, have introduced the concepts of 'private appropriation' and 'collective appropriation', while Holter (1984) has talked of 'forms of personal domination' and 'forms of structural domination'. According to Hearn (1992), however, the concept has a mainly symbolic usefulness, because it evokes the hierarchical dimensions of relationships within the family ('private patriarchies') with reference to a more general model of social relations ('public patriarchies'). It is of interest to review the theoretical debate that has given rise to this position.

Sylvia Walby (1986, 1989) has argued for the existence of six 'arenas' through which the patriarchate deploys itself: capitalist work, the family, the state, violence, sexuality and culture. Hearn (1987) flanks these with six

Table 2.1 Comparison of Walby's (1986, 1989) and Hearn's (1987) approaches to patriarchy

Walby (sites and arenas)	*Hearn (social relations and social processes)*
• Capitalist work	• Reproduction of labour power
• The family	• Procreation
• The state	• Regeneration/degeneration
• Violence	• Violence
• Sexuality	• Sexuality
• Culture	• Ideology

Source: Hearn, 1992: 237.

types of social relations and processes to produce the scheme shown in Table 2.1.

The model is interesting because it seeks to aggregate (rather than synthesize) the different forms in which patriarchy develops and is manifest in society. Note also that a third column can be added in which the nature of the arenas can be re-written once social processes and relations have been 'unmasked' (Table 2.2).

It is therefore evident that patriarchy cannot be reduced to a single dimension: like hegemonic, white and heterosexual masculinity, it is processual in its nature.

Table 2.2 Walby's (1986, 1989) and Hearn's (1987, 1992) approaches combined

Walby (sites and arenas)	*Hearn (social relations and social processes)*	*The arenas in the light of processes and social relations*
• Capitalist work	• Reproduction of labour power	• Patriarchal mode of production
• The family	• Procreation	• Patriarchal relations in paid work
• The state	• Regeneration/ degeneration	• Patriarchal state
• Violence	• Violence	• Male violence
• Sexuality	• Sexuality	• Compulsive heterosexualization
• Culture	• Ideology	• Symbolic forms of masculinity concealment

Masculinity and class: working-class and bourgeois masculinity

Relating masculinity to social class brings us inevitably to the issue of work. A preliminary point is that, in Western societies, work has always been conceived as a crucial aspect of the social life of an individual, but of a male individual, as an increasing number of authors note (Kimmel, 1987; Collinson, 1992; Harlow, Hearn and Parkin, 1995). The factory system introduced a sharp distinction between home and the workplace, and the institutionalization of the wage altered economic relationships within the family (Connell, 1995: 196):

> The expulsion of women from heavy industry was thus a key process in the formation of working-class masculinity, connected to the strategy of the family wage and drawing on the bourgeois ideology of separate spheres. The craft union movement can be seen as the key institutionalization of this kind of masculinity.

In the passage just quoted, Connell refers to 'working-class masculinity'. This is a type of masculinity that has developed in accordance with the notion of the breadwinner, but in contrast to another type of masculinity arising from class relationships: bourgeois masculinity. The latter, although it reflects the assumption of separate productive(male)/reproductive(female) spheres, from the point of view of working-class masculinity is 'unmanly' because it does not involve physical strength and is excessively polite (Morgan, 1992). This has been well documented by Linstead (1985) when he illustrates the importance of humour in organizational cultures – and in particular when he describes what happens when joking and vulgarity are taken to symbolize independence and freedom, as opposed to the more 'reserved' nature of office work. The conformism of managers and their direct dependence on a 'boss' means that they are ridiculed as 'effeminate'. An entirely similar process induces Alvesson (1998: 995) to claim that 'the more effeminate others are, the more masculine you are yourself', the reference being to the 'true masculinity' embodied by factory workers with respect to the bourgeois masculinity embodied by white-collar workers, unable to joke and banter as they work.

A study conducted in a workshop by Collinson (1988) shows how the male workers expressed their gender identity by making vulgar jokes about women (or about sex) and seeking to adhere to the breadwinner model, thereby establishing a direct parallel between 'sexually rampant' behaviour and the image of the 'responsible family breadwinner' (Collinson, 1988: 193), that is, between the power wielded by men in sexual relations and their domestic power. Moreover, humour enabled the workers to share two different forms of masculinity with which they could identify, reconciling the differing male identities that they activated in the (public) workplace and the (private) home.

Within a hierarchy of masculinities (where the lowest position is occupied by homosexual masculinity, for the reasons given above), working-class and bourgeois masculinities constitute two further elements, and thus give rise to a hegemonic, white, heterosexual, processual and sometimes conflictual masculinity.

Masculinity and myth: archetypal and heroic masculinity

Some studies have adopted a Jungian psychoanalytic approach and interpreted the male stereotype in terms of classical archetypes (Neuberger, 1990). In Jung's theory (1964), an archetype is a pattern of behaviour embedded in the collective unconscious. Like a matrix, an archetype provides the reference base for action, and in this it expresses its normative function. Depending on the time and place, some archetypes are accepted and others are rejected. However, they are ever-present and need only be activated by an event or by a person. Finally, archetypes establish only sporadic relations with corporeality in so far as they operate at a subliminal level (Jung, 1964).

Bolen (1989) interprets male behaviour according to archetypes: she attempts, that is, to show that the categories of masculinity often correspond to mythic dimensions. The base models of masculinity are associated with the Greek gods: Zeus, Poseidon or Hades symbolize the dimensions of power and emotionality of maleness, as well as men's unconscious activity. This approach is not normative, in the sense that it does not seek to show that men conform to archetypes, these being merely interpretative keys with which to depict the essential features of masculinity. Moreover, since there is an array of such archetypes, it is possible to inspect several dimensions of the manifestations of masculinities. Finally, male archetypes are not such by virtue of their association with 'men'; women, too, may be guided in their behaviour by a model of masculinities. Rather, they correspond to a symbolic order connoted by maleness.

An archetypal interpretation has frequently been applied in organization studies on leadership (Morgan, 1986; Bryman, 1992). Although these studies are concerned with issues other than those addressed by men's studies, they use archetypes which are invariably male, and they do so because of the influence exerted by hegemonic masculinity on the activity of leadership. One thus finds 'Fathers' and 'Saviours' rather than 'Heroes' or 'Sovereigns': all of which are symbolic of the rational and analytical characteristics embedded in Western archetypes of masculinities (Steyner, 1998). Hence certain aptitudes conventionally regarded as female, like intuition and moral support, are discredited, and a system 'on a male scale' is erected.

Consequently, besides being hegemonic, white, heterosexual, processual and conflictual, masculinity also displays an archetypal nature which is strongly oriented to leadership.

Masculinity and aesthetics: athletic masculinity

Mosse (1996) has examined the formation of masculinity from an aesthetic point of view, conducting a historical retrospective (with particular regard to the modern age) to investigate the main aesthetic forms employed to depict the bodies of men.

The most frequently used model is that of the 'gymnast'. Since Greek antiquity, besides being the almost exclusive prerogative of men, sports have invariably represented the most heroic model of masculinity in the physical sense. An athletic and sculpted body was the counterpoint to the intellect and symbolized the harmony manifest in behaviour that was both morally and physically correct (Mosse, 1996). Mosse's intention, therefore, is to emphasize, not the existence of a particular kind of male corporeality, but the moral imperative of physical exercise for the formation of masculinity. As the relation between gymnastics and military training grew increasingly close, male corporeality began to embody the values of virility, giving rise to the conception of the male body as at the service of a higher ideal – a process which Mosse (1996) labels the 'militarization of masculinity'. The process moved through various stages: training (in both physical discipline and moral obedience), combat and struggle (as a contest 'between men'), the development of courage and will (as the expression of ethical and virile qualities). When this approach is used, one finds numerous other historical examples of the body at the service of masculinity: suffice it to consider fascism and the aesthetic associated with it.

Nancy Theberge (1991) instead draws on Foucault to interpret the institutional organization of sport as a corpus of structured social relations, relations which assume concrete form in bodily action and are symbolized thereby. As in the case of homosexual masculinity, bodily activity is viewed as a field of relations designed to produce differently sexed bodies, where the superior physical performance of men is taken to be symbolic proof of male superiority. This approach is also used by Jim McKay (1997), although he goes a step further. On the basis of a qualitative study of sports organizations in Australia, Canada and New Zealand, and with explicit theoretical reference to Connell (1987, 1995), McKay examines the relations between hegemonic masculinity and emphasized femininity. The latter is a symbolic construct of the female which serves to maintain hegemonic masculinity. It arises in the form of compliance by women with the interests and desires of men, as well as 'spontaneous submission' to them. The relation is 'reflexive', because, if masculinity is to be effectively hegemonic, it must incorporate competitiveness in order to emphasize the inferiority of women, of homosexuals or of other forms of marginal masculinity (Messner and Sabo, 1990). Table 2.3 gives a synopsis of the effects of hegemonic masculinity in relation to the gender regime in sport (adapted from McKay, 1997: 23).

Thus masculinity is now hegemonic, white, heterosexual, conflictual, processual, archetypal, competitive and organizing specific settings for its expression.

Table 2.3 The effects of hegemonic masculinity in relation to the gender regime in sport

Work	Power	Cathexis
Purely auxiliary function of women in sports organizations. Absence or under-representation of women in administrative and managerial posts in sports organizations.	Symbolic glorification of male sports and denial of female ones. Extolling of sports based on competition and strength. Harassment and sexist humour aimed at sportswomen.	Heterosexual relations between male athletes and female cheerleaders. Intensely homophobic nature of sports subcultures.

Masculinity and organizations: managerial masculinity

Organizational studies have grown increasingly interested in gender dynamics over the years (Martin, 1990; Calàs and Smirich, 1991, 1996; Gherardi, 1995, 2003a). The reason for this is probably that organizations, as the arenas of people's everyday action, provide outstanding examples of the processes that underlie such action (Morgan, 1986).

As early as 1977, Moss Kanter detected a 'male ethic' of rationality in organizations. This ethic asserted that organizational needs could only be met by the characteristics usually associated with highly educated men: a practical approach to problems, analytical capacities, a strong orientation to leadership and an ability to ignore the emotional aspects of situations (Kanter, 1977). Following a similar line of thought, around twenty years later, Wendy Hollway (1996) deconstructed and re-read the change from scientific management to human relations as the effect of the competition and succession of different forms of masculinity, and as a specific strategy which she called 'defensive masculinity'.

The majority of studies on gender and organizations, however, concentrated on 'female' dynamics (i.e. the processes of segregation and marginalization which mainly affect women) and only recently has research been conducted on the 'male' in organizations (for a survey see Collinson and Hearn, 1996). These studies view masculinity as a rationale which drives the construction of organizational rationality. However, when a normative model of ration-ality (male, for example) comes to coincide with *the* rationality (in the sense that it is the only one possible), it may become particularly difficult to discern its features. Roy Jacques (1996: 159) uses an effective expression to focus the problem: 'semantic eclipse'.

> In a lunar eclipse, observers on Earth see a small body blocking the view of a much larger one. In a semantic eclipse, a relatively small subset of meanings comes to block sight of a broader set of potential meanings.

For instance, when a mode of rationality normative to Western culture, masculine behaviour, and the modern era is simply called rationality, the only category remaining for the reasoning of other cultures, women, and other historical periods is *ir*rationality or *non*rationality. Only a small area of the domain of rational behaviour is visible; the rest is eclipsed by it.

Masculinity is viewed as a sub-text (Benschop and Doorewaard, 1998) of a system of thought which leaves no room for alternatives. It forces pre-selection among the different ways in which a situation can be assessed and defines the possible interpretations by default. The first problem that arises when seeking to bring out the masculinity of organizations, therefore, is one of awareness. Faced with a masculinity which is often the fulcrum (but rarely the subject) of reasoning, a first direction in which to move might be 'to name men as men' (Collinson and Hearn, 1994). However banal this line of thought may seem, following it brings us to the heart of the problem. Economics and social sciences have always used 'Man' as an abstract concept to denote one gender as much as the other. Yet the symbols employed have constructed a social actor who obeys rationality rather than emotionality, who behaves selfishly rather than cooperatively and who is oriented to the public rather than to the private (Mumby and Putnam, 1992; Gherardi, 1995; Morgan, 1992), thereby rendering masculinity 'invisible'.

On examining a sample of thirty Dutch organizations that had published end-of-year financial reports, Benschop and Meihuizen (2002) have discovered what they call 'presumed gender innocence'. The representation of themselves in terms of Male/Female offered by these companies is largely neutral. Yet careful statistical analysis shows that pictures and images of 'productive' settings, or those of top management, almost invariably comprise a male presence (usually wearing a grey suit and with a 'managerial attitude', the authors note sardonically). Female figures, insofar as there are any, are depicted as supporting figures (if represented together with men) and often in non-work settings (especially in the company of other women), so that they represent a sort of 'counterpoint' to the professional lives of the men.

Cross-referencing managerial practices with the theme of masculinity yields an interpretation of the latter 'as an effect of the interplay of sexual power relations within and between particular practices, rather than an existing *a priori* to those relations and practices in which it is continually reconstituted' (Kerfoot and Knights, 1993: 663). This means, as Brewis and Linstead (2000) point out, not only that masculinity is socially constructed in specific settings, but that it is constantly shifting and emergent, thereby reflecting its inter-textual nature. Masculinities are multiple, and they constantly compete to establish forms and practices, as if they were managers competing to define and gain approval for a corporate strategy. 'A man is not a man without a plan', as Big Boy Caprice in the film *Dick Tracy* puts it, and as Kerfoot and

Knights (1996: 82) ironically declare in order to stress the attraction of modern management to strategic discourse, and how male identity is also something that must be achieved.

Given that masculinity is protean and, like other organizational processes, constantly negotiated, one must know how to recognize its essential features without being distracted by its variety. According to Collinson and Hearn (1994, 1996), there are five rhetorics that covertly support the construction of masculinity in organizations:[3]

1 *Authoritarianism*. Herein resides the aggressive side of masculinity with its intolerance of differences and its endeavour to establish hierarchical relations. Roy Jacques (1997) interprets authoritarianism along the dimensions of domination (as an expression of conformity with a socially accepted model) and marginality (as deviance from that model). The dimension of authoritarianism intersects with gender relations, giving rise to a series of devaluation strategies directed at the female. Likewise, Patricia Yancey Martin (1996), in an ethnographic study, detects a gender-bias with regard to the legitimate exercise of authority: women's work is subjected to a gender 'lens' which often produces a priori judgements.

2 *Paternalism*. This rhetoric extols the importance of trust in personal relations and the worker's 'need' to identify with the company. This type of discourse lies on a continuum of relations centred on the 'law of the father'. Maddock and Parkin (1993) use the term 'Gentlemen's Club' to describe the 'courtesy' with which a typically male mentality is able to entrench itself in hegemonic positions with respect to the female by virtue of the principle of the 'common good'. Paternalism finds legitimacy especially in the protection of the 'weaker' (women, but also other men) against the 'harsh reality' of organizational decisions (Kerfoot and Knights, 1993).

3 *Entrepreneurship*. This symbolic construct concerns the 'conquest of new markets and new territories', so that masculinity is a competitive process which tends to exclude whoever is not 'man' enough to be a 'predator'.

4 *Informality*. The territory of action in this case is the informal relation-ships constructed by men in the workplace, usually around humour, sport and talk about sex. Masculinity is reinforced by a simultaneous sense of unity and differentiation among the men in an organization. Numerous studies have concluded that humour is a device to wield power and to change organizational realities (Dwyer, 1992). Di Tomaso (1989) has highlighted humour's function in excluding and sexually insulting women, while Linstead (1985) and Collinson (1988) have concentrated on the importance of deploying a 'sense of humour' in workplaces in order to join a cohesive group with a specific identity antagonistic to other forms of masculinity.

5   *Careerism.* Like entrepreneurship, this rhetoric relates to the semantic field of competition, but with explicit reference to class dynamics. Success at work is pursued to ensure the economic well-being of the family and to consolidate the figure of the 'head of household', both at home and at work. Fletcher (1998) has conducted an ethnographic study of competitive mechanisms within organizations, showing that, when the value of activities considered to be typically female is acknowledged, those activities are reinterpreted in male terms in order to impede the advancement of those who do not share the values-system on which masculinity is based. More in general, Mumby and Putnam (1992: 474) counterpose the imperative of a success-oriented rationality with the notion of a 'bounded emotionality': 'an alternative mode of organizing in which nurturance, caring, community, supportiveness and interrelatedness are fused with individual responsibility to shape organizational experiences'.

Managerial masculinity is thus an organizational resource to be activated and 'mobilized' (Martin, 1996, 2001) in everyday working life in order to demonstrate one's competence (and assent) with regard to both the contents of managements (for example, the number of men and women present in them and on what conditions) and to their forms (organizational processes, hierarchies, strategies and practices of managements) (Collinson and Hearn, 1996).

Hegemonic, white, heterosexual, conflictual, processual, archetypal, competitive and organizing masculinity is enacted through situated practices which embody gender performances.

Masculinity and the market: entrepreneurial masculinity

Hegemonic masculinity, argues Connell (1995), is also embodied in the figure of the entrepreneur. The reference, however, is not to the Schumpeterian 'innovator', but to the Spanish 'conquistadores' and the 'frontiersmen' of the West. The creation of overseas empires was an entrepreneurial activity in every effect, with the opening of new markets and the start-up of new productive activities (Mendelssohn, 1976), and it was a sexually connoted enterprise. The first Europeans to land in the New World were 'lone' men (soldiers and traders), and if they were followed by women these were always wives or servants. The conquistadores, the synthesis of two occupations pursued by segregated men (the professions of soldier and the maritime trader), were perhaps the first examples of the modern male model (Connell, 1995). Also modern economic rhetoric, for that matter, often described entrepreneurship as an activity geared to the 'discovery of new lands' and undertaken by (male) 'explorers' (Czarniawska-Joerges and Wolff, 1991; Bull and Willard, 1993; Pitt, 1998).

Whilst it can be argued that economic theory has still not furnished a thoroughgoing definition of entrepreneurial activity (Low and MacMillan, 1988; Bull and Willard, 1993), one may nevertheless note that what we know about entrepreneurship derives mainly from the early and classic studies of the twentieth century (Ogbor, 2000): Knight's theory of risk (1921), Schumpeterian theories (Schumpeter, 1934), the theories on 'enterprise creation' of Cole (1959) and Collins and Moore (1964). According to these authors, the distinctive feature of entrepreneurial activity is a capacity for innovation. This, however, is regarded as being essentially a quality intrinsic to persons, rather than simultaneously a set of practices, so that even in the writings of so fine a theoretician as Schumpeter one finds descriptions of the entrepreneur as someone endowed with 'super-normal qualities of intellect and will' (Schumpeter, 1934: 82). Other theoreticians have been even more explicit in espousing a Darwinian and heroic model of entrepreneurship, asserting that:

> However we may personally feel about the entrepreneur, he emerges as essentially more masculine than feminine, more heroic than cowardly. [. . .] His values and activities have become part of the character of America and intimately related to our ideas of personal freedom, success, above all, individualism.
>
> (Collins and Moore, 1964: 5–6)

While this kind of rhetoric has on the one hand attracted much criticism as a discourse constructed by mingling gender themes with American folk-lore and Western ethnocentrism (Butler, 1991; Calvert and Ramsey, 1992; Ogbor, 2000), on the other it has served as a legitimating discourse for all those theories that have assumed the psychological/individual characteristics of the entrepreneur as sufficient elements for a theory of entrepreneurship (see e.g. Baumol, 1993). In this regard, Valérie Fournier and Christopher Grey (1999) conduct a detailed critique of du Gay, the contemporary author most frequently cited by socio-economic studies of entrepreneurship (see e.g. Alvesson and Willmott, 1996; Clarke and Newman, 1997; Grint, 1997). Expressions like 'The character of the entrepreneur can no longer be seen as just one among a plurality of ethical personalities, *but must rather be seen as assuming an ontological priority*' (du Gay, 1996: 181, emphasis in the original) are cited by authors as attempts to 'institutionalize' entrepreneurial characteristics and practices. The assumption underlying such assertions is that individuals have a natural tendency to be competitive, as well as the (physical) ability to work constantly and be geographically mobile (Fournier and Grey, 1999). It is a discursive practice which tends to marginalize those men who do not fit the construct, or those (historically women) who are unable to take part because they are engaged in domestic activities. Taken for granted is a sharp distinction between home and work, with value set on the unique and rational nature of work, while the emotional component necessary to manage interpersonal relations is ignored (Martin, 1990).

Rosslyn Reed (1996) and Kate Mulholland (1996) interweave the theme of entrepreneurship with that of patriarchy. Considering the latter along the two dimensions of private patriarchy and public patriarchy (Hearn, 1992), they see it as an extension of male power from the domestic sphere to the productive one. They argue that capitalist production relations and those internal to the family have reinforced each other by virtue of the control exerted over sexuality and female work. Although men do not constitute a homogeneous class (as repeatedly emphasized), they always have a 'class' interest (in marxist terms) in maintaining power over women. The entrepreneurial literature has never concerned itself with exploration of the power relations comprised in economic structures, instead establishing an automatic relation between the qualities of an entrepreneur (leadership, risk-taking, rational planning) and a model of male rationality (Mulholland, 1996).

However, the construction of entrepreneurship as a form of masculinity has not worked simply through male bodies. It has also and especially come about through the images and representations associated with masculinities, some of them more aggressive and geared to personal profit, others more altruistic and intended to ensure the economic well-being of one's family (Reed, 1996). In the economic rhetorics that have accompanied it, entrepreneurship has been frequently associated (according to the historical period) with the dimensions of leadership and management. The 'entrepreneur' (he who discovers new worlds), the 'leader' (he who exerts control) and the 'manager' (he who imposes the order of rational management) are thus interpreted as archetypal figures with which to find one's bearings in the everyday activity of organizations, and as symbolic expressions of the fears and hopes of performance by the firm (Czarniawska-Joerges and Wolff, 1991).

Hegemonic, white, heterosexual, conflictual, processual, archetypal, competitive and organizing masculinity enacted through situated practices thus also reveals its entrepreneurial attitude.

Conclusions

In this chapter we have delineated the theoretical framework for an approach to gender as a social practice, particularly concentrating on entrepreneurship as a form of masculinity.

We reviewed the issues and positions distinctive of the theoretical debate, defining gender as a performance situated at the point where bodies, discourse and practices intersect. More specifically, we sought to show that the original question as to what gender 'is' has shifted towards what gender 'does', and therefore towards how gender practices are performed. To this end, we compared and contrasted the suggestions of different traditions of research (poststructuralist studies, symbolic interactionism, Italian feminist debate of the 1970s, as well as actor-network theory) which share an interpretation of social practices (interactive and discursive) as acts of 'performativity'. In this way it was possible to propose an analysis of gender relations as an unstable product, situationally enacted, which arranges human and non-human elements into a stable artefact.

We then concentrated on the findings of studies on men and masculinities, the purpose being to show, first of all, how a shift has taken place in the literature from masculinity viewed as an 'essential property' to masculinity as a 'critical issue'. In naming the hegemonic masculinity as an object of practice, while conducting analysis of its ethnic, sexual, institutional, social, archetypal, aesthetic, organizational and economic dimensions, we have contextualized the male practices underlying the processes which give shape to different spheres of activity. Having affirmed gender as a symbolic and relational category, and having dispensed with a view of the female as defined by default from the male, the main contribution of the critical studies reviewed, we submit, is their stress on the fact that masculinity is a standpoint claiming a monopoly on 'objectivity', and that also within masculinity there are a plurality of voices.

The organization of our argument in the form of a spiral has enabled us to highlight various rhetorics, practices and metaphors – sometimes competing and in conflict – in different social contexts and settings of everyday action. The feature shared by the various masculinities discussed is their dynamic and processual construction through situated practices which establish a dialectical and reflexive relation between the symbolic gender order and the gender performances activated by (and in) specific situations. The purpose has been to give visibility to various discursive and interactive practices that construct entrepreneurship as a form of masculinity, thereby marking out (at least from a theoretical and institutional point of view) the parameters and forms of entrepreneurial action.

Now that we have explained the notions that we share or dispute with current theory on the male, the female and entrepreneurship, in the next chapter we shall describe our methodological framework to study gender and entrepreneurship as intertwined practices. That is to say, we shall set out the methodology and research design used to conduct ethnographic analysis of gender as an entrepreneurial practice, and of entrepreneurship as a gendered practice.

3 Doing and saying gender
A methodological framework

In this chapter we present our methodology and our research design for a gender approach to entrepreneurship.

Having set out a conceptual genealogy which enables us to think of gender as a situated performance, we shall now provide the reader with a map on the methodological side which evinces the elements that inspired and shaped our empirical analysis. It should be immediately pointed out that an ethnography of gender as an entrepreneurial practice and of entrepreneurship as a gender practice (or in other words a 'thick description' of the processes that position people as 'men' and 'women' within business practices and as 'entrepreneurs' within gender practices) is an approach still little used in the literature. Inquiries similar to ours are the works by Kondo (1990), who examines the relations that construct people as males and females in a Japanese confectionery factory, and by Fletcher (1999), who studies the processes of subject positioning by six engineers (as 'women' and 'engineers') in a predominantly male organization; but these studies resemble ours more in their 'style' than by virtue of any deliberate methodological choice.

We would also point out that ours is a reconstruction which, in a certain sense, has come about a posteriori. We were not entirely aware of 'where' some of our methodological choices would lead us. Only when conducting our ethnographic fieldwork, when we found ourselves catapulted into unforeseen situations, were we able to bring the meaning or direction of certain of our intuitions into focus. To quote Becker (1994), in research as in life, plans and surprises are inextricably linked, and following casuality can be a research rationale.

A posteriori, therefore, there are three elements necessary to reconstruct our methodological bricolage: two 'classic' studies in the area of symbolic interactionism and ethnomethodology, the debate within post-colonial anthropology in relation to postmodernism, and the concept of 'reflexivity'.

Reflexive ethnography: from the 'red notebook' to the 'toolbox'

Studying gender as performance calls to mind, from a methodological point of view, two studies – 'Agnes' (Garfinkel, 1967) and 'Gender Display' by Goffman (1976) – which are widely cited in the literature on 'doing gender' (Kessler and McKenna, 1978; West and Zimmerman, 1987; Butler, 1990; Gherardi, 1995). Justifiably called 'classics', these studies have exerted an influence on our analysis that should be clarified.

Garfinkel's ethnomethodological study of 'Agnes' (1967) dwelt on the case of a young man who decided to change sex and be recognized as a woman with all the attributes of femaleness, an 'authentic exemplar'. The final section of the chapter is entitled 'Agnes, the doer of the accountable person' (Garfinkel, 1967: 181–5). The interest of this case for Garfinkel is explicit: having chosen to live as a woman although brought up as a boy with a penis (which she had replaced with a vagina) but also with a female body, Agnes was obliged to display the cultural elements of a 'normal' woman in her day-to-day activities, interactions and behaviour. She had to construct her womanhood as a constant concrete accomplishment ordered from within and perfectly suited to circumstances and occasions. The way in which Agnes believed that she 'managed' her sex change revealed to herself and Garfinkel the methods, procedures and operations by which normal sexuality is produced and recognized in everyday life, in behaviour, in conversation and in every type of interaction. This is because manhood and womanhood, as 'natural facts of life', are socially constructed entities, concrete accomplishments in the details of quotidian life, effects to observe, measure and interpret, but also ordinary translations of self into a reality that is grasped and recognized without need for close attention. Agnes thought that she realized the accountability of her womanhood by ensuring that the attributes of normal sexuality were recognizable and readable in her behaviour: that is to say, by behaving according to those attributes in the concrete circumstances of her everyday social life which identified her as an 'authentic exemplar'. What separated Agnes from 'normal' people was that she could not achieve this accountability automatically, without having to think about it. From this point of view, her womanhood was a project realized in collaboration with others, a process of construction and recognition of an image of naturalness. In other words, Agnes had constantly to ensure that her mode of presenting herself did not raise suspicions as to her femaleness and as to the presumed correspondence between appearance and reality, lest she not be recognized as an 'authentic exemplar'.

Recognition of others as representatives of a gender category is therefore based on certain social skills, and these same skills are deployed when we present ourselves to others. The roots of this interpretation lie in Goffman's (1959) analysis of the 'presentation of self in everyday life', which was subsequently developed further in his work on 'gender display'. Goffman

(1976) uses the latter expression to highlight the character of gender as a performance reiterated in accordance with the behaviours, appearances, mannerisms and other contextual factors that we have learnt to associate with the members of a particular gender. We know how to read and interpret gender according to preordained scripts, and failure to respect their canons is a breach of the 'obvious' which appears to others as a deliberate (and therefore somehow socially sanctionable) error in interaction. Whenever we meet a person, we engage in gender attribution; and for a social relation to be successful, it is therefore necessary that all participants should represent, monitor and interpret their own and others' gender displays.

Underscored by both these studies is the fact that gender is a social quality, not a biological attribute, and that it is to be looked for in everyday interactions, read in relation to broader symbolic-cultural domains, and considered as the outcome of mediation and representation work in these various domains. From a methodological point of view, however, we are told very little about how the observations of these studies were structured, about how the researcher behaved, about what alternative interpretations were possible and about the ambiguity inherent in every social interaction. In particular, the notion of gender as 'display' closely matches the more general metaphor of 'theatre' used by Goffman (1959) to interpret everyday life, but in this sense it conveys an image which automatically ties gender to outward appearance. Is it therefore sufficient (as in a theatrical performance) for an individual to appear and to behave as a member of a particular gender for other participants in the interaction to recognize his/her membership straightforwardly? And what if gender competence instead resides in the 'unexpressed', rather than in the display? This seems to be Garfinkel's (1967) position when he identifies Agnes's main problem as her inability to ensure the accountability of her womanhood automatically, so that she had constantly to pay attention to her everyday performances. But in this case, too, why devote so much effort to finding an 'authentic exemplar'? Other scholars today could easily argue that Agnes's authenticity resided precisely in her 'queerness' (Lorber, 1994). Yet others, as we saw in the previous section, might stand the question on its head and argue that identity is the effect of a network of relations which give material form and stability to an artefact (Law, 1994), and that gender is therefore not a substance but an enactment performed into being as heterogeneous practices are engineered into an action net which produces subjectivity and objectivity together (Gomart and Hennion, 1999).

In other words, without wishing to belittle the importance of Goffman and Garfinkel, we would claim that they were heirs to a system of thought that interpreted persons in their 'authenticity', which granted the researcher a privileged vantage point of observation and signification, and which looked for constants that regulated social action. These claims are prompted by studies and ideas arising from debate in two other areas: one more strictly methodological (ethnographic research in anthropology),[1] the other philosophical-epistemological in character (postmodernism). It is to these, therefore, that we shall now turn our attention.

Prologue: realist ethnography and the 'red notebook'

Ethnographic research originated at the beginning of the last century in cultural anthropology and its observation of 'other' peoples and cultures. The first ethnographers were researchers appointed by governments and universities to study the 'natives' of the colonized countries (in America, India and Africa). The distinctive features of ethnography were therefore the observation of persons in their 'territory', and the sharing by the researcher of the entire social environment to which these persons belonged. That the focus of analysis was culture is indicated by the term 'ethnography' itself, which denotes the practice of writing (Latin – *grafia*) about culture (Greek – *ethnos*). However, the first ethnographic studies started from a functional idea of culture as a 'system of integration', and they were influenced by a Eurocentrism which defined itself as 'normal' and accordingly investigated the 'abnormality' of other cultures (Malinowski, 1922; Radin, 1927). It was these studies that more than fifty years later came to be called 'realist ethnographies' (Marcus and Cushman, 1982; Van Maanen, 1988) and whose purpose was the objective and holistic description of the culture of a social group. On the basis of the literature, it is now possible to summarize the construction of a realist ethnography in terms of three main rhetorical-textual features (Clifford and Marcus, 1986; Van Maanen, 1988, 1995; Atkinson, 1990):

1   Priority is given to the ethnographer/author's point of view. Realist ethnographies typically begin with an account of the scholar's arrival in the place where the research is to be conducted. They go on to describe his/her first contacts with the population (often hostile or suspicious) and then the researcher's bewilderment amid a thousand obstacles, which, however, are soon overcome by his/her determination to accomplish his/her 'knowledge mission'. This type of introductory account serves to certify the otherness of the culture observed, to highlight the heroism of the ethnographer and to mythicize the information acquired.

2   The narrating voice is impersonal. After the introductory preamble, the author disappears from the account, his place being taken by a third-person narrating voice and by the actions and statements of the 'natives'. The reader is thus reassured that the research has not been influenced by personal idiosyncrasies, nor by any particular situation, event or 'personage'. Everything recounted by the author is absolutely typical, and a surfeit of minutiae is intended to vouch for the ethnographer's effective presence and the truthfulness of his/her account.

3   The main sensory faculty used is sight. In realist ethnographies numerous events are 'true' because they have been 'seen' by the researcher. Whereas

taste or touch require first-person participation and involvement, sight introduces distance and guarantees objectivity. A speech act may assume different meanings according to the context and therefore requires interpretation, but a visual representation fixes its own margins (spatial and temporal) and thus in a certain sense speaks for itself.

The literature furnishes numerous examples and criticisms of 'realist ethnographies': from the works of Malinowski and Radcliffe-Brown (Marcus and Cushman, 1982) to Whyte's *Street Corner Society* (Atkinson, 1990), to the cockfights described by Geertz (Crapanzano, 1986). However, given that these studies are by now almost obligatory references, we prefer to offer to the reader something more evocative, so as to outline a practical example of the rationale of a realist ethnography.

The *New York Trilogy* by the screenwriter and novelist Paul Auster (1986) contains three spy-stories. In the first of them (*City of Glass*) a detective is hired to keep constant watch on a man: he must covertly follow his every movement through the city and work out the reasons for his actions. The detective keeps close to the man, who never realizes that he is being tailed; he notes the man's wanderings down in a red notebook but is unable to fathom the motives for them. The detective becomes so obsessed that he encamps among the trash cans in front of the house of the man he is stalking, who now begins to spend most of his time at home. The detective tries to reduce the amount of time he spends eating and sleeping to the minimum. He loses all track of time, he lives for months in the street, among the trash cans, waiting for the man to come out of his house. He notes everything he sees in his red notebook. After some time, the pages are about to run out, and the detective is forced (against his will) to leave his post and go to a shop and buy a new one. He takes the opportunity to ring his superiors, who are surprised to hear from him, because the case has been closed for weeks, ever since the man committed suicide by jumping off a bridge. The detective is dismayed: he's seen nothing of the suicide, and his red notebook (which by now is his only contact with reality) says nothing about it. The last sentence in it runs: 'What will happen when there are no more pages in the red notebook?'

The story therefore evokes a model of scientific inquiry based on the conviction that objectivity resides in the detached observation of reality and in its slavish description. It is thought that the data 'speak for themselves' (Van Maanen, 1979), that the researcher is a neutral medium and consequently that his/her fieldnotes exactly reflect events in the world. What is more, these notes certify the existence itself of the real, so that it is as if the latter ceases to exist in their absence.

Post-colonialist ethnography: an obligatory phase

The purpose of this long prologue has been to clarify why, when selecting our methodology, we preferred not to take the classic anthropological studies and the objectivity of a red notebook as our point of departure. Other times, settings and artefacts inspire our inquiry. Our story begins in 1982 with publication of Marcus and Cushman's article 'Ethnographies as Texts' which inaugurated the so-called 'linguistic turn' in ethnographic studies. Our story also finds a setting (two years later) in the School of American Research of Santa Fe (New Mexico), where in 1982 a seminar was attended by all the anthropologists (Clifford, Marcus, Fisher, Crapanzano, Rabinow) who later became the protagonists of post-colonialist anthropology. And our story (again two years later) is embodied in an artefact, *Writing Culture*, a book edited by Clifford and Marcus (1986), which has become the obligatory reference for anyone interested in the production of pluralist, polyphonous ethnographies which give text and language primary importance in construction of a 'scientific fact'.

The point of departure for this new programme of research is stated clearly from the incipit onwards of the article that, twenty years after its publication, can be considered the 'manifesto' of post-colonialist anthropology:

> Anthropologists have finally begun to give explicit attention to the writing of ethnographic texts, a subject long ignored either by conceiving of ethnography primarily as an activity that occurs in the field or by treating it as a method, rather than product, of research.
>
> (Marcus and Cushman, 1982: 25)

The implications of a conceptual recasting of anthropology from a method of research to the product of meaning-attributions are manifold, and they concern essentially three aspects: the researcher, text production, and the question of method as a 'toolbox'. Although it is not our concern to dwell on the debate among anthropologists on these issues, we must at least briefly explain how they have importance for (and are used in) our analysis.

We have seen that in realist ethnographies the researcher/author occupies a 'one-up' position which authorizes him/her to assume a privileged point of view masked as an 'objective' narrative. However, in orienting him/herself amid the dynamics observed, the researcher occupies an explicitly important role; and however much some authors may have argued that they should be entirely 'extraneous' to the reality studied (Dalton, 1959; Roy, 1959), with the development of methodology it has grown increasingly clear that the data presented in an ethnography are influenced by the (subjective) perspective of the researcher and by the rhetorical style adopted during the stage of writing up the data (Marcus and Cushman, 1982; Clifford, 1983; Rosaldo, 1986). It is largely agreed in the literature (Clifford, 1988; Marcus and Fischer, 1986) and by studies on the methodology of social research (see e.g. the

Handbook of Qualitative Research edited by Bryman and Burgess in 1999) that ethnographic writing is always interrelated with:

- the *context* to which it refers and which it artificially (re)creates;
- the *rhetoric* and *institutions* that tie (or oppose) it to specific disciplines or social domains;
- the *gender* of the researcher and the meaning attributed to gender relations in the context studied;
- the *politics* that authorize (or otherwise) particular cultural realities to be represented;
- the *conventions* and *constraints* that govern every historico-social representation.

Thus, while Agar (1980) describes the role of the researcher as that of a 'professional stranger' (an 'outsider' able to attain a more extensive vision of phenomena than that possessed by the 'natives'), the post-colonialist debate problematizes both the concept of 'extraneousness' (i.e. the extent to which it is possible to call oneself 'external' to increasingly global and cross-contaminating contexts) and that of 'culture' (i.e. the extent to which it makes sense to think of a cultural reality in monolithic and homogeneous terms) (Rosen, 1991). As a provisional response to these doubts, numerous scholars have espoused a more narrative, almost autobiographical, approach, thereby inaugurating what is benevolently called the tradition of the 'ethnographic memoir' (Tedlock, 1991), or more sarcastically of the 'confessional tale' (Van Maanen, 1988). In anthropology, works of this kind date back to Casagrande (1960) and thereafter to the writings of Rabinow (1977) and Barley (1983). In organization studies, outstanding examples are the methodological-confessional appendix of Kunda (1992) and Van Maanen (1988). The feature shared by these works is the endeavour of the researchers to emphasize the 'fictitious' nature of ethnography, placing themselves within ethnographic texts as active and 'human' participants, frequently committing gaffes and emphasizing the interruptions and unexpected events that characterized their fieldwork. The objective observations of realist ethnographies have given way to more personal and private considerations of equivocal meaning which lay no claim to absolute validity. The figure of the author is clearly apparent and acts as one of the voices that give shape to the account. Yet, however much this intrusion of the ethnographer into the text may mark a radical break with realist ethnography, there is still a continuity with the latter whereby 'realist tales' and 'confessional tales' are different in form but similar in content (Van Maanen and Kolb, 1985; Prasad, 1998). In both, in fact, the ultimate representation conveyed to the reader seeks to be, if not 'objective', at least 'unbiased'. Whereas in realist ethnographies the reality recounted is 'true' in that it is 'certified' by the researcher's methodology and cool detachment, in the case of ethnographic memoirs the truthfulness of the account is attested by the presence of the 'natives', by their confirmation or denial of the ethnographer's impressions and by the fact that they are 'authentic exemplars' of a cultural context. However, as Czarniawska and Joerges (1995) point out with reference to Rorty (1982), the relevance attributed to the 'actors' depends not on the fact that they know more than anyone else about the context but simply on the realization that they are humans like us. Is this specification superfluous? We do not think so. Indeed, discussion of it will enable us to recover the idea of method as a 'toolbox', to shift the discussion to epistemological matters and re-contextualize it in sociological and organizational terms.

The 'toolbox': postmodernism and reflexivity

When Clifford and Marcus (1986) proposed that ethnographic methodology should be conceived as a 'toolbox', they were making explicit reference to the term as used in the thought of Gilles Deleuze and Michel Foucault. In the work of the latter in particular, the metaphor of the 'toolbox' is used to signify that research is not a system, but rather a tool, a *logic*, an observational lens for inquiry that may develop step by step on the basis of critical reflection on given situations (Foucault, 1972, 1980). In the hands of post-colonialist anthropologists, ethnography is the product of different meaning-attributions to the extent that every ethnographic account weaves together the different views, voices, actions and rhetorics that combine to yield a plausible definition of 'reality' (Marcus and Cushman, 1982). The result of the observation is a polyphonous and cooperative text where the focus of attention is on the ongoing interactive processes:

> A postmodern ethnography is a cooperatively evolved text consisting of fragments of discourse intended to evoke in the minds of both reader and writer an emergent fantasy of a possible world of common sense reality [. . .] It is, in a word, poetry.
>
> (Tyler, 1986: 125)

The emphasis intrinsic in language, the centrality of chance and indeterminacy as fruitful dimensions of social life, the idea of the researcher as a *bricoleur*,[2] the search for a theory which eschews metanarratives and instead constructs itself as a perspective, and the reflexivity inherent in analysis of this kind, these have induced Peter K. Manning (1992, 1995) to trace a linking theme from post-colonialist ethnography to postmodernism to symbolic interactionism in sociology. According to Manning (1992), the meaning of the work undertaken by the post-colonialist anthropologist should be interpreted and contextualized in parallel with and in relation to these two debates. Otherwise it will remain suspended amid fragmented experiences and what anthropologists themselves have not been able to define any more succinctly than 'experimental ethnography' (Marcus and Cushman, 1982; Clifford and Marcus, 1986; Marcus and Fischer, 1986).

According to Manning (1992: 204), there are three issues that epitomize the influence of postmodernism (Lyotard, 1979; Eco, 1986; Baudrillard, 1988) on ethnographic analysis:

- the idea of fluidity – postmodern societies display vast and rapid changes in temporal/spatial relations;
- the idea of reflexivity – images, language and actions are mutually linked and the actor's actions affect and are part of social action;
- the idea of hyperreality – as something that dances with 'reality', produces and consumes signifiers, but lacks precise and easily identified referential functions that serve to fulfil the sign.

It is in relation to these three issues, writes Manning (1992, 1995), that the adjective 'experimental' should be interpreted. Post-colonial ethnographies are an 'exercise in style'[3] (Queneau, 1947): they experiment with rhetorics and literary genres; they play with events by demolishing spatial/temporal categories; they thematize the boundaries that separate (or counterpose) reality and fiction as historical, political and cultural categories; they try to do away with any distinction between observed reality and observer; and they seek to open new spaces of signification in which to contextualize the action of the various participants in the ethnographic *bricolage* (actors, material objects, institutional discourses, and so on). Thus made explicit is the main difference between postmodernism and symbolic interactionism, and therefore between postmodern ethnography and interactionist or classic anthropology. However much postmodernism and symbolic interactionism may share a substantial 'anti-theoretical' stance, together with an interest in the symbolic production of the real and in the processes by which order is negotiated, the focus of the postmodern debate is not on individuals but on the relations which enable them to accomplish the 'position' of 'subject' (Manning, 1995). To paraphrase Foucault (1980) on power, or numerous poststructuralist scholars on gender (Butler, 1990; Calàs and Smircich, 1996), or Law (1994) and Latour (1999) on actor-network theory, from a postmodern standpoint 'being-an-actor', recognizing intentionality in action, being identified as the 'origin' of an occurrence, is not an 'essence' or something that people acquire once and for all; rather, it is a transitive (and transitory) property, ever contingent and precarious, which is located in certain individuals by collective action, more than by individual will. Manning writes (1992: 211):

> The self, as located in an individual who speaks and writes, and who is the 'author' of thoughts and feelings, is secondary to the system within which meanings lie, the codes used, and the voices available from which to speak or write. In some respects the self vanishes.

Manning uses Tyler's (1986) terminology to talk about 'post-modern ethnography'. Research of this kind is called *narrative ethnography* by

Tedlock (1991) and Hammersley and Atkinson (1995), and *critical ethnography* by Van Maanen (1995), while in Italy it is usually referred to as *reflexive ethnography* (Gobo, 1993; Colombo, 1998; Marzano, 1999; Navarini, 2001). Notwithstanding the evident links of these ethnographies with postmodernism, with critical theory (marxism, feminism and the Frankfurt school) and with the linguistic turn in philosophy (Quine, 1960; Ricoeur, 1973; Rorty, 1982), we believe that the term 'reflexive ethnography' best captures the promulgatory force and innovativeness of these studies. Rather than express an intellectual debt to the past or to other disciplines, the term underscores an aspect, reflexivity, which testifies to the 'reflexive turn' that occurred in sociology during the 1990s (Woolgar, 1988; Beck, Giddens and Lash, 1994) and highlights the relationship between organizational studies inspired by a postmodern sensibility (Martin, 1992; Hassard and Parker, 1993; Clegg and Hardy, 1997), feminist theory (Gherardi, 2003a) and ethnographic debate.

In organizational activity, knowing and doing interweave in practical action and common-sense decision-making. The interactive and discursive practices that constitute organizational action at the same time construct organized action, both because 'the essential reflexivity of accounts' (Garfinkel, 1967) is used to create a sense of order in action, and because it reflexively creates the context of action. It is thus essential for those who study organizing processes to use methodologies that constantly interrogate the intellectual assumptions of their research and their reality (Hassard, 1990; Parker, 2001) lest they fall into the trap of 'cultural blindness' (Alvesson, 1993): that is, the inability to focus on certain concepts and organizational practices because they are common to different organizational realities, including that of the researcher. An ethnographer conducting organizational research is engaged in a symmetrical reflective exercise (Linstead, 1993) and seems to share the same distinctive features that Turner (1992) discerned in a 'symbolist researcher':

- S/he is a qualitative researcher who prefers to see things through the eyes of the subject. S/he is interested in meanings, in the process of their attribution, in how they are sustained, in how some meanings prevail while others disappear.
- S/he is a participative researcher, who knows that s/he is part of the production of meaning and of the narration of stories, as both the narrating and the narrated subject.
- S/he is the product of contextual understanding of actions and symbols, not only because they are inseparable but because all symbols are value-laden and meaningful only in terms of their relationship to other symbols.
- S/he is a wanderer among the realms of knowledge who seeks to reconstruct the links among the various levels of reality created by a symbol through individual symbolic production, the collective unconscious and

artistic production: the immanent with the transcendent, the mental with the physical, with action, with transformation.

We would stress, however, that 'reflexivity' is a much-contested term, with meanings that differ according to the discipline concerned (Woolgar, 1988; Alvesson and Skoldberg, 2000; Lynch, 2000), and describing its evolution would require construction of another genealogy. More modestly, we prefer to use two images borrowed from narrative literature to explicate the main dimensions (and 'collateral effects') of our 'reflexive ethnography'.

The first image is provided by Alberto Melucci (1998) who uses the game of croquet played by Alice in Lewis Carroll's *Alice in Wonderland* as an extremely apt analogy to illustrate the concept of 'reflexivity' in the social sciences and to advocate its use in ethnography. Alice's croquet game took place on an 'animated' court (the balls were porcupines, the mallets were flamingos and the hoops were soldiers bent double) with which she interacted. Research fields are equally animated, and the researcher is only 'one-*among*-actors'. We use this expression to denote a twofold process whereby the researcher is directly involved in the reality observed while his or her image as 'privileged observer' is re-located in contexts of action and takes part in the production of meanings: the 'natives' participate and involve the observer in their everyday lives.

The second image is furnished by *Ghosts*, the second spy-story in the *New York Trilogy* (Auster, 1986). Here Paul Auster tells the story of a detective (Mr Blue) who has been hired (by Mr White) to observe the movements of a third person (Mr Black). Blue rents an apartment from whose window he can watch Black, and the first days are tedious: Blue watches Black and nothing of significance happens; White has not told Blue what is supposed to happen, or why he has to watch Black, and this makes Blue even more curious as to Black's behaviour. The weeks pass and Black writes, reads, eats and takes short walks, seemingly unaware of Blue's presence. Blue thinks that Black is waiting for the right moment to 'do something'. He also realizes that he has a long wait ahead of him, given the complete normality of Black's life. After weeks of waiting in which Black continues to spend most of his time in his apartment, Blue is utterly bored. He decides to disguise himself as a tramp and sit on the sidewalk along which Blue goes every day to the shops: his plan is to get to know Blue and thus find out more about the man. The disguise works perfectly. Blue stops Black in the street, and with the excuse of asking him for a hand-out manages to hold a brief but cordial conversation with him. And yet Blue fails to discover anything about Black, since it is he who does most of the talking. The next day Blue returns to his post, still disguised as a tramp, and waits for Black. When Black duly arrives, the brief exchange of the previous day gives Blue the pretext to stop him again and seek to glean some information about what he does. The two talk, but Black is extremely vague in what he says, and Blue is left still mystified about the man's life. The meetings continue for an entire week. Blue notices that Black is increasingly preoccupied and suspects that he is plotting something. During the last of the meetings Blue openly asks Black why he is so agitated, and Black explains. He is a private investigator and he has been hired to tail a man. But this man (says Black) never does anything except sit in a room, eat, drink, make telephone calls and go for short walks. Blue is shaken by the meeting: he has been hired to watch a man who in turn has been hired to watch someone else . . . and if this someone else was being watched by someone else? Auster continues thus (1986: 143–4):

> [Blue] has never given much thought to the world inside him. [. . .] Now, suddenly, with the world as it were removed from him, with nothing much to see but a vague shadow by the name of Black, he finds himself thinking about things that have never occurred to him before, and this, too, has begun to trouble him. If thinking is perhaps too strong a word at this point, a slightly more modest term – speculation, for example – would not be far from the mark. To speculate, from the Latin *speculatus*, meaning mirror or looking glass. For in spying out at Black across the street, it is as though Blue were looking into a mirror, and instead of merely watching another, he finds that he is also watching himself. Life has slowed down so drastically for him that Blue is now able to see things that have previously escaped his attention. The trajectory of the light that passes through the room each day, for example, and the way the sun at certain hours will reflect the snow on the far corner of the ceiling in his room. [. . .] Blue is now aware of these tiny events, and try as he might to ignore them, they persist in his mind like a nonsensical phrase repeated over and over again. He knows it cannot be true, and yet little by little seems to be taking on a meaning.

A reflexive ethnography is therefore one of the possible stories that can be told, 'plausible' more than 'true', 'disturbed' by the constant action of the participants (be these the 'researcher' or the 'natives') and intended to empha- size inconsistencies and contradictions, rather than reality's compliance with a theoretical model. Every ethnography is 'essentially contestable' and 'intrinsically incomplete', to quote Geertz (1973: 29), and it is practically impossible to 'step outside' one's own research experience to adopt a 'professionalized distance', as Silverman (1972: 189) puts it.

The research context, data collection and data analysis

Five ethnographic observations were conducted in order to investigate gender as entrepreneurial practice and entrepreneurship as gender practice. The field for these observations was chosen by applying, not abstract criteria of representativeness (which would in any case have been impossible, given the variety of small-to-medium firms and the small number of possible cases), but rather ones of expected diversity. That is to say, we decided not

to investigate exemplary cases, given that the literature on women entrepreneurs already abounds with histories constructed around 'exceptional
figures'. Our 'theoretical sampling' (Glaser and Strauss, 1967) consisted in
a search for situations in which entrepreneurship was not concentrated
in a single individual, and in which the gender of the entrepreneurs mingled
with the gender inscribed in the product. And it also consisted in a search
for firms belonging to the industrial cultures of both the north and the
south of Italy.

Two cases were production enterprises owned by women. A third one was
chosen as representative of young entrepreneurship and of firms led by a
dominant female figure. The fourth case was a family-owned production
enterprise. The final one was a 'cultural' undertaking. These five firms were
selected in the light not only of their ownership structures but also of their
products, while we wanted to have some sort of 'gender' connotation
(industrial welders and men's shirts as male products, fitted kitchens as female
ones, men's/women's fashion clothing and a cultural magazine as products
with more fluid gender attributions) in keeping with the idea that gender
is evinced not only in organizational dynamics but in the artefacts that these
dynamics produce, and in the interpretations that their producers give to
them.

Table 3.1 sets out the main features of the firms selected.[4]

Table 3.1 Main features of the firms selected

Firm	Product	Corporate form	Year of foundation	No. of employees
Asie Welders	Industrial welders	Limited company (two sisters)	1940	20
Erba Shirts	Men's shirts	Sole proprietorship (one woman owner)	1996	22
Frau Kitchens	Fitted kitchens	Limited company (family-owned)	1974	40
LeCò	Men's and women's leather garments	Limited company (owned by three brothers and a sister)	1990	30
Atlantis	Cultural monthly of gay and lesbian culture	Limited company (owned by five partners)	1982	5

- *Asie Welders* is a company which has been handed down across three generations. Founded in 1940 (as a single-owner firm) by the grandfather of the two women entrepreneurs (sisters) who are currently its owners, it is located in the northern region of Lombardy. The firm designs and manufactures industrial welders. Consequently, its market consists essentially of other firms (Italian and foreign) operating in the engineering sector. Functionally, the company is divided into production and administration. The former employs around 80 per cent of the workforce and is supervised by an engineer, while the latter is run by the two women entrepreneurs themselves together with a part-time administrative assistant. Ownership and management of the business is a well-established component of the women's family background; they began working in the company when it could already count on a relatively solid network of relations and contacts.

- *Erba Shirts* is instead owned by a single woman who started up the company in 1996 with financing provided by the European Community programme for female entrepreneurship. Located in Tuscany, in the centre of Italy, and operating in the textiles sector (men's shirts), the company is divided into two divisions (production and administration). The woman entrepreneur's husband also works in the business. The couple were previously employed by another company (which also operated in the textiles sector), which they then left to open their own firm, thereby transferring knowledge and experience accumulated in around fifteen years of dependent employment. Besides presenting its own collection, Erba Shirts also produces for third parties (for another two European 'designer' firms), and in the course of its first three years has doubled its profits.

- The *Frau Kitchens* company located in the southern region of Basilicata was set up in 1974 as a firm producing hand-crafted fitted kitchens. Initially a sole proprietorship, over the years it has been transformed (with increasing output and turnover) into a limited company owned by the family of the original entrepreneur. The latter started up the firm on his return to Italy after many years working abroad in the woodworking sector. The company is divided organizationally into production, administration, human resources management, marketing and planning. Besides its headquarters, it has another sales outlet in Basilicata and a further two in the neighbouring region of Puglia.

- The *LeCò* company is located in the Salento area of southern Italy and manufactures leather garments for men and women. Initially (the firm was founded in 1990), its customers were a number of companies operating in the fashion sector, but for four years it has worked with an Italian fashion house, which at present is its only client. The business is owned by three brothers and a sister, although its public image is personified by the female entrepreneur, not only in the clothing industry but also in the media. The company, in fact, has been publicized as an example of youthful entrepreneurship centred on a female figure. It was this feature that prompted our selection of it as a case study. The company was started up with funds for the support of young entrepreneurs in the south of Italy, and through reinvestment of capital from a previous firm (owned by the parents) which catered to the down-market segment of the leather goods market. Moreover, when the company began operations, the sister and one of the brothers had already worked in the marketing department of the fashion house to which they now sell their products. There are two departments – production (divided between cutting and sewing) and administration – with twenty-four people employed in the former and six in the latter. During its nine years of activity, the company has achieved constant growth, and has now doubled its output.

- The *Atlantis* company is located in Lombardy, where it operates in the publishing sector. Producing a monthly magazine on gay and lesbian culture, it is a limited company owned by five partners (all men). Three of these partners work on the editorial staff, which consists of an editor-in-chief, two assistant editors, a graphic designer and two features writers, as well as a number of external contributors. Atlantis was set up as a limited company in 1982, initially being self-financed by eight colleagues (men and women), some of whom had previously worked in dependent employment, while others had worked in the 'cultural sector'. For some years the company also published a series of books, which it marketed on its own account. Following a 'schism' in the year previous to our fieldwork, the capital shares had been redefined. This provoked a walk-out by several of the partners, whose shares were bought by those who remained. Consequently, because Atlantis does not benefit from public funding or easy credit terms, and because it operates in a still precarious sector (cultural publishing) in Italy, the company is at present undergoing further financial 'restructuring', although fifteen years of business have enabled it to achieve relative stability.

After these brief outlines of the companies involved in the research, this is an appropriate moment to describe the techniques used in the fieldwork, so that the reader may finally be ushered into the realities observed.

Shadowing and interviewing

Fieldwork in the five companies lasted an entire working week in each organization. During this period, the researcher 'shadowed'[5] the entrepreneur, following him/her step by step in the course of his/her everyday organizational routine and constantly taking notes on the subjects' actions. The choice of shadowing as a research technique seemed appropriate by virtue of the fact that entrepreneurial action is one of those activities which are constantly constructed throughout the day. It does not have rigidly pre-established boundaries (spatial and temporal) and tends to eliminate the dichotomy between public and private. We decided that the ethnographer in our case should be a male, the intention being that we might thus accomplish what the Chicago school calls 'subversion' of the rules (Hughes, 1958). Since common sense identifies gender as a theme pertaining to women, the presence of a woman asking questions about gender might have provoked connivance. Moreover, in the light of what was said when we described our methodological framework, it should be clear that the subjectivity of the ethnographer was as much a resource for his understanding of the reality under observation as for that of the subjects whom he met during the fieldwork, and also for our understanding of what he proposed as the result of his participant observation. An ethnographer, in a reflexive conception of his/her role, participates and observes just as much as s/he is observed and made a participant by the people whom s/he meets. S/he helps to bring about, make visible and collaboratively interpret the 'small events' or incidents caused by his/her presence, and his/her identity is derived and fabricated from the practices, discourses and relations produced in the action space of the fieldwork (Navarini, 2001).

Each day's fieldwork concluded with an (audio) recording of an interview on the following topics:[6]

- the history of the firm;
- entrepreneurial risk;
- innovation;
- the money factor;
- future prospects.

These topics were selected in order to open an interpretative window on the construction that the male and female entrepreneurs put on their activities (and on themselves) as institutional action (and subjects). 'Risk/innovation/ money' is the triptych which, since Schumpeter, has enabled discourse on entrepreneurial activity to articulate itself through logical, temporal and environmental linkages. In recounting their experiences of risk-taking with regard to innovation and capital investment, therefore, people 'narrate entrepreneurship' and incorporate their actions in a sort of 'mythobiography' (Bernhardt, 1985: chap. 2, § 2.1) containing the history and (presumed) destiny of a generic entrepreneurial activity. The purpose of asking about the firm's history and future prospects was to create a moment devoted to the imagination. In this way observation could be made of the time horizon within which the subjects reconstructed and 'activated' past and future action in relation to other issues (whether gender-related or otherwise) which they deemed particularly significant.

Analysing gender and entrepreneurship as doing and saying

We thought it important that ethnographic observations should be analysed by the same person who collected them, because of the importance of his contextual knowledge of material which was essentially descriptive in character.

We decided to narrate the ethnographies as a series of episodes. This was not only a narrative expedient with which to evade the pure temporal sequentiality of the events but also a deliberate strategy to construct units of action/interaction on which to dwell during the stage of theoretical sense-making. In fact, for those who study processes of action/interaction and adopt a qualitative methodology, writing is not formal description but an activity both analytical and creative (Morgan, 1986; Strati, 2000). When 'recounting' a study, a researcher employs a style, a vocabulary and a set of metaphors which further modify the data and theory, so that the very act of writing becomes a 'form of inquiry' (Richardson, 1994).

We then moved inductively from the particularity of episodes, singling out and discussing the concepts and assumptions that arise from them and are subsumed by them. The interpretation, thus, took the form of scientific inquiry that explores ambivalent possibilities and problematizes 'facts that are not necessarily true or which are not true in so necessary a sense' (Eco, 1981: 1050).

When interpreting the interviews, we decided that the ethnographer should not carry out the discourse analysis of the texts. This was because we wanted to exploit the distance between the interpreter of an interview and the person who had conducted it and therefore knew the relational context. We wanted to shift the focus of attention to the text, considering the relationship between gender and entrepreneurship as a discursive practice and treating the narratives collected to be 'impersonal' texts. As a consequence, the requirement that the person who collects the text in the field should coincide with the interpreter of that text does not arise, because the field becomes the text itself.

In the texts analysis we followed two different approaches which jointly yield insight into the meanings and explanations that people attribute to their own actions and those of others: paradigmatic analysis (what is recounted) and narrative analysis (how it is recounted). Our aim was to identify discursive and narrative strategies available to the entrepreneurs focusing on the core meanings of their discourses and the 'process' dimension of their stories.

Conclusions

In this chapter we have delineated the methodological framework for an ethnographic approach to gender and entrepreneurship as material and discursive practices.

We presented the elements of the methodological *bricolage* which we assembled to conduct an ethnography of gender as entrepreneurial practice and of entrepreneurship as gender practice. As said earlier in the chapter, the term *bricolage* is used deliberately, because it links our inquiry with the debate in post-colonialist anthropology and organization studies inspired by a postmodern sensibility, as well symbolizing the plurality of heterogeneous elements that combine to yield a plausible definition of 'ethnographic reality'.

From this derives an image of the researcher which differs from that of the privileged observer and comes closer to that of the collector of fragments of fluid, reflexive and hyperreal accounts. This image is reflected in the ethnographic accounts that we constructed, accounts which situate the researcher within the action contexts observed and are offered to the reader (in the pages that follow) in the form of narratives and episodes on which to dwell during the stage of theoretical sense-making.

4   Company ethnographies

The gendering of entrepreneurship and the enterprising of gender

The pages that follow provide an entry into the realities observed during the five sessions of ethnographic fieldwork, all of which were conducted by the same person, a male, during the first five months of 1999.

The data will first be presented in the form of a narrative, shorn of analytic interpretation, so that the reader may form his/her own impressions and gain intuitions. The extracts in italics represent direct speech transcribed in 'real time'; they are consequently reported exactly (though translated) as they were expressed. Also transcribed – usually enclosed in inverted commas – are a number of statements and questions by the researcher, so that the structure of the conversations is made clear.

After each story, we turn to interpretation of the fieldnotes collected, proposing our view of 'doing gender' and 'doing business' as practical and interrelated activities.

Asie Welders

Asie Welders is a company owned by two sisters who inherited it from their father, who in his turn had inherited it from their grandfather. The company has twenty employees and it manufactures industrial welders.

The company's premises are located in a large open compound. Within the compound stand a number of prefabricated business units (owned by the two sisters, who lease them out) and located in one of these units are the company's administrative offices (its production plant occupies another). There is unrestricted access to the area, therefore, and one need only follow the signs for 'ASIE – Offices' to arrive at a door (always open), climb two flights of stairs and enter a corridor leading to a huge room.

When I arrive I am met by Franca Somma. It is she who tells me about the company. She introduces me to her sister, Enrica Somma (*She's the real businesswoman. I play second fiddle [. . .] If it had been my choice, I would have preferred to be a dressmaker*) and to the engineer (a man), who is ready to explain all the technical characteristics of the welding machines made by the company.

Home versus work

You're split between two camps, in the sense that when you're here you never stop doing the things here, and when you're at home you never stop doing the things there.

The home of the two sisters is close to the factory, *and that's very important for women running a business, because if you think about the travelling involved* . . . Franca Somma explains how she has to take her son to school and then pick him up in the afternoons, and how much time it would take if home, work and school were distant from each other. The two women come in to work as soon as they have taken Franca's son to school. They both accompany the boy because Franca does not have a driving licence; only Enrica does, and it is she who goes to collect him from school every afternoon. On days when she brings the boy into the office after school, the Somma sisters cannot linger too long at work because he has to do his homework.

The sisters live together, in the house where their father, mother and grandfather lived before them. Because of the demands of their children (Enrica has a daughter), the communal running of their household is essential. *Without my mother's help we could never have coped!* They describe, for example, how the grandmother (their mother) looked after Franca's boy when he was a baby, and how she used to telephone Franca at work when he was clamouring to be fed. 'Signora,' the workers would shout, 'the baby's hungry!'

The atmosphere in the company, indeed, is very 'family'. Franca Somma and Miss Sabrina (the secretary, *who doesn't need to work because her husband's the director of a bank*) talk on the telephone, they discuss laws, payments and bureaucracy and there seem to be no rigidly fixed roles.

The engineer: a matter of image

The engineer, on the contrary, never remains seated for longer than ten minutes at a time. He is the only person in the office with a cordless telephone, so that when he is speaking to someone on the telephone, he can move around. Nor is he obliged to remain seated at his desk when he takes a call. Yet, although his cordless telephone is always in his pocket, he is the only person in the office who never answers incoming calls. It is he who discusses the design and engineering of new welders; it is he who travels for the company (to present its machines); and it is he who handles relations with the other engineers and designers (all men).

Moreover, the company has a fleet of cars. The Somma sisters are not interested in the marque: *But that's because we're women . . . The engineer, for example . . . he wants a nice car, because he says 'If I go to Alfa Romeo with a nice car, they'll let me through the main gates; otherwise . . .', and also because he does a lot of travelling, whereas we're always here. I know it's a matter of image but . . . really I couldn't care less, as long as the car takes me where I want to go. More than anything else I want the cars to be new because . . . if one broke down, I wouldn't know what to do.*

As a kind of institutionalization of the engineer, the two sisters are setting up a new company with him, *in which he'll be given the position he deserves, after so many years . . .* The sisters will be the partners and the engineer will be the managing director. *This'll be the first company that we've started; the others we inherited; this is the first that'll really be ours. We hope it goes well.* I ask Enrica for further details. There will be two companies, she says. The first (the current one) will continue to handle the leasing contracts, while the other (the new one), with the engineer at its helm, will continue to make welders. It's a question of image, because a company whose managing director is an engineer has a reputation for being reliable, as opposed to the image conveyed by the two sisters. How come? *Because there are a lot of bogus companies around . . . registered in the name of somebody's wife just to qualify for tax relief. Every so often these companies . . . PUFF! They disappear! If there's the name of an engineer, though . . . Mind you, we don't give a toss . . . but in the market . . . it's like the question of the car.*

The only remark with the engineer, the sisters tell me, is that, sometimes, *he falls in love.* He falls in love with 'strong', rational entrepreneurs who 'conquer' new markets. He trusts them completely and sings their praises; *but then they always let him down!* Either they disappoint him, or they go off with a larger company, or they disappear. And he takes it badly, the sisters say; *he suffers.*

Hirings

The Somma sisters always conduct careful discussion before new staff are taken on, and they also consult the engineer. They now want to hire a new engineer, but they are afraid that this will cause friction with the rest of the staff, none of whom is a university graduate. The issue is directly connected with a marketing decision: whether or not to start selling the company's machines in America. This involves the problem of technical assistance, because if the company sells a machine in America it must provide the necessary technical back-up, and consequently someone will have to go over to the States to provide it. *But there's only the engineer and he couldn't go because* [he's needed here]. Yet the engineer would gladly go to America, most of all in order to see the machines that he has designed being sold in that country as well.

Nevertheless the sisters have decided to hire a technical draughtsman. The job has been advertised and they are beginning to receive the first telephone enquiries. I ask the sisters if they have any preference as to the sex of the 'draughtsman'. *No, we haven't got a preference. At first we talked about him as a man because we've never come across a female technical draughts-man . . . of course there might be some problem with internal relations, like when we called in a woman doctor to examine the workmen . . .* Not that they want a man regardless, *but a woman is inevitably going to have children. And as long as you've got someone off work in the administration, it doesn't matter, because the administration is much the same. But if you've got a draughtsman off work for long periods, perhaps when you're finishing a machine . . . well, you just stop working.* The sisters explain to me that:

- sooner or later women have children;
- children are very important to women;
- the work that these women do is not particularly rewarding;
- *and so what do you want, we work like this because we're working for ourselves . . . but it's obvious that as soon as the baby has a temperature . . . who's going to see the mother at work any more!*
- hence it is nothing to do with *prejudice*; it's a practical problem *in that a woman can't offer the same guarantees as a man.*

However, the problem does not arise, they say, because *it's only men who are ringing about the job in any case.* Those who enquire are sent a questionnaire to be completed with entirely routine information (education, experience, present job and annual salary), and on this basis the decision is taken on whom to call for interview.

By chance, I overhear a telephone call from someone interested in the draughtsman's job. On conclusion of the conversation, Enrica Somma (it is she that spoke to me before) tells me that she is surprised that the caller was worried about being 50 years old. *A 50-year-old workman, no, I'd never take him on, unless he was super-super-super skilled, something that . . . well, after a while they tend to get a bit doddery. But a technical draughtsman, even if he's 50 years old . . . he still sits in front of his little computer and he draws his pretty lines . . .* I ask Enrica to elaborate on the difference between a technical draughtsman and a workman. She replies that a technical draughtsman is like a university professor because *he works with his head, not with his body. Builders or foundry-workers, for example, do a kind of work which physically . . . takes it out of you . . . but you should work with your brain . . .*

Pursuing a career versus staying at home

Franca Somma continues to make telephone calls while Enrica stamps forms and deals with paperwork. It seems, however, that most of their work consists in answering the telephone, in that all incoming calls are answered and redirected by the sisters (when Franca answers the phone, she introduces herself as '*la signora Somma*', whereas Enrica tersely announces '*Asie Welders*').

'But isn't doing the telephonist's job boring?'

Yes, but a telephonist is usually a woman, she has children and she's always off work . . . so . . . And men don't like this kind of work!

'Do women like it?'

Yes, it's like being a shop assistant. Because women prefer jobs where they don't have to think, where they shut up the shop in the evening and then forget about it. And then women are better at talking on the phone, something that men are no good at. For example, when you're getting customers to pay it's much better if a woman calls, because she's more persistent, she knows how to handle people better . . . and then women are pains in the neck: when they get something into their heads, they won't let go.

A package arrives from the bank. *Mrs X at the bank, she's an example of a woman who's got herself into a position of power . . . a viper of a woman. She had a baby, she stayed at home for six months and then went back to work . . . as if to say that if you want to get ahead in your career you can't stay at home for a year and a half (or two) like lots of women do. Though the result wasn't so good, not for her, nor for her son, nor for us* (laughs).[1] The package from the bank contains two diaries for 1999. I ask whether they haven't arrived a little late (it is by now mid-January). *Yes, but we're not 'important' customers, so that they only send them when they've sucked up to everyone else . . . we get those that are left over* (laughs).

Secretaries versus entrepreneurs

Someone telephones about modifications to be made to a welding machine. Enrica Somma tells the engineer to ring the person back and explain the situation (the technician is off sick and the technical department is entirely taken up with testing a new machine). But the engineer is reluctant to make the call and reiterates to Enrica the situation that she has only just described to him. As Franca Somma and I watch, she explains to me that it is the engineer who should phone, because the customer believes that he has spoken to a secretary and might therefore think that he is being fobbed off.

According to the Somma sisters, being mistaken for a secretary sometimes proves useful, because it enables them to follow negotiations from the inside while appearing to be outsiders: especially because they often have insufficient information to gauge a situation, so that being taken for secretaries gives them a chance to acquire it. *We've got an excuse because we're women.*

By way of example, they mention an episode when a customer telephoned (somewhat irritated) about a malfunctioning machine and Franca Somma put him off until the engineer arrived. By the time the engineer did so, the situation had resolved itself. When the customer spoke to the engineer, he asked him to *apologize for me to your secretary* (she laughs). They tell me about another occasion when it was the engineer who pretended to be a secretary (imitating a woman's voice) to get someone who kept ringing him 'off his back'.

Franca Somma gives me another example: there are two firms, both equally good, offering the same product, except that there is a difference of 20 euros between their prices. Obviously, she wants to buy the one that costs less. *Only that if you're the owner you're a skinflint; if you're a secretary (so you're pretending to be someone else) then you're . . . 'careful'. [. . .] That's the point: I couldn't care less about money, but I think that as a businesswoman I should care about it. And so I'll haggle over even 5 lire, I'll create such shenanigans . . . only on a question of principle, though* (laughs).

Enrica, after answering a telephone call for the engineer (who should have rung the caller but has not), and after making excuses for him, tells me: *yet if we were secretaries, we wouldn't feel guilty about these things; we'd say 'the engineer isn't here', period.* I ask for more explanation. They say that a secretary only follows orders and therefore doesn't feel embarrassed or awkward at saying to the caller that the engineer (or the owner) is not there. By contrast, the sisters feel embarrassed because they're not the secretaries but the owners, *so that we can't act as if nothing has happened.* They tell me about their relations with 'shabby' businessmen. For example, there was one that had made an order and then didn't pay. Franca telephoned him, and he used his secretary to stall her. After a while, her patience ran out (*because being busy is all very well, but after a while it was obvious that he was doing it on purpose*) and she complained vigorously.

Housewives versus entrepreneurs

One day, two well-groomed men come into the office, both wearing blue suits and ties. They have to sign an order and consign it to the production department. Franca Somma intercepts them and asks what they want, but she does not introduce herself. She shows them into another room and goes off to fetch the workman, but finds that he is busy with some other people. While the two men are waiting, she asks them for the name of their firm, and also for their own names, but she does not introduce herself, nor do the two men enquire as to her identity.

On another occasion, a woman comes into the office and asks Enrica Somma for 'dottoressa Somma'. *What's it about?* It's about some paperwork. Only then does Enrica recognize the woman, and immediately sends her off to her sister. Who is this woman?

She's the wife of one of our tenants who used to have a business partner, but then they fell out, and he set up a company with his wife . . . and now his wife goes around trying to get a handle on how things work . . . she goes around gathering information because . . . her ideas about administration are a bit, well, elementary. But . . . you know, you can't come into a business office carrying your shopping bags like she does, I mean . . . it's fine by me . . . but it's a question of image . . . we're not a street market here. As regards the split between the two partners, the sisters tell me that one of them has decided to invest in Poland. They think that the markets in Eastern Europe are distinctly advantageous, because there is an abundance of skilled workers and labour costs are very low. *But we shan't be going East.*

'Why not?' *Well, we're housewives.*

Asie Welders: an anti-heroic story

The first of our stories describes a reality poised between the two worlds of business and the family: which accounts for our decision to present the experience of the two businesswomen in dichotomous terms.

The first of the two terms in the dichotomy (business) is a goal to achieve; the second (family) is a heritage impossible to relinquish. Here, however, we shall concentrate on the dialectic between this dichotomy and its implications for gender and entrepreneurship.

The patriarchal element

The patriarchate constitutes the sub-text for the entire organizational history of Asie Welders. The company was created on the initiative of just one man (the grandfather of the two female entrepreneurs), and he devoted his entire life to its nurture. Thereafter the company became the family's 'inalienable' property, handed down from one generation to the next, acquiring the significance of something made exclusively *for* the family – as Mrs Somma repeatedly emphasizes.

The two businesswomen seem to interpret their business activity in entirely these terms. It is apparent in all the ethnographic episodes illustrated, where Enrica and Franca Somma seek to play down their role as women in the organization, an organization, moreover, which manufactures industrial welders and therefore operates in a sector historically and implicitly connoted as male. All those with whom the two sisters have dealings in their day-to-day work – whether employees or businessmen – are of male gender. The only exception is Miss Sabrina; but she, they say, only does office work, and anyway (as stressed in one of the very first conversations) she has no need to work because her husband has a good job. In this sense, it is significant that all the examples of occupations cited by the two sisters have a man as their 'natural' incumbent (the builder or the university professor).

The engineer, of course, enjoys all the privileges attaching to his masculine status within the company, occupying a rent position which advantages men and masculinities in the entrepreneurial activity. He is the acknowledged 'authority' who deals with all aspects of the design work and the organization's external relations. Above all, no one ever questions his actions, which are taken to constitute the 'norm'. The engineer is also attributed business acumen that the two sisters fail to recognize in themselves. His aptitude for business is manifest in his close concern for the company's image vis-à-vis its various interlocutors, and in his (excessive) faith in those, like him, trying to expand their range of action (and who invariably let him down).

Against the background of this gender sub-text, more detailed analysis of certain of the episodes recounted will shed sharper light on the events observed in Asie Welders.

Balancing home and work

A large part of the entrepreneurial activity of the Somma sisters is conditioned by the imperative of maintaining a dual presence at home and at work. Their acknowledged 'responsibility' for another organization (the family) forces them to set limits on their lives in the company, which are frequently subject to time constraints and deadlines.

In the first episode (as well as in that of the 'Hirings'), the Company takes the form of an utterly impersonal entity, with its own and impelling exigencies, indifferent to any private aspect of a person's life – be it pregnancy or advancing age. The assertion that a 'woman can't offer the same guarantees as a man' is thus merely a matter of what is most expedient for the company: there can be no prejudice when choices are imposed by the 'impartial' dictates of the production cycle.

Maternity seems to be one of the most sensitive issues faced by a working woman and an organization. From the point of view of the two female entrepreneurs, maternity is a 'natural' part of a woman's life; but precisely for this reason it is a source of uncertainty for the organization, because there is no guarantee that the timing of her pregnancy will match the time frame of the persons involved in corporate planning. But, then, giving priority to the company over the family may prove to be the worst strategy (as documented by the episode entitled 'Pursuing a career versus staying at home'). Long periods of absence from work mean that the person is no longer considered an organizational resource, while giving priority to the company evidences that the woman is indifferent to the effects of this on her 'natural' organization, namely the family.

In order to juggle these various aspects and needs, the two businesswomen have blurred the confines between the domains of work and family so that they can move smoothly between them. They stress that the 'communal' management of day-to-day life enables them to organize the two domains without having to dichotomize them (and themselves) too drastically. Moreover, they also find it easy to alternate physically between them, given that their home is close to the company's premises. Thus taking Franca's son to school is simply a staging post along the way to work, and going to pick him up is a daily chore that sets the cadence of organizational time.

From this point of view, the male presence of the engineer serves the purpose of exonerating the sisters from any need to 'represent' the firm in the market. Such activity would require them to undertake frequent business trips around the country, which would be impossible to reconcile with important aspects of their daily lives (like the woman they mention who came into the business carrying her shopping bags). It would also require their compliance with certain canonical and aesthetic principles of consumption in the business world (like driving the right car, for example).

A matter of visibility?

A rather curious aspect of corporate life at Asie Welders is the reluctance of the Somma sisters to be recognized as businesswomen. Although what they say about the advantages of not performing a particularly visible organizational role is true (because they can turn the ambiguities of the situation to their own advantage), it is equally true that an organizational position is nevertheless attributed to them: everyone who enters the premises takes them to be 'secretaries', in fact. The process is exemplified by the episode entitled 'Secretaries versus entrepreneurs':

1   Not being identified as entrepreneurs provides an alibi: it enables the sisters to shed numerous responsibilities inherent to business activity, both commercial and financial.
2   Not being identified as entrepreneurs provides them with a motive: the people with whom the sisters have dealings would expect them to behave in a certain way if they saw them as entrepreneurs. It also provides the sisters with justification for 'not doing what an entrepreneur should do' and also for 'doing what an entrepreneur should not do'.
3   Not being identified as entrepreneurs yields an advantage: that of being privy to what is going on in all the intermediate phases of a negotiation. Although these phases may not have a crucial bearing on the eventual outcome, being in on them enables the sisters to monitor developments.

In all three cases, however, the non-identification of the sisters as entrepreneurs is apparently determined less by any particular action on their part than by the association of their femaleness with the role of women in business organizations. And this seems to be a socially shared process, given that, when the engineer had to 'dodge' someone on the telephone, he did not resort to any particular stratagem but merely imitated a female voice. The situation is ironic to the point of paradox: the Somma sisters (although they are the entrepreneurs) are not required to do anything in order to conceal their role; they need only speak on the telephone; the engineer (who is not the entrepreneur) must instead resort to stratagems to demonstrate his 'extraneousness'. As if to say that, while it is difficult to combat the socially shared image of women in organizations as 'secretaries', it is even more difficult to counteract that of men as 'entrepreneurs' (or managers), precisely because it is not explicit but taken for granted.

Defining oneself by default

Apart from the 'strategic' advantages of not being taken as entrepreneurs, it is unclear why the sisters should play down their importance in the company to such an extent. The formula with which Franca introduces herself and her sister ('She's the real businesswoman, I play second fiddle [. . .] If it had been my choice, I would have preferred to be a dressmaker') is overly self-effacing, given that both of them have degrees and they contribute equally to the running of the company. However, if analysed carefully, this curious introduction is indicative of two aspects taken into account by Franca Somma when defining her notion of entrepreneurship.

In the first part of the sentence Franca states that there exists a shared image of the entrepreneur. Besides relating more to a man than a woman (as illustrated by Enrica's explanation of why they have decided to register the company in the engineer's name), this image conveys an ability to be ruthless in dealing with others. Franca Somma is indeed able to behave in this way (as when she protested vigorously to a defaulting customer), but she does not see this as something that comes naturally to her. It is this that prevents her from seeing herself (and being seen) as a 'real' entrepreneur. The same applies to matters of money (see the episode 'Secretaries versus entrepreneurs'). Franca Somma is not interested in money. However, as an entrepreneur she feels that she should be, and in a manner that demonstrates her position in the market and her close attention to the financial aspects of bargaining.

In the second part of the sentence, the stress is instead on the choice of becoming an entrepreneur. For Franca Somma, hers was not a genuine choice because she inherited the business from her father. She would have preferred a much more 'female' occupation, that of dressmaker, for example. However, the contrast between the image of the 'entrepreneur' and that of the 'dressmaker' is not obvious: from a purely economic point of view, dressmaking is a market sector, and as a form of self-employment 'dressmaking' could easily constitute entrepreneurial activity. Hence, the image used by Franca functions by evoking other scenarios to do with traditionally male occupations ('entrepreneur') rather than female ones ('dressmaker') and with domains of competence and interest determined on the basis of gender membership.

In both cases Franca Somma interprets her experiences as an entrepreneur 'by default' with respect to a (male) standard of what is 'normal entrepreneurship'.

An anti-heroic story: the dis-entrepreneurs and the dual presence

During one of our first telephone contacts with Asie Welders, the Somma sisters reacted to our announcement of the topic of the research by warning us (ironically) that what we would find in their company was an example of 'dis-entrepreneurs', rather than of an entrepreneurship standing as an alternative to the male equivalent. The reason adduced was that in recent years the company had shed increasing numbers of employees.

With hindsight, this description seems to relate more to deliberate non-compliance with certain assumptions about entrepreneurship and male corporate performance – principally that of the entrepreneur as the 'solitary hero'. Asie Welders is run by two women who do not act particularly aggressively or competitively, either on the market or within their company; two women who find no difficulty in delegating responsibility, and who do not aspire to the 'conquest' of new market shares. Their entrepreneurial experience has value to them above all in its significance for their private lives, and their reference parameters are family values much more than business ones. All this obviously contrasts with the image of entrepreneurism as a 'heroic' quest, and thus makes it easier to unmask its masculine features.

Here, we submit, the main process by which gender and entrepreneurship are constructed resides in the dual presence patterns that characterize and situate the action of the two female entrepreneurs. Firstly, they characterize it in the sense that they sanction the indivisibility of gender and entrepreneurship as symbolic activities: performing entrepreneurship involves a gender positioning, and, depending on how gender is performed, entrepreneurial action acquires different dimensions and levels of legitimacy. Secondly, they permit fluid and constant movement between different spaces of signification (home/work, reproduction/production, secretaries/entrepreneurs, housewives/working women) facilitating breach of the boundaries of the symbolic gender order according to the occasion. Gender and entrepreneurship are therefore a theoretical dichotomy whose dividing line is constantly blurred, crossed and denied but then reconstructed a posteriori by the joint action of several actors.

Erba Shirts

Erba Shirts is a single-proprietor business owned by Mrs Erba, who started it up with a grant from the European Community fund to promote female entrepreneurship. The firm produces men's shirts and has twenty-two employees. Mrs Erba's husband also works in the firm. Before they started up the business, they were both employees in another company, which also manufactured shirts.

The company's premises are situated close to the centre of a village in the province of Arezzo. The company's name and logo are inscribed on the glass door, with the announcement 'production and direct sale of shirts' underneath. There is a bell, but there is no need to ring it because the door is always open (when somebody is on the premises). Scattered around the lobby are bolts of cloth, some large boxes, framed shirt-collars and strips of material, shirts displayed in a cabinet, a panel bearing the inscription 'stages in the manufacture of mother-of-pearl buttons', and a poster with the company logo.

As I enter, I am met by Mrs Erba, who introduces me to her husband. Once inside the building, I immediately find myself in the production department, which contains: an enormous table (for cutting); two parallel rows of benches (around twenty in total), each with a sewing machine; a coffee machine; heaps of fabrics; a small office closed off by panels and indicated by the sign 'Office'.

The workers (all women) wear overalls stitched with the company's initials.

Mr Erba is compiling the new autumn–winter pattern book, which is about to go into production. His work consists in coding the patterns and cataloguing them in the new collection according to the quantities requested by customers. The phone rings frequently and it is always he who answers.

Mr Erba asks about my research. He says that in his opinion research of this kind is pointless, because without experience it's a waste of money. Instead, he tells me, it's companies like his own that should be helped: newly formed businesses which if they had a 'little' incentive, could really make a 'great leap forward'. Not least, he says, because if you risk your own money, you're somehow committed; if you receive financial help, *you're not afraid*, like he and his wife had been three years previously when they went into debt to start up the business. *We took the risk because we believed in what we were doing . . . then, all right, I knew my customers, the type of product, I had the women . . . Because you say 'I'll open a production line' . . . but if you haven't got the right women, you can't open a line.*

He then talks about the 'settling down' of a business. He claims that companies like his can never settle down except when they are in decline. Maybe financially they can, he says, but the market is so volatile that you have constantly to adapt, even by changing business form. He adds that they are planning to create a couple of new offices. *One for her* (Fiore, the secretary) *and a larger one for me, where I can do all the things that you can see me doing here.*

Mr Erba must now go off to his mother-in-law's house, taking some shirts for their final 'cleaning'. I stay in the office and talk to Mrs Erba.

She is supervising the stitching work. She has to do this, she tells me, because no other member of staff has the requisite skills. She says that she knows all the stages of shirt production, and in fact it was she who 'trained' the workers; and in any case they should be versatile, so that they can work on several stages of the production process.

The 'women'

The 'women' are initially hired for a period of three weeks (on trial, with relative notification to the Labour Office), after which they may or may not be taken on permanently. *Some of them are better suited to the work, others less, and this you can spot immediately.*

At ten o'clock work suddenly stops: some of the women go over to the coffee machine, others have brought something to eat, others smoke. One of them (the most 'expert', who had also worked in the previous firm) stands up: this is the signal that the others have been waiting for, keeping an eye on her as ten o'clock approaches. The only woman not to take a break arrived late for work this morning.

Mrs Erba chats with a group (the most 'old'), and apart from the fact that she is not wearing an overall she is indistinguishable from the other women. Mr Erba instead carries on with his task of checking the fabric. The break lasts for ten minutes. I am struck by the compactness with which the women move: they do not return to their work stations in 'dribs and drabs' when they finish their coffee or cigarettes; instead, they all sit down at their machines in unison.

At half past five the scene repeats itself: the women who have finished work stand up, take off their overalls and light cigarettes; the others hurry to finish what they are doing. The women have been organized into couples for the cleaning. Those whose turn it is today immediately set to work, while the others clear their work stations and place their chairs upside down on the tables. Within five minutes most of them have left (as they walk out of the building, the women shout 'Ciao donne!' to each other). Mrs Erba gives instructions to some of them (as they leave) about the work to be done the next day, according to the weekly schedule. One of the women has to be paid, and Mrs Erba makes out the cheque.

When the girls have left, our real work begins (with reference to the fact that the Erbas often stay on at work until dinner time, or even later).

'Why men's shirts?'

I ask Mr Erba why they decided to make shirts for men, rather than women.

Women are much more difficult, much more careful about fashion. Orange is in and they want orange, then yellow is in and you have to give them yellow, then embroidery is in and you have to given them all those squiggles. A man no . . . once you've changed his collar, he doesn't care about all that crap.

A man's shirt is a fairly standard item of clothing, so the pattern may change as far as the collar is concerned, but not much else. By contrast, if the company decided to produce women's shirts, it would have to open a special department, with staff to attend the fashion shows and to conduct market research. *Unless you decide to produce for someone else, but in that case they send you the buttons, they send you the cloth and the patterns, and you assemble them, and that's it.* Mr Erba instead wants the shirts that leave his factory to be his 'own', even though some of his output is sold under another firm's trademark.

A couple of days later, I happen to meet the 'fashion adviser' of this other firm (*they have a fashion show in Hamburg like the one organized by Pitti in Milan for men's clothing . . . and our shirts are there!*), whom the Erbas invariably consult over the patterns to put into production. He explains to me that shirts are extremely important in the clothing sector, second only to suits (jacket and trousers). He adds that, although the trend is now towards more casual styles, *try to imagine an orchestra conductor or the 60-year-old CEO of a multinational who turns up in a jacket and a T-shirt . . . whatever the fashion . . . it's a bit difficult.* The customers of the firm for which he works are *professionals aged between 30 and 45. If they're over 45 they're from a higher social class, considering that one of our shirts costs around 15,000 euros in the shops!*

Seeing the examples, I ask him whether the shirt is a typically male garment. *Not at all! At least for the last twenty years, there's been a great demand for women's shirts which has gone completely unsatisfied. The problem is that shirt manufacturers, by culture, make shirts for men, and so they won't even consider making shirts for women.*

The English correspondent

Rob, the English correspondent for a shirt company supplied by the Erbas, comes into the office. Fiore tells me that also about to arrive is a girl from London who handles their relations with foreign customers. Rob is received by Mr Erba, but neither of them has sufficient command of the other's language for any effective conversation to take place. The agent/interpreter is due to arrive in half an hour's time, so Mr Erba has to 'invent' something in the meantime. They go into the office and Mr Erba shows Rob some fabric samples. They smoke cigarettes. Mrs Erba is with them, but only for the time required for her to smoke a cigarette as well, and to compliment Rob on his shirt.

Mr Erba takes Rob round the production room, showing him what the women are doing and the prototypes of shirt collars about to go into production. The interpreter arrives, carrying her 8-month-old son in her arms. She starts talking to Rob. Mrs Erba asks if she can hold the baby, and so the interpreter must divide her attention between Mrs Erba who is talking (in Italian) about the baby, and Rob who is talking (in English) about shirts. Mr Erba (who was been making a telephone call[2]) comes back into the production department and starts discussing matters with Rob, communication between them now being possible with the interpreter present.

They go off to a nearby bar for a coffee. When they leave the bar, Mr Erba describes to Rob (through the interpreter) the 'restructuring' that he has in mind. They are standing in the car park in front of the building, while Mrs Erba stands watching them from behind the glass doors, the baby in her arms. As soon as they enter the building, Mrs Erba 'passes' the baby to her mother and returns to the production department.

Mr Erba, the interpreter (holding her baby) and Rob settle down in the office, and Mr Erba asks Rob if his company has opened any new sales outlets. On learning they are about to open one in New York, he jokes: *Let's form a company you and me and go sell shirts in Florida . . .* The discussion now becomes technical: they talk about fabrics and colours, when to send them, the size of the bolts of material, and so on. Rob shows Mr Erba some shirts that he has brought with him, and explains that he wants Erba Shirts to 'copy' some of their features. But suddenly the interpreter's baby is sick and she has to leave for a moment to clean him up.

The baby passes back to Mrs Erba, who returns to the production department and hands him over to Fiore, because she has to continue stamping the button-holes in the shirts. In the meantime, with perfect nonchalance, Mr Erba shows Rob some fabrics.

Erba Shirts: an ordinary case of entrepreneurship

The case of Erba Shirts can be interpreted from various points of view.

A strictly organizational reading of the company would highlight the relationships among the people involved in its daily productive activity. The impression would thus be gained that Erba Shirts is one of those many organizations based on a functional division of labour.

From an entrepreneurial standpoint, the story of the company can be cited as an example of how market choices carry an implicit connotation of gender deriving from the specific market sector towards which those choices are addressed.

Finally, from an institutional point of view, the company can be described as one of those (rare) situations in which the woman assumes responsibility for a business and the man acts as her assistant. This would therefore be an amusing case in which the wife takes the husband's surname in civil matters, and the husband takes the wife's surname (which is the name of the company, with which everyone identifies the couple) in business.

These three views of the company are not mutually exclusive; indeed, detailed analysis of events will show that they all relate to processes of gender construction.

The organizational dimension: when gender is ordinary

The workforce at Erba Shirts is entirely made up of women, except for a single male worker. All the female workers are involved in production, where they stitch the shirts, apart from Fiore who is employed in secretarial work. The only man also works in production, but in the cutting section. In their informal conversations, Mr and Mrs Erba refer to the female workers simply as the 'women'. This is not to devalue them from a professional point of view: Mr and Mrs Erba repeatedly stress the importance of having 'reliable' people in production – because of the precision required by the work, and because of the pressures that build up at peak production periods. And in any case, as documented, the women themselves salute each other with 'Ciao donne!' when they go home.

Mr and Mrs Erba, therefore, do nothing more than repeat something that in their corporate experience is entirely 'normal', namely that the personnel in the production department of a shirt factory is overwhelmingly female. They repeat, that is to say, one of the functional divisions (of gender) inherent to occupational representations: the one whereby, in the dressmaking industry, sewing work is conventionally considered to be women's work. Sewing is a domestic chore typically performed by women, and it evokes the qualities of 'precision' and 'neatness' attributed to female archetypes. 'Cutting' work, by contrast, has always been a male preserve in the European dressmaking industry. Historically, it was the tailor (*il sarto*) who designed the clothes, did business with customers and organized production. Indeed, the *Zingarelli Dictionary of the Italian Language* (1999) gives two different definitions for the nouns *sarta* (female) and *sarto* (male), defining the former as 'a woman who cuts and assembles clothing, especially female' and the latter as 'one who makes bespoke clothing' and as the 'designer and executor of patterns for a fashion house'. This is not simply a matter of differences in declension; rather, it is a gender construct which positions men and women in different contexts and ascribes different abilities to them. This differing construction of meanings still persists in Italian, so that the image of a 'sart*a*' evokes a more domestic dimension, while that of a 'sart*o*' evokes work which is more conceptual or technical in its content.

At a micro level this distinction is also reflected in the work of Mr and Mrs Erba, and in the division of tasks between them. Table 4.1 gives a schematic representation. This functional division of tasks reflects the differing experiences accumulated by Mr and Mrs Erba when they worked as employees in another company. In this sense, there is nothing anomalous about the arrangement; indeed, it is an entirely 'rational' one. Yet it marks out dichotomies between planning ability (male) and the practical management of everyday routine (female), between relations with the organization's

Table 4.1 Schematic representation of the daily activities of Mr and Mrs Erba

Mr Erba	Mrs Erba
Gives instructions on which fabrics to cut.	Supervises production.
Prepares the shirt patterns.	Trains the workers.
Cuts the shirt-collars and the tails.	Stitches the collars.
Deals with customers and suppliers.	Handles relations with (and among) the women workers.
Designs the collection.	Cuts the button-holes.
Organizes deliveries.	Moves shirts from one worker to the next.
Handles external relations.	Attends to domestic matters.

'outside' (male) and its 'inside' (female). It consequently reflects experiences and knowledge gained on the basis of gender membership, imbuing them with the ordinary functional (male) division of organizational tasks.

The choice of market: when gender is at work but cannot be seen

As an item of clothing, a shirt carries an intrinsic gender connotation: not because it is worn more frequently by men than by women, but because it relates to settings that are socially and symbolically connoted as male.

As the 'fashion adviser' aptly points out, the question of why the company produces shirts for men rather than for women is redundant, because a shirt is intrinsically male. It is worn together with other male items of clothing (jacket and trousers), and it situates the wearer within a sector of relatively formal and public relations centred on masculinity (the examples given are those of an orchestra conductor or the chief executive officer of a multi-national company). It is a sector which demands compliance with certain standards and permits deviations from the norm only in details (the collar of the shirt), provided that these variations do not alter the socially shared meaning of the ensemble. Should they do so, we enter another sector: that of female fashion, which Mr Erba interprets in terms of flux and uncertainty.

Curiously, gender is invisible in the case of masculinity but utterly obvious in femininity. Where men's shirts are concerned, in fact, stability is imparted by the fact that men's clothes are not 'subject to fashion', and the stand-ardization of clothing implicit in work relations is taken for granted. By contrast, the difficulties that arise in the market for women's shirts are due to the influence that fashion exerts on the female population.

On this reading, men and women are assigned radically different roles in the market: the former are represented as reliable and involved at first hand, the latter as passive consumers. This is a gender-driven process, in that a diversity based on socially constructed relationships is used to erect a symbolic edifice which reinforces that diversity by tying it to biological features. The legitimation enjoyed by women in our society to dress in much more 'varied' manner than men (probably because of their different social roles) acts to their disadvantage by becoming symptomatic of female unpredictability.

The institutional standpoint: who is 'the entrepreneur'?

Mrs Erba is the registered owner of the company: it is she who carries entire bureaucratic and fiscal responsibility for the business. Yet, although she represents the company formally, it is Mr Erba who is universally regarded as its 'mainstay' (this being the expression used by Fiore). And indeed, as illustrated by various episodes, it is the husband who handles relations with the public (customers and suppliers), and it is he who takes responsibility for corporate planning.

The episode 'The English correspondent' shows very clearly that Mr Erba is the pivot of the firm's business relations: we observe him as he deals with a customer, shows him the company's current production, discusses future commercial arrangements with him and imagines setting up a new business with him. Mrs Erba is only intermittently present, being constantly called away to the production department, and also because of the presence of the baby, which renders the situation even more chaotic.

The presence of a baby, moreover, clashes with the productive setting. A child makes demands that conflict with organizational routine and hence may interfere (as happens in the episode recounted, in fact) with the ordinary course of entrepreneurial activity. Furthermore, childcare pertains more to the private sphere, while productive settings are usually regarded as public and 'grown-up'.

This symbolic clash is resolved by a gender-driven process: in particular, the performance by the actors involved of certain gender 'scores'. In other words, when certain events at odds with an entrepreneurial context occur (trivially, fussing over a small baby), interpretation of the appropriate 'gender display' (Goffman, 1976; see also the discussion in the section in Chapter 2, 'Gender: a situated performance in the intersections between bodies, discourses and practices') may help re-establish equilibria which would otherwise break down. These are equilibria that relate to the presence of men in public situations and to the 'preference' of women for private ones: what would have happened if Mr Erba had looked after the baby? In the situation described, moreover, the actors take pains not explicitly to consider the presence of the baby as a source of problems. Would it have been possible for a baby's behaviour to prevent the company from working?

Respect for gender equilibria, therefore, enabled redefinition of the entire episode by restoring the appropriate (male) connotations to entrepreneurial activity.

Erba Shirts: an ordinary case of entrepreneurship

In recounting the story of Erba Shirts from three different points of view, we have sought to show how (and to what extent) gender plays a part in attributing meaning to situations which – if interpreted in purely entrepreneurial terms – would engender uncertainty and inject ambiguity into the situation. Gender dynamics, especially from an organizational point of view, define prerogatives and create linkages among work skills, gender characteristics and the functional division of tasks.

As regards entrepreneurial activity, and the choice of product in particular, we have tried to describe how certain gender characteristics result in subsequent choices being taken for granted, according to the practices and customs of the particular market addressed.

As for the institutional 'question' – or the question of who is actually the entrepreneur in a situation where the registered owner of a company does not take part in product design but prefers to attend to 'everyday' matters – we have seen that 'doing business' and 'doing gender' are closely interrelated and indeed define each other.

In all three cases, the (male) gender of the entrepreneurial system pre-selects among the options available, making some appear more viable than others only because they correspond to archetypes deemed more appropriate (male or female). From this point of view, the main process involved in the reciprocal production of gender and entrepreneurship is the dialectical enactment of 'ceremonial' and 'remedial' work (Gherardi, 1994). When the actors concerned fail to respect the 'ceremonial' aspects of doing business, activating a correct gender score may be an efficacious 'remedial practice'. We believe that this process is already apparent in the story surrounding the start-up of Erba Shirts. Given a public policy which provides incentives for employment growth in a specific sector ('female entrepreneurship'), and thus drastically sanctions the dividing line between male and female spaces, the Erbas realized that only one of them could legitimately take part in this 'ceremony'. And in effect, the fact that the firm takes the name of Mrs Erba, although everyone regards Mr Erba as epitomizing the business, and the fact that he appears institutionally in the position of 'collaborator', is a remedial practice intended to enable the equal opportunities ceremony to continue. Thus exactly replicated are the distinctive features of the 'ceremonies' of more general entrepreneurial action (cultivating public relations, forming strategic alliances, defining the gender component that positions the product in the market, enhancing the corporate image and personifying the company) that sanction the division of male and female tasks and transpose them into organizational roles. Viewed thus, the pivotal role of Mr Erba, the absolute non-intrusiveness of Mrs Erba, the choice of a product with marked (but invisible) gender characteristics, as well as Mr Erba's aversion to public policies for new enterprise creation in specific sectors alone, can be interpreted as remedial practices necessary to ensure that Erba Shirts' business is effectively imbued with an invisible masculinity that symbolically sustains entrepreneurship – even in the case of a firm which institutionally and statistically belongs to the category of 'female entrepreneurship'.

Frau Kitchens

Frau Kitchens designs and produces fitted kitchens. With forty employees, it is a limited company whose shareholders are all members of the same family. The company was initially a single-proprietor firm owned by Mr Primo. He was then joined by his wife, who helped him to run the business. Their three adult children are now partners as well (although two of them will not work in the company until they have finished university).

The factory is located on the main road between Bari and Matera in the southern Italian region of Basilicata. It is immediately visible from the road because of the enormous sign in front of the building, and the large number of flags bearing the company's name and logo along the roadside.

There is only one entrance to the factory: the offices lie to the right of it, and the display and sales area to the left. On entering, visitors find themselves in the reception area (with plants, a long counter painted blue, low couches and tables strewn with magazines). Behind the counter a woman (Lucia) is busy answering the phone (which rings constantly).

I introduce myself and am told that Mario Primo (Mr Primo's son) is on the premises but busy in a meeting. I am (politely) asked to wait. While I do so, I take in my surroundings and note:

- an enormous reproduction of Giuseppe Pelizza's *Quarto Stato* hanging on the wall behind Lucia;
- a photograph of a venerated (alleged) miracle-worker: Padre Pio;
- a notice stating 'Salesmen received on Friday mornings';
- the telephone directories for the main towns in the South;
- a plaque inscribed 'Basilicata Business Award – 1991', and a statuette in the form of a stylized male figure: 'Basilicata Business Award – Men and Companies – 1991';
- company brochures scattered around the counter, as well as leaflets on the company's credit facilities.

Ten minutes after my arrival, a woman enters the main door and looks at me curiously. We greet each other: we have never met before and we do not introduce ourselves. But her curiosity is evident (two hours later I discover that she is Mrs Primo, mother of Mario Primo and the wife of Mr Primo).

Lucia continues to answer the telephone. One caller asks for Mr Primo. Lucia replies that he has not yet come in to work and transfers the call to Mrs Primo, who is already in the office.

While I wait for Mario Primo I note another detail: the kitchen units on display have not simply been assembled; they have been 'set' with saucepans (on the hotplates), dishes and glasses (on the draining boards), while bowls, jars and flowers have been arranged on the shelves. I ask Lucia who decorated the kitchens: she doesn't know, but says that whoever it was had permission from the head of marketing. She then tells me about the criteria used when deciding on kitchen décor.

'Classic' kitchens, she informs me, shouldn't be too 'showy'. Pastel colours should be used, and materials like porcelain, because they give a bit of colour. She then tells me that she once decorated a fitted kitchen designed for single persons living on their own: a single plate, a single glass, a steel saucepan, a candle, some wine, a napkin: *because this gives the modern feeling that I suppose single people have.*

Lucia's role is to ensure 'customer satisfaction': consequently, she must always be polite to callers, watch what she says (because 'perhaps' is always taken to mean 'certainly') and try to understand the customer's problem so that s/he can be referred to the right person.

The meeting with Mario Primo

After I have waited for about an hour and a half, Mario Primo finally appears. We introduce ourselves and go up to his office on the first floor. He introduces me to several of his colleagues (one of whom is Francesca, head of sales, at present his fiancée and soon to be his wife). He is able to do so because all the sales staff have assembled in his office for a meeting: Mario has just completed an overhaul of the company's computer system and he has been explaining the new set-up to them.

The company has a sales staff of ten people, whose importance to the firm Mario immediately emphasizes: they are, he tells me, the company's 'inter-face' with its customers. Sales personnel are carefully selected, but of greatest importance is their training. It's vital that they have a clear idea of the company's philosophy (a medium-priced quality product designed specifically for the customer) and can convey this philosophy to the customer (anyone who buys a product from the company has the right to complain whenever and however they want). Above all, they must be able to figure out who actually decides on the purchase. He gives me an example: it's usually married couples who come into the salesroom, and sometimes they bring other members of the family with them as well. *And when you've got ten people in front of you it's a shambles because if you can't work out who actually decides on the purchase, you've lost the sale. You know that only one of those ten people is going to take the decision to buy, and if you don't treat that person properly, I can assure you he or she is not going to buy your kitchen.*

I ask about the type of customer targeted by the company's marketing. He answers as follows:

- couples;
- whether young or middle-aged, they must be 'well-off';
- if they are a young couple, they are probably about to get married; they want a nice kitchen, but not too expensive, given that they have other expenses;
- a middle-aged couple is likely to have grown-up children no longer living at home, *so they've decided to invest in the kitchen they've always dreamed about.*

As regards marketing strategy, Mario tells me that it is focused on the delivery of full customer satisfaction. Production is based on a series of 'pieces' (units) assembled into a range of models which can be dismantled, reassembled, extended or reduced according to the customer's wishes.

Over the next few days, as I watch the staff completing forms with the measurements of the kitchen units ordered by customers, I notice that all the orders are made out to men. *The one who decides is the woman, but when it comes to money . . . The man's name is written on the order form, and the woman backs off. It's a tricky business . . . you have to understand their relationship – in terms of power, that is. Because you often spend the whole* afternoon talking to someone, and then he shuts up and the other one takes over, and you realize that you've got it all wrong. Mario makes a comparison with his current (premarital) situation. *It was Francesca who went around looking at furniture and all that stuff on her own. Then she told me about what she had seen, because I was the decision-maker, I was the expert. And when they* (the salespeople that Francesca had talked to) *saw me, they said 'But who's this!' . . . we played . . . just for once we were on the other side.*

Mario Primo's office

Mario Primo's office is no different from – that is, no more luxurious than – those of the other managers: medium-sized, a clock, a map of Puglia and Basilicata, a calendar and a crucifix on one wall, two small landscapes on the other.

When Mario is in his office, the door is always open and no one knocks before entering. Arranged on his desk are a computer, a calculator, a pen-holder, some files, a photograph of Francesca, some folders and a telephone. On one side of the desk is his chair (padded, with casters) and two chairs (comfortable but without casters) on the other. Opposite the desk is a plan of the factory, in its present state and as it will be after restructuring (the company is about to erect another production shed). Hanging on the same wall is a huge aerial photograph of the factory. Each of the offices, including Mario's, has a window giving onto another office, which has a window through which the next office can be seen, and so on. These windows are set in line so that from one office it is possible to see (at least partially) into three others.

Leaning on a cabinet, I notice an ABC-book (with the English alphabet) and ask Mario about it. He tells me that it was a present from a consultant, prompted by the fact that Mario doesn't speak English and (perhaps) should learn the language. He adds that he'd like to bring in a puppet of Homer Simpson which someone gave him last week . . . *but it's tacky and it wouldn't be professional.*

To delegate or not?

Mario Primo checks the order forms compiled by the sales staff. They are the first to be processed by the new computer program and must therefore be carefully scrutinized: *to make sure that the sales staff know exactly what to do [. . .] I used to check all the forms myself, but I couldn't do it very thoroughly. We had to rely on the sales staff . . . we had to rely on them a bit too much.* Mario is therefore simply making a double-check: *when we're up to speed there won't be any need for this.*

Mario must now go off to a meeting to decide on the design of the new production shed. *Of course, I could decide not to go and tell them 'I'll see you in a week's time', but then I'd get the building with a week's delay.* He tells me this constant shuttling among tasks is extremely stressful. *Yesterday, for example. I did a hundred and one things, I was here until eleven o'clock* (in the evening), *but even then I didn't get the job done (and this morning the new order forms are already here) . . . this other work is still waiting . . . they say that routine is stressful, but this feeling that you'll never manage to get anything finished . . .*

It's a matter of delegating . . . I don't know if I'm a masochist and I want to do myself harm . . . I'd have preferred to concentrate on the financial plan for the new sales outlet today, go to Bari, or Potenza, contact the construction company about the new shed; next week there's a trade fair and I don't know anything about it. But now I've started . . . I only hope I can hold on for another couple of months.

When Mario leaves the office he bumps into Mr and Mrs Primo, and I witness a (rare) 'family scene'. Mario's mother tells him to decide where he wants to go on honeymoon. To Mario's answer that he does not have the time, she says that she can 'hold the fort' for a week. *I appreciate the effort,* he replies.

The designer

The designer is a young woman who has worked at Frau Kitchens for six months. She was previously employed by a furniture company in the neighbouring province of Bari.

She starts the conversation by drawing a comparison: where she worked previously they watched market trends very closely; here the main concern is with the customer. Her previous company 'took risks'; here they stick more closely to tradition. This has caused her some problems because she is sometimes told to design kitchens which strike her as 'a bit odd', and then Primo says that he wants them to be more 'normal'. A kitchen is 'odd' if it has an irregular shape, with projecting parts and vivid colours. It is 'normal' if it has a regular shape, relatively neutral colours and is simple to assemble.

I ask her if when designing a kitchen she has its future user in mind. She replies that she does: she thinks about a woman, and adds: *For example, here we don't design kitchens for single people!*

'What would a kitchen for a single person be like?'

Certainly without glass-fronted cupboards, because he'd never clean them. And then, I'd never put a shiny aluminium hood above the cooker because it would always be smeared with fingerprints. I've seen it at home, with my brother, when something's dirty he says 'Yeah, right, you do it' . . . he's not interested.

The sales staff

I talk to Mario Primo about the sales personnel. What, I ask, is the difference between a salesman and a saleswoman?

I prefer the women . . . they're more careful . . . probably, if all my sales staff were women I wouldn't be bogged down in all this (the reference is to the company's new computer system).

'And what about relations with customers . . . is there a difference between men and woman salespeople, according to you?'

Well, the decisions are made mostly by the women (i.e. women customers). *So a salesman is better . . . he gives a sense of security to the woman; he knows how to charm her.*

Accordingly, I decide to talk to the sales staff, which is made up of five people: Mr A, Mr B, Mr C, Mr D and Miss E.

I speak first to Mr a. He tells me that anyone who comes into Frau Kitchens knows exactly what awaits them, because of the care devoted by the company to its customers. He says that he sometimes spends a whole day designing a kitchen, and it's this personalized service that customers find so pleasing. *It's always the woman who decides on the purchase, because the man keeps out of it, he doesn't want to make the decision . . . he's not interested. If it's a young couple . . . then the man may check over the details . . . but more to see whether . . . yes, it's always the woman that decides.*

I then talk to Miss E, who has worked for the company for ten years. It is she, together with Mrs Primo, who 'decorates' the kitchen units for display, enhancing their features with objects and ornaments. All the kitchens in the display area are 'for couples' because couples constitute 99 per cent of the firm's purchasers. It is, she says, always the woman who is most interested, but eventually the man gets interested, too, especially in the technical details – the electrical appliances, for example. The choice is usually made jointly, unless the couple are accompanied by their families, in which case they choose what their parents have decided. She does not think that there is any difference between a salesman and a saleswoman: although, perhaps, *with a kitchen, which is an article for women, if you're dealing with another woman then you feel more comfortable, because she may have had more direct experience of working in a kitchen.*

'Do you think that yours is a job for a man or a woman?'

According to me there's not much difference. As I said, men have a taste for colours and furnishings, too. To see what I mean . . . take a car . . . that's much more a man's thing . . . because car engines . . . I mean, although I really like cars . . . when it comes to technical matters . . . I ask C and D the same question (about whether they consider their work to be male or female).

C: *I don't see any difference, although it may be that kitchens are more closely associated with women. But, then, with the work getting more and more technical, according to me, a man . . . with specialist knowledge can make up for not being a woman.*

D: *I don't think there's any difference. It's a job that men and women can do equally well.* I explain that the difference between male and female is not solely a question of biology. There are cultural stereotypes involved as well. *Yes, I see what you mean, but . . . you know, I wouldn't read too much into it. Also because it's basically about technical things . . . I know the little dodges to show a housewife that she can trust me. For example, putting the worktop between the sink and the cooker, the dish-rack on the right (unless the woman's left-handed), the fridge at a distance from the hob, for safety . . . These are all things that a housewife knows already, only that she's never thought about them . . . so when I point them out to a woman, she sees that I'm a professional and trusts me.*

C: *Anyway, according to me, when you go into a store which sells kitchen units, you expect to find women working there. Though a really attractive saleswoman . . . might make the other woman jealous, while a man can reassure the woman with his knowledge and make friends with the man, playing on the fact that they belong to the same sex.*

Mario Primo's method for 'handling situations'

Mario tells me that he has to go out for an appointment. He says that he could take me with him, *but I don't want this person to 'clam up'. You know, it's a bit tricky.*

He returns after a couple of hours and seems reasonably satisfied with the outcome of the meeting, which I subsequently discover was with a regional official to discuss a business grant for Frau Kitchens. Mario complains, however, that in order to obtain the grant he has to submit a report, and hence must spend the afternoon checking a series of documents. The telephone rings: the caller wants information about the functionary who will shortly be visiting the company. Mario says that he found him *a bit stuck up . . . but when we got chatting he relaxed a little . . . He doesn't know much about it . . . he may be useful if he trusts us . . .*

[On conclusion of the telephone call] 'Do you think that a businessman should be trustworthy?'

I think it's vital! For example, there was a person due to start work at the beginning of the month. But the accountant couldn't get the paperwork done. He deliberately did it for the company, of course, but then he had to make his excuses to the person . . . who in any case wouldn't have missed out on anything. But I'd given my word and . . . for me that's extremely important. At a personal level, even before work comes into it.

The next morning I find it impossible to see Mario: he has to talk to people (privately) before his afternoon meeting with the functionary from the regional authority. Most importantly, Mario has called in a business consultant to simulate the interview. The plan is for the consultant to act the part of the functionary and 'interrogate' Mario in his role as applicant.

I ask Mario how he thinks the meeting this afternoon will go. *There's someone coming to do a job that he's never done before. I discovered that yesterday. I went over to find out what he was like. People who don't know how to do their jobs are the most dangerous. Because they clam up and won't give anything away. So I'm going to be friendly, I'll get him to trust me . . . apart from anything else because I haven't got the skill to . . . Then, we've prepared a set of documents: two copies of some of them, because we've already given them to him, but we'll probably have to get him to look at them again so that we can explain things properly. I'd have preferred to deal with a technician. I'd feel more confident, because we've done the work and he could assess it better. Not that it's a situation where you're exposed and have to . . . bluff it out.*

Before leaving Mario to his meeting, I notice that he has tidied up his office. There are no longer files scattered on the desk. All the material has been neatly stacked, and the rest of the desktop is empty, apart from some technical drawings on prominent display. The functionary is a quarter of an hour late, and Mario uses the time to check the final figures on the computer.

When the meeting ends, I ask Mario how it went. As he expected, he replies, the functionary *didn't know what we were talking about; he didn't know what marketing was. He just did what he had been told to do.*

The meeting with Mr Primo

During my first day in the company, I spend the entire afternoon watching Mario Primo and two technicians as they work with the computer, checking an interminable set of codes for the program just installed. As they talk, various individuals come into the office with problems to be dealt with. I cannot help noticing that all these people are men. The only woman who enters the office, and then only from time to time, is Mrs Primo; but she only puts in a brief appearance, and without saying a word.

In the course of the afternoon, however, I notice a man whom I am unable to identify. Nobody speaks to him, and he speaks to nobody. Indeed, he is almost entirely ignored; nor for his part does he seem to be interested in anyone in the office. He walks constantly to and from the production department, and I imagine that he is a storekeeper, or something similar.

The next day, I ask Mario Primo if I can meet his father, at least to thank him for allowing me into the company. But Mario answers that he doesn't even know if his father is on the premises.

During the afternoon, the same man from the day before walks into the office next to ours, this time in the company of two other persons from the production department. From his tone of voice (although I cannot hear what he is saying), he seems to be someone in authority. However, the fact that the three of them are occupying the designer's office (temporarily free) suggests that they are from the production department and are using the office for a brief discussion. Then the office public address system announces a telephone call for Mr Primo, and I see the phone being picked up (in the next room) by none other than my 'mystery man'. I ask Mario

Primo for confirmation, and he says, yes, the man is his father. Despite my (low-key) insistence, I fail to have myself introduced, and Mario stalls me by saying there'll be plenty of other occasions.

The next day I arrive somewhat earlier than usual. I go up to the first floor, where Mario Primo tells me that I shall have to wait a quarter of an hour because he is busy talking to a designer about the new plant.

While I wait, I hear a voice calling 'Mr Primo'. I turn round and see . . . the Director himself! I jump to my feet, and with three steps I cross the corridor and come face to face with him.

'Good morning, Mr Primo, I am Attila Bruni, from the University of Trento'.

Bruni?

'Yes, we spoke on the telephone about my research, and you were kind enough to put me in touch with your son . . . well, I wanted to introduce myself . . . and thank you for letting me come into your company . . .'

. . . (quizzical, bored expression)

'. . . You often have these situations where you talk on the telephone, but then you fail to meet . . .'

. . . (quizzical, bored expression).

(I begin to run out of things to say, and his silence is certainly no help) '. . . I've met your wife . . . I met her . . . (I do not know what to say) . . . I was wondering . . . Well, I was wondering whether it would be possible for you to find me half an hour for an interview. I'm here until Friday . . .'

. . . (quizzical, bored expression).

'I'd be very grateful if you could tell me the story of this company . . .'

. . . (quizzical, bored expression).

'Yesterday your son went over the main stages, but I was interested in the overall idea . . .'

THE IDEA! Well done! (enthusiastic expression, interested tone of voice).

'It's the idea that's decisive in the end . . .'

The idea is everything in the life of a man (he links arms with me). You have an idea and on that you base an entire life . . . Yes, we'll find the time, you'll see.

And there our meeting ends.

Over the next few days, whenever our paths cross, greetings are exchanged. Yet Mr Primo is elusive, and I do not want to be rude by harassing him over the interview. For the time being I watch him, noting that he always moves around on his own, between production (on the ground floor) and administration (on the first floor), mobile phone in his pocket, gazing into the distance. He is most frequently approached by the staff from the warehouse and the only person to whom I see him talking (both of them use the informal 'tu') is the head storeman (Roberto, his nephew). Although he has his 'director's office' on the second floor (the only office with a nameplate), he also has a 'station' in the technical office so that he can supervise work in the production department next door. It is a 'station' in the sense that it is not a desk but a reception counter with a raised front section which conceals the person sitting behind it.

On the last day, *in extremis*, I manage to interview Mr Primo. The interview does not take place in his office but in that of the designer, who is away. I do not record the conversation because he resents the presence of a tape recorder.

He tells me that a business idea is something that you have inside you, and that it requires *great determination, great sacrifices and much courage*. He started off as a worker in a German factory which manufactured wooden brush-handles. He then returned to Italy and set up as a cabinet-maker. He decided to produce hand-crafted kitchen units, which (thirty years ago) did not require skilled labour. He chose the name of the company – Frau Kitchens – in memory of his sojourn in Germany, and to avoid using his own surname.

The names of the kitchens

I want to find out who decides on the names given to the kitchens. I talk to the head of marketing. He tells me that 90 per cent of them are chosen by Mrs Primo, but not according to any logic. I ask why they all have female names, and he replies that it's standard practice in the industry, because kitchens have implicitly female connotations. But then I discover that one of the firm's models has a male name: 'Clinton'. The head of marketing says that the name was chosen by Mr Primo: the kitchen was designed when Clinton was elected president, and Mr Primo took it in mind to 'entitle' it that way (the next model was the 'Hillary'). There should have been another 'couple' – 'Thelma' and 'Louise' – but 'Louise' sold badly (the kitchen not the name) and so only 'Thelma' was left.

I ask Mario Primo for further explanations. He tells me that some kitchens take the names of the daughters of staff members; others are named after minor Italian starlets. 'Clinton' is the only male name, but it was acceptable because it denoted an important person. This, says Mario, is the criterion: finding a name which is immediately recognizable and can therefore be remembered easily. And male names? According to Mario, they don't work, because kitchens are articles 'for women'. *Sofas, maybe, they can have male names, or watches, even better. But just think if someone asks you 'What's this kitchen called?' and you answer 'Giovanni'! . . . it wouldn't sound right . . . because it's* la cucina *(feminine in Italian) and a sofa is* il divano *(masculine) . . . and that's different.*

I run into Mrs Primo and ask her about the names. She tells me that she chooses almost all of them herself, and that she associates them with events, precious stones, or flowers, according to the type of kitchen. *'Clinton' was chosen because it was an important, imposing kitchen. The 'Hillary' was more cute, and therefore needed a softer-sounding name.*

Mrs Primo

Intrigued by the constant but muted presence of Mrs Primo, I ask her if she will give me an interview. Her office is on the second floor, situated between the meeting rooms and Mr Primo's office.

When we have climbed the stairs, I notice that the only door with a nameplate on it belongs to Mr Primo, 'General Manager'. Mrs Primo's door is ajar. Her office has a splendid view across the surrounding countryside. There is a photograph of a boys' football team, and next to it a sports trophy. The office is relatively bare, but nevertheless comfortable. There are a pair of cupboards (on the right) and a desk with a chair on the one side and two chairs on the other. Placed on the desktop are a pen-holder, a telephone and a table calendar (there is another one hanging on the wall).

The interview gets under way and I ask Mrs Primo about the history of the company. Her immediate response is: *Have you already asked my husband?*

After the interview, we return to the first floor. But over the next few days I continue to gather information about Mrs Primo's role in the firm, which intrigues me greatly, given her constant but marginal presence in the organization's everyday life.

For example, during my first morning I observe the final stages of the meeting with the sales staff. The head of marketing talks about 'aggressive techniques of market penetration' and announces that Mr Primo has overcome his misgivings and decided to produce a down-market kitchen for sale at a competitive price (*because for the sales people, price is an argument as well*). Mrs Primo speaks as soon as he has finished (Mr Primo is not present) and says exactly the reverse. Frau Kitchens is a brand-name which is and always has been synonymous with quality, and they cannot fall short of that standard.

Moreover, during a conversation with the head of marketing, I notice that a meeting is in progress in the next room. Present are Mario Primo, his mother and a couple of engineers. The mother sits at the head of the table, with the engineers and Mario along its sides. I ask the head of marketing what is happening. He tells me that it is always Mrs Primo who takes charge of this kind of negotiation: *I often consult her myself, about all sorts of things. And anyway, what do you want, she saw this company being born, she knows everything better than anyone else, even better than Mario Primo. She can solve problems that you couldn't even imagine . . .*

On my last day, I am in the technical office and ask all the people present (collectively and provocatively) if they think I shall ever be able to interview Mr Primo. They laugh, exchange glances, joke at my question, as if I've failed to understand whom I'm dealing with, yet the atmosphere is cheerful and noisy. But then Mrs Primo comes into the room. They fall silent, compose themselves. One of them removes a sweet paper from his desk; another empties the cigarette stubs from his ashtray. None of them speaks; they listen in silence as Mrs Primo gives instructions.

Frau Kitchens: a matter of honour?

The case of Frau Kitchens exemplifies those situations in which an entire firm is devoted to conveying a certain image of its product and of the market segment in which it operates. Indicative in this regard is the fact that the statements made by the actors concerning the company's business and values are all perfectly consistent. However, this is not due to some sort of persuasion or coercion by management, but rather to the difficulty of perceiving viable alternatives to what has 'traditionally' always been the case.

When the product is gendered: the fitted kitchen as the custodian of tradition

The market for fitted kitchens is resistant to innovation, and this is because it reflects a set of social customs. In the collective imagination, the kitchen is primarily the place in which certain social (as opposed to culinary) situations occur. Managing to impose a 'new' type of kitchen (for single persons living alone, for example) would require inducing change in the modes of kitchen use (as described by the designer).

It is this feature that more or less explicitly provides the basis for all the activity and corporate strategy of Frau Kitchens, which accordingly grounds its distinctiveness on a different feature: that of customer care. The latter, explained Mario Primo at our first meeting, does not simply mean giving advice; it also involves matching customers' expectations. Frau Kitchens' clientele consists almost entirely of families, and these families have expectations as to the product on offer and as to the service provided: a personalized service in that it respects what we may call 'family equilibria'. Neglecting either of these expectations would mean losing a customer.

Fortunately, however, both Mario Primo and the sales staff invariably encounter the same types of 'equilibria' in their customers. Frau Kitchens' market mirrors a reality in which responsibility for the management of domestic spaces is assigned to women, and the management of the family's finances to the man, while the parents of both are empowered to influence the final decision. This is therefore a reality with pronounced gender features, in particular:

- a dichotomization of the 'spaces' of competence according to gender membership;
- the construction of practices and symbols that enable this dichotomy to develop in everyday routine;
- the family as a means of control.

We shall now conduct more detailed analysis of these aspects in the entrepreneurial activity of Frau Kitchens.

Dividing up the 'spaces': a question of competence?

During the episode entitled 'The sales staff', Mario Primo states (from an organizational point of view) that he prefers women, because they are more 'careful'. However, given the features of the company's target market, it is more prudent, he says, for potential purchasers to be handled by men, because they give customers a sense of security and they know how to be 'charming'.

The matter is given further specification during conversations with the sales staff. The salesperson/customer relationship is a delicate one, especially when the negotiation centres on an object (a kitchen) with gender connotations. A female salesperson may prove to be more 'reliable' (in the sense of 'credible'), and she may also be able to exploit her 'direct experience' to her advantage. Yet if she is 'charming', she may provoke the jealousy of the housewife on the other side of the table. A male salesperson, by contrast, is less reflective of the customer's gender expectations, but he can compensate for this by demonstrating his technical expertise, thereby both reassuring the female customer and colluding with her husband.

It is the gender element that gives meaning to this representation of the salesperson/customer relationship:

- The initial assumption is that men and women have different roles in the management of 'domestic affairs', of which women have practical experience, while men carry out some sort of 'supervisory' role.
- A set of attributions designed to emphasize differences is constructed on this assumption. Men are interested in technical aspects and make rational choices, while women are more malleable and are susceptible to 'charm'.
- The different worlds of gender membership thus defined give rise to different relational mechanisms. The relationship with (and among) women is based on emotionality and is intended to reassure; the relationship with (and among) men is more distant, or at any rate regulated by more objective parameters.
- The relationship between the salesperson and the customer (whether a man or a woman) is managed on the basis of the gender membership of each. This entails adoption of language and a demeanour that match the person's gender position within the organization to which s/he belongs.

The process just outlined exemplifies what Joan Acker (1990, cf. chap. 2) has described as the production of gender within organizations. The creation of divisions (hierarchies, powers) on the basis of gender profiles is followed by the production of symbols and thought patterns which evince, justify and counterpose these divisions. At this point, interaction and gender positioning among individuals become key features of everyday organizational action. The final outcome of this process is what Acker identifies as an organizational logic predicated on male times, bodies and expectations.

A posteriori, it is precisely this structure of relations that we identified at Frau Kitchens, and discussion of it enables us to move to the second aspect of gender which influenced the company's organizational and entrepreneurial activity.

'Doing business': where times and modes are (male) gendered

If we give a different reading to the case of Frau Kitchens, one couched in temporal terms, we note that the dimension time is both absent in the company and of fundamental importance to it. It is absent because the activity of Mario Primo, the members of his family and his colleagues is incessant, unremitting – almost as if it is performed in a single temporal flux. It is of extreme importance because a 'lack of time' seems to be one of the most problematic aspects of the entrepreneurial lives of Mario Primo and Frau Kitchens.

Mario Primo performs a wide variety of work tasks: he coordinates the sales staff; he handles relations with institutional actors; he even plans the company's future. The episode 'To delegate or not?', in particular, shows that entrepreneurial time squeezes out any other variant (private time, for example), and that personal preferences must be ordered according to the dictates of the corporate time frame. This entails, for example, that individuals must be willing to subordinate their private time to organizational dynamics – as when Mario Primo gave priority to the business over his honeymoon.

These varieties of time are accompanied by certain 'modes': primarily the non-emotionality with which particular episodes are handled – a case in point being the episode when Mario Primo tells the researcher what he expects to happen at his meeting with the functionary from the regional authority. On that occasion, the relationship (entrepreneurial and organizational) established by Mario Primo with the functionary was poised between two different domains. On the one hand, Mario Primo complained about his interlocutor's lack of expertise, which prevented any technical assessment of his project presentation. On the other, the functionary's lack of expertise was a resource, because Mario Primo could set the relationship on a different footing, that of trust, provided he could convey a 'reliable' image of himself.

Entrepreneurial activity (i.e. an application for a grant) thus becomes something akin to espionage, the outcome of which is determined by the amount of trust that the entrepreneur is able to establish. A 'trust relation' is put forward as the only possible remedy for the interlocutor's lack of expertise. This interlocutor, however, expects to be presented with a set of technical data. The 'trust' is therefore constructed on proof that the two parties share common practices and a particular approach to problems that can be defined as rational. The 'trust' is therefore grounded on Mario Primo's adherence to an abstract and socially shared model of entrepreneurship. The latter is constructed around the (gendered) symbolic elements of 'possessing competences' (at the organizational level) and 'keeping one's word' (at the interpersonal one).

All these times and modes are presented, and perceived, as natural aspects of entrepreneurial activity. However, the model of entrepreneurship that they depict is the one akin to the cold and rational sphere of the male, where the 'Entrepreneur' is a public (male) figure in constant relation with other actors and perpetually ready to sacrifice himself to such needs and such unforeseen eventualities that may arise.

The 'familiar' element: the importance of tradition

We have seen that Frau Kitchens' customers have bonds with their families that give the latter considerable influence over the final decision. We have also seen that this is one of the distinctive features of the fitted kitchen market, given that social traditions constitute one of its symbolic referents. We shall now try to show how the 'traditional' element, too, influences the entrepreneurial and organizational activity of Frau Kitchens.

Firstly, tradition has a direct influence on the final product. The designer explains that the company pays close attention to customer needs, and that this entails the design of 'normal' kitchens. The comparison that she draws with the company for which she previously worked suggests a further aspect, one of interest from the entrepreneurial point of view: striving for the 'market' (an abstract entity) requires a competitive and ruthless approach, whilst a focus on the 'customer' (a flesh-and-blood person) requires a much more emollient posture.

Secondly, Frau Kitchens has a history with markedly 'traditional' features. Mr Primo, the founder of the company, started off in dependent employment. He then set up as an independent craftsman, and eventually formed his own business. He thus embodies the traditional (male-gendered) image of the person who progressively achieves his or her goal by hard work and strength of will. This image is reflected in Mr Primo's account of his story as an entrepreneur, marked as it was with 'determination', 'sacrifices' and 'courage'. Again by virtue of this image, a business idea acquires an entirely particular significance, being represented not only as a 'stroke of genius' but also as the element which imbues the entrepreneur's life with meaning, making a 'man' of him and marking out his 'destiny' – a destiny reflected in the company's name (in honour of its origins) and in the day-to-day tasks that require Mr Primo to supervise production work personally, so that he does not even have the time to occupy his director's office.

The names of the kitchens: how tradition pays homage to (female) gender

Tradition assigns different fields of action to the male and female. Whilst it helps to preserve the implicit asymmetry between the two terms, it is also the process which legitimates the female and gives visibility to it within a world where 'normality' is constituted by the male.

Fitted kitchens, for example, in that they are 'female' articles, are valorized by being given female names which are immediately recognizable to the public and exalt their gender characteristics. This is the logic explained by Mario Primo (in the episode 'The names of the kitchens'), and it is according to this logic that an 'important' and 'impressive' kitchen is given the name of a man: as in the case of the 'Clinton' kitchen, which, although it belongs to the male world of politics, has its female counterpart in the 'Hillary'. In this example, from a symbolic point of view, although the female element (a Christian name which therefore denotes a person) is placed in a marginal position with respect to the male one (a surname which therefore calls attention to the family), it is absolutely necessary for definition of the relation between the two.

This paying homage to gender is also reflected in the organizational activity of Frau Kitchens, where women tend to occupy female roles (the example of Lucia suffices) and men occupy male ones (in that the majority of the employees are of male gender).

The case of Mrs Primo is interesting. Her figure is difficult to bring into focus when one reads the ethnographic report. In fact:

1   We meet her in the first episode, but her image is already out of focus. The outsider notes only a formal distance between her and Lucia, and her evident curiosity in the stranger (the researcher) sitting in the entrance lobby. Mrs Primo appears and then disappears, moving among the offices without uttering a word.

2   When we meet Mrs Primo again, she is in the company of her husband and son, talking about the latter's honeymoon. The fact that she is discussing an 'organizational' matter from both the private point of view (it is her son's honeymoon) and the corporate one (Mario Primo will be absent from the company) adds further confusion.

3   In another case, a female member of the sales staff is talking about the décor of the kitchens. Decorating the kitchen units on display is a key presentation technique, but the involvement of Mrs Primo in the process seemingly stems purely from the fact that she is a woman.

4   Finally, it emerges that it is Mrs Primo who has chosen the names of almost all the kitchens. The curious aspect here is that the matter is mentioned as if it is of entirely no consequence, as if choosing the name of a kitchen has nothing to do with organizational decision-making.

Careful inquiry was therefore required to ascertain that Mrs Primo was always present at meetings, that she was closely attentive to the company's image and that she was a figure that the workforce regarded as important. These elements are clearly apparent in the three episodes (those concerning Mrs Primo) with which the Frau Kitchens case concludes. The common denominator among them – as with the four other episodes in which she appears – is that nobody explicitly identifies Mrs Primo among the organizational and entrepreneurial actors, even though everyone constantly meets her, observes her and acknowledges her capability and authority.

In her performance of a variety of roles, and in her self-presentation as 'la signora Primo', the woman standing at the side of the man entrepreneur, Mrs Primo bears out the traditional view of women as essential for the management of everyday routine but perennially obscured by the male. The most frequently cited example is that of patriarchal societies (like Italy's) in which masculinity is extolled for its 'productive' force, while women are given responsibility for the management of (also economic) domestic matters, but without value being set on this work.

Frau Kitchens: a matter of honour?

The case of Frau Kitchens maps out the intimate linkages among product, market sector, and entrepreneurial and organizational activity.

What is interesting from the gender point of view is that this represents one of those cases in which the traditional component is present to such an extent (in the product, in the company's target market and in its day-to-day work) that spaces are created in which maleness and femaleness can develop independently, with no attempt made to find connections or complementaries between them. Here maleness displays its distinctiveness in precisely its ability to obscure the female and render it invisible. Not that female action is devalued; rather, it is simply ignored – except in specific areas where maleness would find it embarrassing to justify or explain its presence.

The suspicion prompted by these observations is that the female is not exalted because maleness has some sort of 'honour' to protect, lest it lose its acquired privileges and lest the traditional parameters used to interpret reality break down. The process observed in this case is that of preserving the 'rent position' (Bruni and Gherardi, 2001) enjoyed by masculinity at Frau Kitchens, as in many other settings. In the case just examined, in fact, the symbolic space of masculinity is given a competitive advantage whereby everything male is over-valued and transformed in terms of a social ability specific to a particular class of persons ('men'). The man who emigrated in the 1960s and returned to his village to set up a small firm with the money earned abroad; the entrepreneur who still works in the machining department when he could delegate the manual work to others; the son of the firm's founder who makes the definitive 'rational choice' of reorganizing the business according to managerial principles: in all these stories, the fact that the protagonist is a man provides a guarantee for the authenticity of the process and the result. From a symbolic point of view, 'doing' masculinity is here an intrinsic part of the life of a successful business. The representation of the salesperson/customer relationship (for example, but see also Mario Primo's speech on being 'credible') depicts masculinity as an ability involving tacit 'knowing-how' (La Cecla, 1999, see chap. 2). The symbolic space of the female is subject to the opposite process: what women do is made recognizable by the fact that it is not a male practice and is therefore not perceived as a corporate resource. In a work setting connoted as male territory, the problem of social comparison (Festinger, 1954; Berger and Luckmann, 1966; Tajfel, 1981) with a group – women – perceived as socially distant may not arise for men. However, the presence of women and their self-confinement within the bounds of the 'female' attests to the authenticity of the process and to respect of gender balances.

LeCò Fashion

LeCò produces leather garments for a well-known fashion house. A limited company owned by three brothers and a sister, it has thirty employees. The business was set up with a grant to support entrepreneurship in the south of Italy, and by reinvesting capital from a tannery owned by Mrs Creta's parents.

The company's premises are located on the main road between Otranto and Uggiano in the southern region of Puglia. There is no sign to the factory and, unless someone gives you instructions, it is impossible to find, even though it stands next to the road. The building has two storeys and is somewhat 'imperial' in its appearance, with marble columns and a ponderous design. The intercom buttons (with a video camera) alongside the front gate are marked only 'Offices' and 'Residence': the owners of neither the offices nor the residence are named.

It is Mrs Creta (the businesswoman that I am to 'shadow') who comes out to greet me at the front gate; Mrs Creta works full time for the company, while her brothers have other business interests as well, and are often absent. I ask her why there is no sign outside giving the name of the firm. She says that there is a nameplate beside the intercom, but it's faded with the weather. *I've asked Simone* (her brother) *to do something about it several times . . . I should call somebody . . . But we don't want a big sign on top of the building, nothing like that. Also because the factory is already big enough, so . . .*

Located on the ground floor of the building is the production department, while upstairs are the office, the stitching and ironing department, the showroom (where I see some paintings left to dry[3]) and Mrs Creta's apartment. The keys are left in the lock of the office door – and also in that of Mrs Creta's apartment – but staff always knock before entering.

Just as I am introducing myself to Mrs Creta, we are approached by a man who did some work on the factory when it was being built. Mrs Creta has called him about some drainpipe leaks which are staining the marble on the entrance. They have known each other for some time and they talk as friends. The conversation is relaxed, even though each of them has a point to argue. Mrs Creta asks the man to give her an estimate (for what appears to be rather complicated repair work). He replies: *We'll have to see your mother . . . because she talked about it . . . and your father . . .*

Mrs Creta: *That's right, the most pernickety ones* (laughs).

I see a clothesline on the balcony at one of the windows of the sewing department. I ask Mrs Creta about it.

Yes, I have the fortune/misfortune to have my home here [. . .] I'm one of those people who puts heart and soul into what they do . . . and then I tend to give vent to my emotions . . . in fact, I had to get away for a while . . . At first, she had promised herself to move away as soon as possible, but then she got used to living on top of her work, and now she has no desire to go and live in a block of flats.

The office

The office is 'inhabited' by three people: Mrs Creta, Roberta and Antonio. Three open doors give onto smaller rooms (one of them is used for meetings, another is the office where Mrs Creta's father works, while the last one is shared by Roberta and Simone). There is also a closed door linking the office with the machine room, where the patterns are designed by computer.

Arranged on each of the three desks in the office are a computer, a telephone, a pen-holder, paper, fax forms and a calendar. The room is lit by neon, but an enormous window opposite Mrs Creta's desk lets in brilliant sunshine and affords a distant glimpse of the sea. The room also contains a photocopier, a typewriter, a whiteboard screwed to the wall, a plant, a radio recorder, the monitors for the four surveillance cameras arranged around the building, and a video intercom. Attached to the walls are messages, faxes, photographs, and photocopies of newspaper articles on CoNa fashion shows (CoNa is the firm for which the family produce their leather garments).

'With women you can mess about more; but with men . . . you're more restricted'

Mrs Creta shows me some items from their collection. Apart from differences in size, I notice that the women's garments have zips made in colours and shapes not usually found on men's clothes.[4] How come?

Because women are more scatter-brained than men . . . more vain than men, but I think that's natural . . . and so they spend more money . . . probably . . .

'In what way "natural"?'

(Mrs Creta's mother is taking part in the conversation. Since they say essentially the same things, the speech that follows is reported as if produced by a single person.) *Women have to change outfits all the time; it's part of their nature. If a woman puts on a dress in the evening, she won't wear it again the next morning . . . because women always have to change . . . though they might wear the thing again later . . . But men don't feel this need;*

they think more about their cars . . . but not about their clothes. Also because men have only one way of dressing . . . a jacket, a tie, a shirt . . . and these are classic items which always look right.

Mrs Creta cites the example of her husband: a lawyer who takes pains to dress in a certain way, making sure that his shirt is always ironed and his jacket is always neat. *Also because of the work he does. But he doesn't buy a lot of clothes, because he's not interested.* The same applies to her father. Not only is he uninterested in clothes, but in certain periods (when work in the factory is particularly intense), *I have to force him to go to the barber, because otherwise he looks like a mad scientist. I have to send him out to get shoes . . .*

The mother adds that it is especially important for women to have a 'fine wardrobe', so that they can display their status and feel more security. *Also because . . . at a party, let's say . . . the men don't look at each other so much . . . at what they're wearing . . . but the women . . . they notice immediately; they're much more observant.*

'Why are you all women here?'

I address this question to Mrs Creta's mother, given that the only man in the company (apart from her sons and her husband) is Antonio, and that the work could just as easily be performed by men – as regards not only the machines but also the cutting room and the computer. She tells me about her experience with a young man in the cutting room.

She had been the one to flank him at the beginning; she explained what he had to do and checked his work. But when she saw that her presence made the man uncomfortable, she decided to have him flanked by another worker, although she continued to time his work rate. The workman exploded when he overheard Mrs Creta's mother telling the forewoman that she would make him recoup the time he had 'wasted' (the man was rather slow) in the form of unpaid overtime. He began to shout and swear, claiming that he was physically unable to work any faster. She sacked him on the spot, telling him that she had no intention of working with someone who refused outright to learn and 'adjust'.

Mrs Creta, on the contrary, would prefer to hire some more men. *Because there are too many women in this company . . . I like a balance . . . women are very good workers, but they've got problems to do with their . . . nature as women. There's not much of a work culture around here . . . when they get pregnant . . . well, when they find out that they are pregnant, after a couple of weeks they go on maternity leave . . .*

A little later Mrs Creta talks to her mother about hiring another girl in the production department, in view of an expected increase in orders. It transpires that someone has already been recommended to her mother by a friend, whom she now rings and asks for the girl's telephone number. Mrs Creta's mother says that she wants to train three new female workers, so that she can move another woman to the stores. Mrs Creta replies that her father doesn't want a woman in the stores, because of the physical strength needed to stack and move boxes full of heavy leather garments. *Leave father out of it, I'm the one who organizes production*, is the mother's rejoinder.

I ask if she has ever thought of hiring a man in the production department. *Yes, but there's this sort of prejudice against a man sewing . . . or cutting . . . There'd be less back-biting, though . . . There are some periods when the girls all get on well together, and others when they fall out . . . women are more likely to bicker.* Ten minutes later, the person calls back to say that the girl she mentioned has just accepted another job.

The mother immediately telephones the girl and lists the good reasons why she should prefer the job with LeCò. She emphasizes the company's solid financial situation and the experience she would gain in a specialized field. She then suggests a ruse for backing out of the other job offer without causing offence.

Mrs Creta's typical day

Mrs Creta's work in the office is extremely mixed. A large part of it involves handling relations with suppliers, customers, the CoNa management and the workforce. As a consequence, Mrs Creta has a variety of different scenarios to deal with during her working day. I note down episodes which convey the atmosphere in the office.

One afternoon, the atmosphere in the office is fraught because a delivery has not been made on time. Mrs Creta tries to find out what has happened to their package, and realizes that the error has been made by the shipping company. She telephones the company's complaints department but gradually loses her temper as she is shunted among internal extension numbers. She decides to ring her direct counterpart at the company headquarters in Lecce. After complaining to him and explaining the reason for the error, she writes a fax in protest.

Even with CoNa, with whom we have friendlier relations . . . we've learnt that it's always better to send a fax . . . because if something happens . . . I mean, in this case nobody wants to take responsibility, they're all passing the buck. And so it seems that it's our fault, that LeCò is inefficient . . .

She asks her father for advice. *Papa, what should we do about this package?* (The father) *Send a fax 'for the attention of'* (a manager at CoNa) *. . . and then see whether they don't take five minutes . . . if not, I'll ring them myself* (irritated) *It has to be a toughly worded fax; if not who's going to pay for the stock?*

On another occasion, Mrs Creta receives an order from a boutique (the firm also supplies individual customers). However, the fax does not specify the patterns requested; instead, it simply states 'like the ones you sent last year'. Mrs Creta must figure out whether the items from 'last year' were part of the summer or winter collection. She looks through the order book, and as she does so informs her mother and a female worker about the problem. The worker goes off to the production department to fetch the patterns from last year, so that they can work out what the boutique wants. Mrs Creta asks her mother whether she thinks they can complete the order in time. The mother takes personal charge of the problem, and goes to the production department to find out how much leather there is in stock. Mrs Creta asks her father about the price of the models from last year, but he cannot remember. I ask her if it is always the father who decides the prices. She says *yes, it is*; indeed, he wouldn't trust anyone else to do it. She tells me about the time when he was in Pisa, and flew back just for the afternoon to draw up the new price list, and then immediately caught the evening flight back to Pisa.

The last episode arose when the patterns for the new collection have been sent to Milan. Some days later, Mrs Creta sends a fax asking which of the patterns should go into production, and which should be discarded. The reply fax is unclear, although it says that another will follow, and that this one will be 'definitive'.

Three days have passed and the fax has still not arrived. Given that LeCò has to know exactly what items are to be made if they are to start up the new production phase in good time, Mrs Creta decides to call the CoNa offices in Milan. She discovers that they have decided that all the patterns must go into production, but have not bothered to inform LeCò of the fact.

Mrs Creta immediately sends a fax to the CoNa manager responsible (Emma), with whom she has a good relationship – although (according to Mrs Creta) she is one of those people who tend to avoid or put off problems, rather than solving them. In fact, she says, this is not the first time that a situation of this kind has occurred with Emma, which makes her even more irritable.

A little later, Mrs Creta's mother and Simone come into the office, and she tells them what has happened. At the same time:

- Mrs Creta telephones some of the women workers to tell them to come in to work tomorrow. While telephoning, she decides that she hasn't got time to organize her daughter's birthday party for next week: better postpone it for a couple of days.
- She telephones her daughter to tell her that the party has been postponed.
- She sends a fax to a customer who doesn't want to pay for an order and, simultaneously, she writes to CoNa to inform them of the matter.

Mrs Creta and the firm

I note down the following remarks by Mrs Creta with regard to the firm:

- (On inheritance) *Since the company was set up for the children as well . . . My dream is to let my parents enjoy life more . . . still working, but more relaxed.*

- (On her work in the company) *I first worked in sales . . . from the ages of 18 to 26, I looked after the CoNa sales campaigns . . . then I had a baby . . . the company was set up . . . and I devoted myself to what was mine . . . You know, when you have a child, your life inevitably changes . . . because you have responsibilities that you can't evade . . . I came back to the company almost by accident, I slipped back into it . . . but I'm happy with my lot.*
- (On the company's 'image') *We're an odd company [. . .] Even with me, they expect la Signora . . . at the bank, for example, I've had difficulties . . . now they know me . . . because I'm simple, but at least I am myself . . .*
- (On the company's 'spaces') Mrs Creta tells me that she wants to use the showroom for her daughter's birthday party. She talks about a party that she organized last year. She covered all the sofas and closed all the bedrooms and the offices, leaving the showroom open. *I got everyone involved. The aunts and my mother prepared the salads and the cakes, and then I got the women workers to stitch the covers for the sofas.*

Public relations

I ask Mrs Creta if it is she who handles all the company's external relations.

Yes, I suppose so . . . not all of them. Those when you have to be a bit more ruthless . . . for example with the delivery people, those you have to push. Or the office in Milan . . . but I consult my father first if I can . . . so that I don't carry all the responsibility . . . if I can, I divide it, so I can have an easy conscience . . . even if afterwards . . .

I ask how important public relations are for a business person.

She tells me that she has no natural bent for public relations: she's had to learn. *It may be because I've always been a bit headstrong . . .* (laughs) *if you want to have good relations with other people, you've got to be polite at all times, but . . . that doesn't mean just saying 'Good morning/Good afternoon' . . . I always say these things, but there's more to it than that.* She explains that she always tries to get on well with others: because it makes your work easier . . . *The banks, for example, I find it impossible to deal with them because they look at the figures . . . and you have to win them over!*

[. . .] *You sometimes get these customers who are so arrogant . . . and I show them my claws . . . but then, I'm a hard case . . . maybe because I grew up with three brothers . . . so the tough guy is me!* (laughs) *But I've learnt, I've even changed my character, because by nature . . . I've never had many friends . . . at school I had one friend, but the others . . . I'm a bit anti-social, I know that I'm awkward and . . . I mean, I've learnt that you can't always be ruthless . . . it's a bit like a husband and a wife: I have to compromise on certain things, otherwise sooner or later one of us gets crushed. And experience has taught me a lot of things . . . the fact that I ran the sales office in Milan for CoNa . . . and then when I handled relations with the tanners for my parents, I found out a lot . . . and I've always followed my father, you know, with the banks . . . having my parents close has been an enormous help to me.*

LeCò: between tradition and innovation

Analysis of LeCò's story reveals a manifold and dissonant reality which is difficult to arrange into any systematic order.

In so far as the company operates in the fashion sector, it is explicitly involved in the discourse on gender. However, because it is engaged in the production (not the design) of clothing, the Male/Female distinction is perceived as a 'technical' question which concerns the measurements, rather than the 'wearability', of the company's models. Moreover, the company can count on the long experience accumulated by Mrs Creta's family in the leather goods market (her parents ran a tannery) and the fashion business (Mrs Creta had previously been head of sales at the firm for whose trademark LeCò produces). The company's organizational dynamics therefore display an explicit 'relational' character which involves its personnel not only in their work but in their emotions.

Dressing as an entrepreneur

Apparent in the first conversation with Mrs Creta and her mother (apart from their personal considerations on men and women) is a 'common-sense' wisdom on how men and women dress.

Dressing (and by implication undressing, too) is an activity more female than male, in that women 'have to change all the time', whereas men are 'not interested' (they are more interested in cars, for example). Note that this is not simply to create an antithesis between men's and women's attitudes to clothes; rather, it is to refer to a world of symbolical meanings. In the conversation reported, the public context used to frame women is the 'party', while that used for men is 'work'. In other words, men and women are contextualized in radically different social settings. 'Work' and 'party' constitute two opposing worlds of meaning, in that:

- they are mutually exclusive;
- the former is 'regular', the latter 'sporadic';
- the former abides by generally endorsed standards, while the latter allows for more 'eccentric' behaviour.

Different modes of behaviour are thus attributed to the public presences of men and women, and this has implications for the ways in which they dress. Wearing a 'jacket, tie and shirt' is a tactic adopted to forestall any conflict with the (male) gendered world of entrepreneurial activity. In the same way, having 'a fine wardrobe' enables a woman to hold her own in the (female) gendered milieu of a party.

In their choice of clothing, therefore, men and women are appreciated to the extent that they blend with the worlds in which they are situated.

Contaminating spaces

As Mrs Creta declares, and as borne out by the situations observed, her life has been marked by a close correspondence between private and business choices. One factor undoubtedly responsible for this is that the two spheres have coincided: for example, by virtue of the physical closeness of her home and her work. Yet on numerous occasions during the ethnographic field-work it appeared that Mrs Creta's entrepreneurial activity was instead determined by random events: she herself says that she had 'slipped back' into the company. This is not to imply that she is indifferent to the company's future; indeed, she declares that she cares deeply about it. Rather, it is the reconciling of different interests that constitutes the distinctive feature of Mrs Creta's work and reveals a (male) gendered assumption of entrepreneurship.

In recounting (and living) her life, Mrs Creta is not concerned to present herself as someone who inhabits two distinct and independent spheres. Quite the opposite: her ability to juggle such diverse aspects is a resource which makes her organizational life more manageable (and liveable). Indeed the term 'organizational life' is probably restrictive, in that it comprises more 'global' affective relations, personal expectations and life projects.

The episode that most clearly illustrates this feature is 'Mrs Creta and the firm', which concludes with a small example of Mrs Creta's attitude to the company. On one occasion she had organized a party using the firm's premises as a container which symbolically mixed two contexts – work and the party – contexts which, as we have seen, are contradictory. The company temporarily loses its 'austere' nature alien to the lives of the people who work there and becomes a place in which activities other than strictly 'productive' ones can take place. Thus gainsaid is the stereotype of the lone entrepreneur, and of the firm as a quasi-sacred creation to be venerated: entrepreneurship is not necessarily monolithic; it can be shared with others and is of varying nature.

Handing down customs

Mrs Creta's entrepreneurial experience is clearly buttressed by the presence of her family. Her parents (although they are not formally involved in the company's activities) frequently feature in corporate episodes. In the situations recounted to convey the multiplicity of relations in which Mrs Creta as a businesswoman is involved, intervention by the father, or by the mother, is often crucial – not because they provide practical solutions to problems but because they indicate the 'approach' that Mrs Creta should adopt. The episode 'Why are you all women here?' (for example) evidences the decision-making power exerted by Mrs Creta's parents over the hiring of new personnel, a power exercised not over individuals but over the approach to be used in the recruitment procedure. Similarly, in 'Mrs Creta's typical day', she asks her parents for advice based on what she knows to be their distinctive knowledge. They tell her whom she should contact, they lend a helping hand, they advise her on the tone that she should adopt and they point out where the responsibility lies.

In all these cases, therefore, Mrs Creta's parents are a source of experience, rather than of authority. Their main concern is to place their experience of entrepreneurial behaviour at LeCò's disposal, behaviour which they describe in terms of respect for deadlines agreed, for pledges made and for power relations established.

The 'Family', however, is the arena in which affective, rather than productive, relations are developed, and it is in this sense that it acts as an important antidote to the system just described. In the episodes cited, in fact, the family's support is described by Mrs Creta as assistance in the emotional management of organizational life. 'Company' and 'Family' are thus closely bound up with each other. This is not a novel finding, given that almost all small businesses in Italy are owned and run by families. It is interesting, however, because it conflicts at the symbolic level with the (male) rhetoric to the effect that 'doing business' requires 'renouncing' one's family, or that maternity may be damaging to a company's business.

LeCò draws a large part of its 'strength' from the participation in the company by all the family's members, with merit allocated to each of them according to his/her competence and his/her degree of involvement. The latter is interpreted in its 'productive' dimension, but even more so in its 'affective' one, as the support provided for the 'states of mind' that arise in the course of entrepreneurial activity.

What is conveyed, therefore, is the importance of the 'Family' as the *locus* of memory and as the archetypal (and thus, inevitably gendered) model of relations to which to aspire.

Experience as the salient feature of entrepreneurship

We have just seen the importance attributed to 'experience' at LeCò. However, when describing her behaviour in handling the company's public relations, Mrs Creta highlights an aspect of 'experience' that has thus far not been mentioned. The experience on which she relies, she says, does not consist in a stock of technical knowledge, but rather in a 'relational' posture which she describes as follows:

- being headstrong;
- being polite;
- being cooperative;
- being arrogant;
- being tough;

- being aggressive;
- being obstinate.

Some of these modes of behaviour are deprecated ('being arrogant'); others are recommended ('being cooperative'); yet others are seen as unpleasant but necessary ('being aggressive'). All of them, however, define relations evocative of gender in that they refer to either male or female symbolic domains, according to the behaviour expected of an entrepreneur. Moreover, they are relations experienced on the basis of Mrs Creta's (female) gender, both within her family (her 'toughness' is cited as being at odds with her 'femaleness' but in accordance with a childhood surrounded by males) and in business (for instance when it is necessary to be 'ruthless', which is appropriate to an entrepreneur of either gender). They are ways of 'footing' (Goffman, 1974): 'keeping pace' with behaviours shared and valued in a social setting, aligning oneself within a frame of events that embeds interaction arrangements. Note, however, as Goffman (1980) stresses, that footing is not to be thought of as a mechanism which statically orders people within a series of practices; rather, it is a way out of those practices. As Mrs Creta pointed out, once one has 'kept pace' with the movements of the participants in a particular framework, it is possible to activate other frames or to upset the rhythms of the present one.

LeCò: between tradition and innovation

The case of LeCò depicts a reality rich with gender features. However, giving systematic account of these features is difficult because they spring from very different relational processes, ones driven by familial rather than commercial dynamics.

A further aspect to bear in mind is that, due to the close relations between family and firm, it is not easy to confine Mrs Creta's activity to one of these two domains. This proves to be a resource in situations when she receives sufficient affective support from her family so that she does not face the market alone, but it is also a normative element imposed on her work as a businesswoman.

The overall impression gained of LeCò is that of a company seeking to carve out not only a place in the market but also a space of relations. This is an 'innovative' endeavour to the extent that an attempt is made to inaugurate new modes of entrepreneurship. But at the same time it is an endeavour that reflects the archetypal image of the family as paramount. Mrs Creta's business activity thus symbolically indicates the possibility of a dialectic between the spheres of tradition and innovation. This dialectic relies on the process of footing (Goffman, 1974, 1980) just described in the previous section. In Goffman's thought[5] (1974, 1980), in fact, footing processes are ambivalent: they enable people to align themselves within a predetermined frame and disrupt its coordinates, because once 'in step with it' they are able to disturb its rhythm and deviate from its path. The action of Mrs Creta, and of LeCò in general, can be interpreted in terms of footing: LeCò's activity is explicitly focused on aligning itself with a family archetype, but, once aligned with this archetype, it activates traits of gender and entrepreneurship that do not stand in a static relationship. What Mrs Creta cites as the salient feature of her entrepreneurial ability – experience – is nothing but the ability to take the stances of others and situate them in different contexts and practices.

Atlantis magazine

Atlantis is a limited company owned by five partners which publishes a monthly magazine for gays and lesbians.

The editorial offices are located in Milan, in the basement of a block of flats. You find the street, ring the intercom, cross a courtyard, descend the stairs, go through a door (always open) and find yourself in the office. It took me a couple of days to realize that, although there were several rooms, there were no doors (four linked rooms). Nor were there personal desks (apart from Mr Air's) or 'dedicated' telephones: when a call came in, all the telephones rang together.

Mr Air arrives at nine o'clock, he makes a couple of phone calls and then has a cup of coffee. The office is empty. Mr Air switches on the computer: he has to finish paginating an article by Mr Water (the graphic designer). Mr Air is the chief editor. He arrives first in the morning, because he has the only set of keys, and it is he who turns on the central heating and the coffee machine.

Twenty minutes later the two assistants arrive (Mr Fire and Mr Wind, who are a couple). There is no fixed 'clocking-on time', but rather a time-span during which the staff has to come into work (*As you can see our working hours are quite flexible . . . But I should work on my own; I reckon I'd be better off. Why? I'd be responsible for what I do and I wouldn't be accountable to anyone . . . very simple* (laughs) . . . *It's obvious that I can't* (laughs)). Mr Air must go out, so he gives instructions to the other two. The conversation is laconic, but this may be due to the Monday-morning effect. I watch and for the moment keep my distance.

A routine morning

We set off for the printers. We take the bus because Mr Air does not have a driving licence. He talks to me about his relations with the printers. He's changed firms frequently, and the owner of this one is also his partner: he publishes the magazine. His premises are not far away and are within easy reach; Mr Air hands over his material and we leave.

We get back to the editorial office, where Mr Air, after he has made a couple of phone calls to people he failed to contact earlier, sits down next to

Mr Wind and follows the impagination of the magazine. When the phone rings it is almost always Mr Air who answers.

We go out again, this time to the bank to pay some bills. I take the opportunity to ask about the magazine's corporate set-up. First it was a partnership; now it's a joint-stock company. Previously there were eight partners who worked on the magazine. But this created a *public-sector* mentality. *Each of us had his own row to hoe . . . and he was only concerned with that, there wasn't any interest . . . he was only interested in one job and in earning a steady salary.* They split, and now there are five employees (plus contributors), of whom three are partners. Mr Air believes that their company bears little resemblance to a 'Company'. *Companies usually have a more hierarchical structure, more centralized, whereas here you've seen . . . there's almost no structure.* He also tells me that he would like an entirely independent administrative board which would conduct audits and monitor the work. *Because, all right, I can get away with it . . . but there are others . . . who should be checked up on.* 'Can't you do it?' *Yes, but it's also me who gets the hassle!* 'But you're the chief editor?' *Yes, but as such I should be worrying about the next issues* (annoyed) *. . . instead of being here in the bank making payments.*

An almost private matter

The decision to launch a publishing venture has intersected with Mr Air's private life. His desire to do something that is not merely a 'job' (Mr Air dislikes 'working' in the purely productive sense) and his choice of politics 'in private' (Mr Air no longer votes) are all aspects bound up with the magazine. *Atlantis was also a way to come out, to come to terms with my homosexuality.*

In 1986, for example, Mr Air (together with others) opened Querelle, the first gay club in Milan: in the mornings he worked in the magazine offices, in the evening at the club. But he had to quit after a year because of the stress.

I report a series of phrases and brief observations which convey an idea of Mr Air's relationship with Atlantis:

- Mr Air would like to take a holiday: a week in a place where it's hot. His brother has a travel agency and has found him a real bargain. But he can't tear himself away from work. *I'm sure that if I went off for two months, the magazine would fold.*
- On Wednesdays the Atlantis editorial office closes earlier because Mr Air takes himself off to the cinema at five o'clock, given that ticket prices are reduced on Wednesdays.
- Mr Air doesn't consider himself a 'true journalist'. What is a 'true' journalist? *It's someone you tell 'Write me an article by three o'clock', and he writes it for you, but me . . . I'm not like that . . . I need to think about things a bit . . . and then journalists write such garbage!* (laughs).

- Having finished registering invoices with Mr Fire, Mr Air says to him: *Fire, can you go and check the post for me?* Fire gets up and goes into the other room. But as soon as he is out of the door, Mr Air yells. *Fire! Come here!* Mr Fire returns. *Don't leave your stuff like that . . . all over the place.* And Mr Fire tidies up the files on his desk. *Fire . . . have you telephoned that woman about the coffee?* No, he hasn't. *Huh, Fire . . . OK . . . all right, I'll call.* A brief pause and then: *Fire, have you paid the rent?* (There would be nothing odd about this question if it concerned the magazine premises. But Mr Air is asking about the rent for his own flat.)
- Not including hard core material in the magazine is an aesthetic choice for Mr Air. *Pornography . . . strikes me as an alternative, rather than something complementary.* I ask him about the first issues. *The first issues, yes, they were a bit more mixed, also because fifteen years ago the lesbian question didn't exist, and in fact at the beginning Atlantis was a 'gay culture monthly'* (the title is now 'gay and lesbian culture monthly'). *Then I wanted to get round this lesbian question . . . that is . . . they're 5 per cent of the readership. With this equal opportunities business we'd end up by having five lesbians in the office . . . to make up the quota . . .* (laughs).

The saga of the front cover

Mr Air wants to use a photograph of the catalogue of a well-known fashion designer on the front cover of the next issue. But he has to get permission. Mr Air knows the designer because he too is gay. But he is difficult to get hold of. Although Mr Air has been leaving him messages for days, he hasn't called back. *It's really tough having to insist . . . to keep on trying . . . you look so weak.* He fails to get through. The girl on the telephone has said that the designer is going to be extremely busy for the next two days and she can't put him through. But let us proceed in order.

In May, when the first issue of the magazine came out in revamped format (all in colour, more pages, glossy paper, folding cover), the fashion designer (who is gay) telephoned Mr Air to congratulate him on the new graphic design. A month later Mr Air asked him for an interview, and in reply received only a catalogue and a handful of press releases. They wrote an article nevertheless. They also managed to sell advertising space to the designer, but at a quarter of the usual price because his marketing advisers said that that magazine was *too politicized.* 'What is politicized about it?' *I don't know. People who work in marketing, they flick through magazines, they don't read them.* And so we come to this month, when Mr Air asks for permission to print a photograph of an old copy of the catalogue on the magazine cover. *Yes, no, I don't know*, nobody gives him an answer. Mr Air is re-routed to a marketing manager (*some 25-year-old who's been to bed with . . . because it's always the same old story*), who makes himself simply impossible to find. But how is the cover photograph chosen?

We used to choose a photo of a good-looking boy . . . a nice face . . . a beautiful body. Now we try to choose something which . . . well, it should be right for the cover . . . we still don't know whether it sells more or less copies . . . although according to me it's not that Atlantis's readers . . . but, you know, for the sake of image . . . you have to. To continue the conversation, I say somewhat provocatively '. . . and anyway, a lot of newsagents still classify Atlantis among the porn magazines . . .' *I've nothing against pornography!*

The saga of the advertising

I talk to Mr Fire. Before the split he was in charge of the bookshop; then the bookshop was taken over by the group that had left and he moved to the editorial staff. He handles advertising and relations with advertising agencies, although in reality, he explains, there are very few contacts with the agencies. The magazine relies more than anything else on a network of contacts (with various homosexual organizations) built up over the years. Yet it is precisely the advertising agencies that the magazine needs, because they offer longer and bigger contracts on which long-term investments can be made. But (Mr Fire explains to me) you have to know someone in an agency; otherwise it's difficult to convince them. Moreover, Atlantis carries 'porn' advertisements (sex shops, hot-lines, hard core videos), and some people are reluctant to have their product appear alongside a sex shop. Others are even more reluctant for their product to appear in an avowedly gay magazine.

Mr Fire would be willing to remove the hot-line advertisements if he could be sure of filling the space with other advertising. But he can't do this a priori; if he does, the magazine will fold. But what irritates him most is that no one ever says outright 'No! Because you're a gay magazine!', and everyone ducks the real issue. And yet (he says), there does exist a gay lobby in Italy, in both fashion and advertising. *Dolce and Gabbana, for example . . . they're gay, they put themselves forward as gay, they have products which draw on homosexual imagery . . . but it is people like them that give us the greatest problems . . . so I'm pessimistic and I say that there's no sense of community . . . and then just imagine how much it would cost D&G to buy space in Atlantis: with the money they spend on organizing a party we could live for a year!* He believes that everything is made more difficult by the fact that a gay market does not exist in Italy, apart from saunas and night clubs. There are no restaurants, no beauty products, no bookshops, no theatres, no cinemas. But what should a gay restaurant have? *Nothing specific . . . it should be opened by two gays . . . create a particular ambience . . . a place which caters to the gay community.*

The surprises of ethnographic research

One day, the person that I am 'shadowing' says to me: *Have you got a boy-friend or are you single?* Seeing that I'm a male I realize that he thinks that I am homosexual. He is wrong, but the question catches me unawares, and I begin thinking about how being considered an 'insider' might help me access information about the group. They all know that I am there to do ethno-graphic research, and I assess the possibility of 'sharing' the reality in which I find myself while not belonging to it. As it happens I have no partner at the time, and so I simply answer that I am 'single'. The conversation stops there, for the time being. I know that he thinks I am gay, but I cannot understand why. I find this odd but not particularly embarrassing. What I do find embar-rassing is the fact that I have done nothing to prevent him from thinking I am gay (but nor have I done anything to make him think otherwise), and this in the name of 'research' and 'managing to become part of the reality observed'. Yet it is strange that I am able to 'mislead' a homosexual. In a sense it is a problem of culture, and here a brief aside on my 'image' is required. I have long hair (tied back), a chin beard and an earring (just one), I wear cardigans and slacks, and I am what is usually called 'soft-spoken'. This is not the first time that someone has thought I am gay, but it has usually been heterosexuals who have done so. This is because (I presume) my 'image' matches the stereotype produced by Western heterosexual culture of homo-sexuals. And this is why a homosexual who knows his 'culture' (and who does not have long hair, an earring or a goatee, and is decidedly more 'in-your-face' than I am) often takes me for what I am not. Moreover, I have homosexual friends, both gay and lesbian, and none of them has ever mistaken my heterosexuality. Which I therefore presume is reasonably obvious.

In the days that follow, because I am in close contact with the person for entire workdays, I find myself discussing just about everything with him – politics, films, travel, hobbies, and so on. We obviously do not think in the same way, but there emerges a world which both of us to some extent share, at least at the level of key-words.

On my last day, during the final interview, we begin to talk about the situation of the gay community in Italy and how nice it would be if things were otherwise. I want him to tell me something about the relations between male, female and homosexuality. If there exists a (cultural) construction of male and female, I am interested in whether and how homosexuality is likewise constructed. I realize that this means that I must ask a declaredly homosexual person about prejudices against homosexuals, and I also realize that this is not a particularly 'polite' thing to do. In fact I do not know how to put the question to him. But then I remember that he thought I was homo-sexual as well, and at a certain point ask: 'But the other day, for example, why did you ask me so confidently if I had a boyfriend?'

Why?

'Well, I'm usually asked if I have a girlfriend . . .'

Yes, but you can see!
'You can see what?'
That you're homosexual.
'And how can you see?'
Well, a straight would have settled the gender question simply by doing research on women. And then a straight would never have been interested in the homosexuality issue in particular . . . and he would never have managed to get so far into the editorial offices as you have done . . . And so on, but with the oddity that the more the conversation continues, the more his remarks about heterosexuals grow insulting. I listen, merely smiling and nodding from time to time. And I begin to grow uneasy; not because I am heterosexual and he is insulting heterosexuals, but because he does not know that I am 'straight'.

I have spent eight hours a day for five days with this person. We have eaten together, chatted, and he has been as helpful as possible . . . and in the end I am duping him. And I also realize that if he hadn't taken me for a homosexual he would never have talked to me as he is doing now, and that my justification for leading him on is the 'valuable information' that I am gathering. Which is a pretty 'weak' justification in terms of relations with another person.

. . . but you are gay, aren't you? This is the final phrase in his explanation of why he thinks I am gay. As a question it leaves no room for evasion; the answer can only be yes or no. I am extremely embarrassed, because saying 'yes' will be an outright lie, while saying 'no' will reveal that I have been dishonest with him.

'No.'
Ah, how strange, I could have sworn . . .
'Yes, I know . . . yet . . . no, I'm not homosexual.'
So . . . have you got a girlfriend?

'No, I really am single.' It is unpleasant to face someone to whom you have just admitted that, although you haven't been lying, neither have you been telling the truth. Of course, I could explain the value of being considered an 'insider' for my participant observation. But this does not seem a good excuse from a human point of view. Indeed, it seems shabby. The problem is that when he asked me (three days ago) about my sentimental situation, and I decided 'not to tell a lie' (but *not* in the sense that I told the truth), I never imagined that the situation would come up again. I can guarantee that there was nothing premeditated in my behaviour. I did not know what was going to happen some days later, nor did I know whether I would be able to handle the interviews without committing 'heterosexual' gaffes. But I think I managed to do so.[6]

Atlantis: does heterosexuality matter?

The case of Atlantis is important not only because it exemplifies an aspect of entrepreneurship but also because it highlights an assumption that in the other cases remained invisible because it was taken for granted: the presumed heterosexuality of organizations and of entrepreneurial activity.

In the fieldnotes, it seems that homosexuality structures organizational identity and the experience of people involved in the company: life and work choices are apparently determined by occupying a dimension fashioned by one's sexual orientation. The latter, however, is never treated together with the gender issue, with the consequence that homosexuality apparently 'transcends' the Male/Female.

Homosexuality and Heterosexuality as dimensions parallel to the Male/Female

Although homosexuality does not seem to interweave with gender dimensions, the ethnographic fieldwork does not reveal a setting shorn of socially shared meanings of Male/Female, either at the organizational or, even less, the personal level. Emotional aspects are invariably treated (and dismissed) as 'weaknesses' (for example, when Mr Air complained about seeming weak to the person he was trying to contact during 'The saga of the front cover'). In the same way, an abstract and 'rational' model of organizational planning is often extolled (for example, when Mr Air talks about 'running' the editorial staff). The reference models (the 'true' Company, the 'true' journalist) appear to be the classic ones, unless they are discredited by other clichés (the 'true' journalists who write 'garbage', or the 'true' marketing managers who merely flick through magazines before deciding whether or not to advertise in them). The figure of Mr Air himself, as a businessman, is not at odds with the canons of male entrepreneurship: even if the climate of the editorial office is 'collaborative', Mr Air tends to present himself as the pivotal figure (for example when he says that if he went away for a week the magazine would fold).

The problem, then, is to understand the relationship between Homo/Heterosexuality and the Male/Female dichotomy in the case of Atlantis.

From what has been observed, the relationship seems to be a 'parallel' one, in two senses:

1   The Homo/Heterosexuality dichotomy seemingly operates 'in parallel' with Male/Female. A homosexual order is just as much taken for granted as a male one, and homosexuality is intrinsically 'better' than heterosexuality (in the same way as the male discredits the female). In the organization studied, people's roles are legitimized by their homosexuality and their opinions on homosexuality (just as happens in those organizations where masculinity is the sub-text of people's careers). Thus

the processes that sustain the two dichotomies seem to move along the same track. Mr Earth's attitude, when he stresses his difference from the 'softies', provides a sufficiently emblematic example of how the values scale of the Male/Female can also operate in a homosexual setting.

2   Seen from another standpoint, Homo/Heterosexuality and Male/Female are two parallel lines which never meet. The former is based on sexual practices, the latter on a set of socially shared meanings. Hence it follows that the former has mechanisms of inclusion and exclusion which are much more 'objective' than those of the latter and, consequently, while Male/Female may be (and in effect is) constantly subject to negotiation in interpersonal relationships, Homo/Heterosexuality still remains an essentially static dichotomy. When Mr Air says that they will be forced to hire lesbians by 'equal opportunities' legislation, what he is not questioning is female homosexuality. In other words, Mr Air is using the female counterpart of his homosexual practice, not of his gender position.

The 'communitarian' dimension of homosexuality

Some dichotomies typical of the Male/Female are not employed to describe experience in this 'parallel' movement; while others, rather than being contested, simply become meaningless.

The interweaving narratives of public and private that emerge from the fieldnotes constitute the Public/Private dichotomy as nonsensical from a homosexual point of view. Homosexuality has apparently induced the 'inhabitants' of the Atlantis editorial office (in particular Mr Air, when he says how important running a business has been for his 'coming out') to cease distinguishing between the two dimensions and to merge them together. The label 'homosexual', moreover, although it concerns the (private) use that people make of their bodies, has its more immediate repercussions on the (public) lives of these people.

Homosexuality is a label more than a category. This was especially evident in joking among the editorial staff (also directed at me), when 'homosexual' could be a humorous epithet when inappropriately applied.

However, the ethnographic data raise the issue of 'appropriateness'. Although the label 'homosexual' is considered to be misplaced when applied to a person's attitudes, it was used to define Atlantis's market sector and public. And even more contradictory is the fact that this market and this 'public' (in the words of the actors) do not exist but are based on suppositions and hopes that have no counterpart in reality.

The subtle distinction is probably due to the (grammatical) use of the word 'homosexual':

•   The term 'homosexual' is inappropriate when it is used as a general noun ('the homosexual'). In this case it is viewed (and employed) as a 'stigma'

(Goffman, 1963), a static label unable to comprise the differences and coexistences in the reality that it seeks to circumscribe.

* The term 'homosexual' is appropriate when it is used as an adjective ('the homosexual person'), and therefore to refer to one aspect of a person's life. In this case it is understood (and used) in respect of its 'local' aspects situated in the experience and opinions of the persons concerned.

In organizational terms, this distinction seems to determine the standpoint adopted. The distinctive feature of Atlantis is that it is situated in (and caters to) a market and people *one* of whose characteristics is homosexuality, though this cannot be defined homogeneously. For example, the total absence of emphasis on the political dimension of a business like Atlantis is due, we believe, to the view of homosexuality as only *one* aspect of a person's life-course, without it being lumped together with other choices. This was particularly evident in 'The saga of the advertising', when the 'community' took the place of the 'movement'. Talk about a 'gay community' authorizes the speaker to emphasize the reciprocal help relations that 'should exist' among homosexuals, while eschewing political notions like 'power' or 'conflict'. At the symbolic level, the idea of a community relates to much more situated dimensions able to merge the public and the private into a loose-knit system of relations realized (Mr Fire hopes) in the market. It is likely that a person is able to express his or her sexual orientation independently of his or her political persuasions. Or better, if this is feasible for a hetero-sexual, there is no reason (as Mr Earth points out) why it should be 'odd' for a homosexual.

Finally, belonging as a homosexual to an organization which produces a product for a homosexual public is only a coincidence of events (and intents) like those that link a group of heterosexuals engaged in producing a product for a heterosexual public. These are 'loosely coupled' events which have only some features in common. The organizational practice that springs from them seeks legitimation in the market, not through construction of a political space.

The nature of the market

The intention of Atlantis is to legitimate its identity as a company in the market. The ethnographic accounts (particularly the two 'sagas') show an idiosyncratic nature between the market and the 'orientation' of Atlantis as a company. The reason for this clash is not clear: it does not depend on aesthetic factors (Mr Air has been complimented on the magazine's new graphics), nor on political ones (the magazine does not follow any particular political agenda). The only feature explicitly (and repeatedly) cited is the magazine's anomalously homosexual orientation, and as it regards not the personal choices of the members of the editorial board but the determination to assert this orientation in the market. The anomaly thus arises less from a subjective choice than from the insinuation of doubt into hegemonic masculinity and into one of its canonical assumptions: the (compulsive) heterosexuality of physical desire and practice.

Sexual practices are dimensions that the patriarchate assigns to the private sphere, and their public discussion may upset a gender order that is already unstable. Presenting oneself 'for what one is' implies respecting the loci of affirmation of oneself practices. If these are homosexual, they must a fortiori remain private: they cannot be affirmed, not even in a free and impersonal market. The market, it seems, is heterosexual in its orientation, in accordance with the maleness that underpins entrepreneurial and organizational dynamics.

The role of the researcher: what does being 'single' mean?

As illustrated by the episode 'The surprises of ethnographic research', calling oneself 'single' in a setting where the presumption of heterosexuality is inoperative may be 'ambiguous'. Consider again the process that led to Mr Air's conviction that the researcher was homosexual:

- *Yes, but you can see! . . . That you're homosexual!* The researchers' outward appearance, although physically in keeping with the male gender (he sports a beard), is also contaminated by features that might be related to the female (he has earrings and long hair). His outward appearance, in association with his role as a researcher, is therefore somewhat ambiguous. Hegemonic masculinity rejects ambiguous and 'contaminated' identities like, for example, gayness (Connell, 1995, 2000). Mr Air took it for granted that the researcher knew this; and in some way this awareness was shared by both of them.
- *Well, a straight would have settled the gender question simply by doing research on women.* Here, a 'straight' is somebody who takes for granted that, when talking about gender, one talks about the female (worse, about 'women'), with the male (i.e. 'men') being treated as obvious or normal, exploiting the advantages of a culture which a priori assumes the masculine as given. In this manner, maleness is made invisible, removed from critical reflection and continues to be the prime term, the one in relation to which the other is defined by default. In Mr Air's discourse, a 'straight' is someone who took the Male/Female dichotomy for granted and exploited the advantages of thinking 'in masculine terms' in order to 'settle the question by doing research on women'.
- *And then he would never have been interested in the homosexuality issue in particular.* The dominant model of sexual desire, what Connell calls 'cathexis' (1995), is one of the most covert assumptions of masculinity, justified as it is by being 'biologically normal'. It seemed strange to the person interviewed not only that a 'straight' could interrogate masculinity but also, and especially, that he would be interested in sexual

(we would say bodily) practices in organizations. In other words, if he found it difficult to understand that a 'straight' could be interested in the gender processes underlying organizations and the market, he found it even more incomprehensible that a 'straight' would want to investigate one of the most covert aspects of organizing: compulsive heterosexuality. Although it may make sense to talk about 'female leadership', it does not make sense to talk about 'gay leadership'.

- *And he would never have managed to get so far into the editorial offices as you have done* . . . Bodily practices are not necessarily sexual practices. They belong to the broader category of interrelational practices that sustain them. His discourse evinces that this relation is very close, so much so that those who do not engage in these practices are not accepted by their organizational community.

Thus, the implicit elements on which his discourse was grounded were respecting aesthetic (and external) categories of Male/Female; assuming the coincidence (or otherwise) of gender identity with biological identity; taking for granted the model of socially shared bodily practices; proving membership (or otherwise) of a community.

These are probably the same criteria that the interviewee applied to himself when he was no longer recognized as a member of the male heterosexual community. But he was also implicity revealing to the researcher the shared gender assumptions of the organizational culture to which he belonged, showing that his non-compliance with them automatically placed him in other communities. Calling himself 'single' caused such confusion in his interlocutor that he committed the error of interpreting the researcher's non-recognition of a gender rule as signalling indulgence in 'other' sexual practices. He probably thought it normal that somebody interested in homosexuality, and knowledgeable on gay issues, should also be a member of the homosexual community, taking it for granted that sexual orientation in organizing was not under discussion. Likewise, the researcher committed the opposite error of interpreting their membership of 'peripheral' categories of masculinity as proof of one (and only one) difference: it was obvious to him that his heterosexuality required no justification, or clarification, and that it could never be the subject of confusion or deception, taking for granted that 'research' has nothing to do with sexual practices.

Thus, both of them were trying to cancel their difference, thereby falling into the 'gender trap' (Gherardi, 1995) of the mutual exclusiveness and internal homogeneity of different gender identities. In seeking to distinguish themselves from the gender order of their respective organizational cultures, they were both reaffirming one of its cardinal principles: the cancellation of difference and the assumption that what is 'diverse' must be internally homogeneous.

Atlantis: what is the importance of being heterosexual?

Various themes emerge from the foregoing discussion, in particular:

1   Homo/Heterosexuality and Male/Female are distinct and 'parallel' categories. It is impossible to talk about one without talking about the other, just as it is not possible to discuss one without dissecting the other. The processes by which organizational sexualities are constructed and attributed follow this double track. They direct attention to the interconnections and rigidities associated with it and propose a 'communitarian' dimension for sexual practices.

2   The processes by which practices acquire meaning operate through the Male/Female dichotomy, but from a homosexual point of view. The outcome is ambivalent (more than ambiguous) because the reality produced seems entirely shareable, although some of its features are utterly unpredictable (from a heterosexual standpoint).

3   Market, business activity and organizational reality are bound together by a common 'taken for granted' (Schutz, 1932): that is, a normative model of (hegemonic?) masculinity. At Atlantis, this process operated through organizational dynamics constantly poised between the mechanisms of dominant sexual desire and the search for a 'space' within a 'Male' grounded *also* on a specific form of cathexis.

The inclusion of a homosexual enterprise in the research sample thus enabled us to account for the heterosexual assumption of the market, but of the researcher too, evidencing that the dominant model of sexual desire is constantly present in the negotiation of organizational practices. But the inclusion of a homosexual enterprise also brought with it the (covert) hope that this would represent an occasion for destabilizing the symbolic space of (heterosexual) masculinity, in accordance with the literature (Hocquenghem, 1972; Mieli, 1980; Gonsoriek and Weinrich, 1991; Weed and Schor, 1997) and with our personal political beliefs. However, perhaps because Atlantis did not pursue a political agenda, and perhaps because (like any other enterprise) it was obliged to build a reputation in the market, we cannot say that this was the case. Gender seemed to perform the role of a commodity: an item like any other to be sectioned, capitalized upon and marketed. What we found, therefore, was a process of 'gender commodification', in the sense that the symbolic space of gender was exploited as terrain on which to (re)construct market relations. For that matter, was it not the same process that prompted the member of our group who carried out the fieldwork to capitalize on his external appearance and engineer a misunderstanding over his sexual preferences for the sake of research?

Conclusions

The foregoing re-reading of corporate stories prompts a number of concluding remarks.

The first relates to one of our principal premises concerning the conduct of an ethnographic study of entrepreneurship as a gender practice and of gender as an entrepreneurial practice. The stories that we have recounted describe a space in which gender and entrepreneurship do not belong to distinct practices and symbolic domains; instead, they mark out the limits, opportunities and meanings of organizational action. Masculinity finds legitimation, and is realized, in certain of the practices that sustain entrepreneurial activity; and, reflexively, entrepreneurialism is symbolically realized also through gender performances. Hence derives the rationale of these concluding remarks, which do not seek to draw demarcation lines between gender and entrepreneurial practices but instead emphasize the continuities between them. The entire work of re-interpreting the ethnographies therefore followed the criterion of extrapolating processes which characterize the practices that construct gender.

A second consideration concerns the structure of patriarchal relations that seemingly subtends all the stories recounted, albeit in different forms. The situations in which patriarchy was most evident are probably those of Frau Kitchens and Asie Welders, the latter already 'handed down' across three generations, the former now passing from the first generation to the second. In these cases, gender dynamics and the role attributed to the 'Family' are constitutive and structuring parts of entrepreneurial behaviour and organizational dynamics. In the case of Erba Shirts and LeCò, the patriarchate takes manifest form as 'tradition'. In the former of the two companies, gender dynamics operate covertly, giving rise to a pre-selection among the options available which masks maleness and femaleness (and the features associated with them) with the rhetoric of 'normality' and the 'taken for granted'. In the case of LeCò, tradition again takes concrete form in the 'Family', not as a source of authority but rather as the archetypal model of relations to which to aspire. The editorial office of Atlantis is not susceptible to this interpretation, however, for it is the only case in which family and tradition are absent from the history of the company and its members. Nevertheless, Atlantis, too, is affected by the dynamics of hegemonic masculinity, given that it must constantly cope with a market that embraces a model of heterosexual physical desire and practices.

Although the patriarchate constitutes the system of symbols and practices that sustain masculinities in the organizations, there is also a destabilizing factor apparent in all the cases observed. In none of the firms analysed does one find the figure of the 'lone' entrepreneur, and none of the stories has a single protagonist. On the contrary, the large number of people involved in running the businesses sometimes made it difficult to identify who the 'real' entrepreneur actually was. This finding directs attention to the situated nature of entrepreneurial activity, which never consists of abstract models but intersects with numerous other dimensions (public and private) in the lives of organizational actors. It therefore highlights the relations and processes manifest in entrepreneurial and organizational action, emphasizing that these come about, not in an impersonal space governed by the laws of abstract economic rationality, but in the concrete arena of quotidian behaviour.

We therefore asked ourselves what a meta-ethnographic interpretation of the processes observed would be, an interpretation able to encompass all the ethnographic work, following actions (the practices that construct gender and entrepreneurship) and not actors (the firms and the entrepreneurs). We singled out five main processes, which we now describe to the reader as summarizing and concluding theoretical reflection on our ethnography.

A first process common to the various businesses studied relates to the fact that gender and entrepreneurship are performed by constantly shuttling between different symbolic spaces. Gender and entrepreneurship are constructed through the dual presence that characterizes and situates the action of the male and female entrepreneurs studied. We wanted to associate Asie Welders explicitly with the idea of crosswise presence, because the process was particularly apparent in that business. But it is possible to put this construction on all the situations characterized by fluid and continuous movement between different spaces of signification (home/work, reproduction/ production, secretaries/entrepreneurs, housewives/work women) which facilitates breach of the boundaries that mark out the symbolic order of gender and entrepreneurship according to the occasion. One thinks in this regard of Mrs Erba who, while instructing her female workers, also talked to her cleaning woman about domestic chores. Other examples are the constant mingling of public and private, family and firm, distinctive of the organizational routine of Frau Kitchens and LeCò (albeit with different overtones); or Atlantis, where the magazine merged public and private experience together. Thus, gender and entrepreneurship are a theoretical dichotomy whose dividing line is constantly blurred, traversed and denied, but then jointly reconstructed a posteriori by diverse actors.

The second process of gender and entrepreneurship construction also moves in this direction. It concerns negation of the crossing of symbolic boundaries, so that sanction is given to separation. When actors behave in breach of the 'ceremonial' aspects of doing business, or when critical situations arise and order must be re-established, activating a correct gender score may constitute an efficacious 'remedial practice' – to the point, for instance, that the two (female) owners of Asie Welders were persuaded that their engineer (a man) should perform the role of the entrepreneur while they pretended to be secretaries. Note that the process also operates in reverse, as in the case of Atlantis, where demonstration of strong orientation to the market served to restore the balance between symbolic universes thrown out of kilter by transgression of heterosexual practices. This is the notion of the dialectical enactment of 'ceremonial' and 'remedial' work that we used to summarize symbolically the case of Erba Shirts but which forms the backdrop to all the 'ceremonies' of entrepreneurial action and doing gender that sanction the division between the male and female spheres – including, as at LeCò, the 'clothing ceremonies' required of men and women so that they do not cut poor figures in their respective organizational/entrepreneurial and gender milieux.

The same process is apparent in the radical dichotomizing of tasks according to gender membership at Frau Kitchens. In this case, however, there is a further feature that merges with the 'boundary keeping' intended to protect the positional rent enjoyed by males in numerous settings, and which we used as the label for the firm. 'Doing gender' and 'doing business' are therefore tied together by a tacit knowledge which imposes further boundaries and further constraints on action. Unlike 'remedial' and 'cere-monial' work, in fact, 'boundary keeping' concerns not only the assertion of different symbolic fields but also their defence. Representative of this process are those episodes in which action is intended to preserve an acquired space: for instance at Atlantis, where business practices were designed to institution-alize a market sector on the basis of shared sexual practices. 'Boundary keeping' processes are evident in all the situations observed at Asie Welders, where the two female entrepreneurs established the boundaries of their entrepreneurial action of the basis of their 'womanhood'. And a further example is provided by the episode when Mr Erba ignored the flurry of activity caused by the presence of a baby to maintain the boundaries of his male action and the separation between different spheres of activity.

The fourth process is what Goffman (1974, 1980) calls 'footing' and which we noted in Mrs Creta's behaviour. Footing, as we have seen, has two func-tions: it enables people to adjust their stance within a particular frame, and it provides an occasion for them to disrupt its referents, because once 'in step' they are able to disturb its rhythm and deviate from its path. In the case of Mrs Creta, footing enabled her to align herself with a male symbolic order and to disrupt static gender scores. In the case of Mario Primo it instead took the form of his endeavour to give a male and managerial thrust to organ-ization of the business, and (in everyday routine) to translate conversation into different symbolic spaces of masculinity, according to the interlocutor. At Asie Welders, footing was an ironic process by which the two female entrepreneurs aligned themselves in gender terms (as women-secretaries) and thus resolved the doubts of external actors as to their presence in the company. Footing work also seems to characterize the situations observed (for example) in the Atlantis editorial office, where management sought to 'keep in step' with the market, regardless of the consequences for organizational and gender practices.

The final process that strikes us as important is 'gender commodification'. By this we mean the exploitation of the symbolic space of gender as terrain on which to (re)construct market relations, as exemplified by Atlantis. In the case of Asie Welders, for instance, it was a process of gender commodification that persuaded the two female entrepreneurs that women were less 'reliable' than men, given the alleged 'impartiality' of the production cycle. But we also found examples of gender commodification in the stories of Erba Shirts and Frau Kitchens, where the symbolic spaces of male and female were a production factor to be allocated in the most efficient manner possible, a process which acted reflexively on everyday organizational practices.

Having described these five processes, we wish to propose a final metaphor which conveys a summary image of them. If we conceive 'doing gender' and 'doing business' as symbolic spaces marked out (and occupied) by the action of those who engage in these practices, the joint production of gender and entrepreneurship seemingly proceeds as follows.

At first, the two spaces closely interweave: home and business merge and it is difficult to draw a clear demarcation line between public space and private space. At this 'mobilization' stage, distinctions among the various symbolic fields (public, private, male, female, gender and entrepreneurship) are only of relative importance, and boundaries are easy to cross. But when numerous actors interact and set about establishing some kind of order (especially when a critical or ambiguous event occurs), the process of cross-wise presence described earlier is obstructed. The actors involved activate a dialectic between ceremonial and remedial work which prevents any breach of boundaries, thereby sanctioning separation between the two spaces. This phase is followed by 'defence' of one's own symbolic space. Confined to a specific territory (whether male, female or entrepreneurship), the actors seek to forge alliances with the other occupants of their space and engage in a process of 'boundary keeping' which protects the benefits that they have acquired and preserves their space against trespass by 'outsiders'. It is now that footing work renders the symbolic spaces more or less open and receptive to new practices, or new participants, and constructs the parameters of territorial belonging. One consequence of this process is 'gender commodification': if 'doing gender' and 'doing business' acquire concrete form through the progressive separation of spaces (symbolic and of action), then the commodification and exploitation of one's own symbolic territory appear to be a practical consequence. However, thus obscured and removed from scrutiny is the complexity of the processes observed, which appear to be the neutral consequences of two spaces purportedly pertaining to different symbolic dimensions.

5   Gender and entrepreneurship as discursive practices

In this chapter we shall examine the relationship between gender and entrepreneurship as discursive practices by analysing the discourses and narratives collected in the form of interviews during the fieldwork.[1] Consequently we shall invite the reader to enter an analytical dimension which differs from that of the previous chapter in that the focus of attention will be on the text and no longer on the interaction.

In recent years, discursive and narrative practices have aroused a growing interest both in the area of organizational studies and in that of gender studies. The relationship between gender and discourse has been the centre of attention of many scholars (Dundas Todd and Fisher, 1988; Bergvall, Bing and Freed, 1996; Walsh, 2001), who showed how gender is socially constructed through discursive practices (Weatherall, 2002; Litosseliti and Sunderland, 2002; Holmes and Meyerhoff, 2003), highlighted the power relations connected to, and reproduced by, such practices (Wodak, 1997; Walsh, 2001; Thornborrow, 2002) and promoted a critical and deconstructionist perspective (Bergvall, Bing and Freed, 1996; Wodak, 1997). A relevant contribution to the debate comes from organizational studies, where several scholars focused on discursive and narrative practices of gender construction in organizations and in organizing (J. Martin, 1990; Parkin, 1993; Gherardi and Poggio, 2001, 2003; P. Martin, 2003).

Discourse analysis, like organizational theory, has arisen from the interweaving of a variety of disciplines – sociology, psychology, philosophy, linguistics and literary studies – and from the diverse theoretical traditions of ethnomethodology (Garfinkel, 1967), semiology (Barthes, 1964) and poststructuralism (Foucault, 1973). While on the one hand this heterogeneity highlights the importance of text analysis and shows that organizational discourses and narratives are able to yield crucial insight into organizations (Czarniawska, 1997a), on the other it accounts for the large number of discourse analysis methods at hand for the study of organizational phenomena (Potter and Wetherell, 1987; Keenoy, Oswick and Grant, 1997).

Conducting discourse analysis of the accounts and narratives produced by people belonging to an organization requires the researcher to single out the discursive and textual strategies used by them to give meaning to their actions, to their interactions and to the context in which they operate (van Dijk, 1985; Potter and Wetherell, 1993). A variety of routes can be followed, and it is difficult to identify standardized rules or procedures. By way of a preliminary simplification, one may distinguish among the methods employed to analyse discourses and narratives in organizations according to the specific focus of the analysis:

- *What is recounted in organizations: discourses as artefacts.* Cultural studies of organizations – in particular those conducted from a symbolic-interpretative standpoint (Hatch, 1997) – consider discourses to be 'artefacts' which can be used to understand and interpret a culture, and to identify its dominant values and norms (Piccardo, Varchetta and Zanarini, 1990). This approach therefore views discourses and narratives as objects, products and indicators – amongst other things – of a particular organizational culture. Analysing them, the researcher seeks to identify the social discourses available to the individuals in a given organizational and social culture at some particular time (Gavey, 1997).
- *How it is recounted in organizations: discourses as processes.* When this type of approach is used, attention shifts from discourses and narratives as objects to the actual process of narrating. By means of narrative, organizations gain new members, and these new members acquire their organizational identities. Organizations, in fact, use narratives to reproduce their collective memories and to embed new members and new histories in that process, while individuals come to assume that the stories narrated in the organization are their own stories, and to view their own stories as particular examples of the exemplary narrative of the organization (Linde, 1998).

These two focuses of analysis can be associated with the two methods of narrative analysis outlined by Polkinghorne (1995) on the basis of the distinction drawn by Bruner (1986) between paradigmatic and narrative knowledge. According to Polkinghorne, paradigmatic analysis endeavours to identify categories and taxonomies. It seeks to uncover themes and concepts shared by the stories collected by the researcher and to develop general knowledge from particular stories. If we use the example of a data matrix, we may say that the researcher moves vertically, extrapolating nuclei of meaning which traverse the various narratives and discourses collected. The concepts used may derive from already existing theories, or they may be deduced inductively from the data (as in grounded theory). Narrative analysis, by contrast, is concerned to identify the plot and the rhetorical devices that act retrospectively to combine the elements of a story together and give them meaningfulness, producing nexuses of sequentiality and causality as parts of a temporal development which culminates in the finale of the story. In this case, the main purpose is to reveal the uniqueness and complexity of individual narratives and cases.

In the first part of the chapter, discourses about entrepreneurship are treated as 'artefacts' and subjected to 'paradigmatic' analysis in order to highlight the main cores of meaning around which they are developed. The second part of the chapter concentrates on the stories of entrepreneurship, showing their 'process' dimension by means of a 'narrative' form of analysis.[2]

The 'ingredients' of entrepreneurship: risk, money, innovation and gender neutrality

In order to analyse the discursive construction of an entrepreneurial subjectivity, our conversations with the interviewees centred on certain 'discourse *loci*' – or, as Barthes would put it, certain *figures* recurrent in the literature on entrepreneurship (Schumpeter, 1939; du Gay and Salaman, 1992; Amit, Glosten and Muller 1993; du Gay, 1996). A figure is a *locus* (*topos*) which is in part codified, like a sign, and in part projective (like an image or an account), 'a modest supplement offered to the reader to be made free with, to be added to, subtracted from, and passed to others' (Barthes, 1977: 5). The three *topoi* selected were risk, money and innovation. The texts that we collected were analysed with a view to revealing the manner in which the accounts relative to these three topics constructed the subjectivity of the entrepreneur discursively.

We are fully aware that the interpretation offered is the result of textual cooperation among the interviewees, the interviewer and the analyst.

We shall first examine how the themes of risk, innovation and money were developed in the discourses of the male and female entrepreneurs interviewed, drawing on models already standard in the literature to show how the accounts of the interviewees were part of a widely endorsed discourse on entrepreneurship. However, when we analysed the texts, we endeavoured to go beyond the meanings intentionally expressed by the interviews, on the assumption that discourses are practices characterized not by linearity but rather by ambiguities and contradictions, and that every discourse is framed by a specific power relation. We shall highlight the tendency – apparent in the accounts of both men and women – for the gender dimension to be erased, so that entrepreneurship is depicted as neutral with respect to it. We shall then concentrate on the accounts in which the three themes (and more in general the concept of entrepreneurship) help define gender attributions and competences. Finally, we shall discuss the way in which – crosswise to the three themes analysed – the interviewees set gender and entrepreneurship in relation to each other.

Business risk

Many dictionaries associate the meaning of the word 'risk' with possible harm or danger consequent on the unpredictability of events. In some cases the specification is made that risk may be connected with 'rash' behaviour.

The etymology of the term from the medieval Latin *reseclare* = 'cut' refers to the perils incumbent on the subscriber to a contract consequent on arbitrary or imprecise cuts or divisions: which therefore indicates the threat arising from the uncertainty (the 'not knowing') that characterizes the economic relationship with the 'other'. The accounts of the male and female entrepreneurs interviewed during our fieldwork depict risk as constitutive of entrepreneurial activity: it is impossible to be an entrepreneur, it seems, without assuming risk. An entrepreneur is a risk-taker by definition, and entrepreneurship is defined as the willingness to take risks. Indeed, were entrepreneurial activity not to involve risk, there would be no economic reason for engaging in it.

> There is no safe business because there would be no risk involved in it. Then everybody would do it, and it would lose all its interest because there'd be too much competition.
>
> (M31)[3]

An entrepreneur is therefore someone who is willing to face the consequences of assuming risk; but in the accounts that we collected risk was more often associated with responsibility than with hazard or gambling. It was invariably defined as a constant and unavoidable part of entrepreneurial activity, but the risk assumed by the entrepreneur was distinguished from the risk attendant on other types of self-employment because it entailed a social responsibility.

> A lorry driver is not an entrepreneur, mark you. He's a self-employed worker. That's very different, because he only takes risks that affect himself. [. . .] If he gets up in the morning and doesn't want to work, that's up to him; but here, if I don't turn up one day, there are twenty women who won't get their wages. A lorry driver is more like one of the women at the machines.
>
> (M35)

In this excerpt the entrepreneur positions the self-employed worker as the 'other'. He emphasizes that – unlike a self-employed worker – the entrepreneur assumes responsibility for other people as well: if the business goes badly, the jobs of the people who work for it are in jeopardy. Interestingly, in this extract the absence of the risk associated with social responsibility is exemplified by reference to the entrepreneur's employees ('the women at the machines'), who are also the same people for whom he assumes the risk (the 'twenty women who won't get their wages'). In this way the entrepreneur interviewed constructs his identity in contraposition to that of his employees, emphasizing a relationship of protection/dependence.

In some cases the contraposition between the subjectivities of the entrepreneur and the employees is expressed through the representation of the latter as part of the company's fixed costs structure, i.e. as an element of rigidity in entrepreneurial action which prevents it from adapting flexibly to changes in the market. But there is a third group of subjects with respect to which risk is used to position the entrepreneur's subjectivity: the customers. The entrepreneurs describe their relation with customers as an asymmetrical one, where greater discretionary power (with respect to products and payments) is concentrated in the hands of the latter.

> Our image is a clean product, well made and delivered on time. As soon as you fail to deliver on time, you lose a customer.
>
> (W32)

Unpredictability mainly concerns the behaviour of customers when it comes to paying. Several interviewees mentioned the mounting problem of delayed payments, which significantly increases their margin of uncertainty.

> Today, a customer you considered good ten years ago because he almost always paid his bill at the end of the month, today doesn't belong to the 'good' category any more. You put him among your risky customers, because he tends not to pay at the end of the month. Today, being an entrepreneur means taking on a huge amount of risk. The risk is always there and it's always very great, because a customer who pays you like clockwork today . . . tomorrow, for some reason or other, even one beyond his control, may not pay you and so he cuts you off at the knees.
>
> (M35)

It is therefore important for the entrepreneur to be able to rely on a broad customer base, so that s/he does not depend exclusively on any single client and may maintain a broad margin of discretion. Those whose customers are small firms or private individuals apparently enjoy an advantage: they can diversify their receipts and need not depend entirely on one single customer.

> Our advantage . . . what gives us a certain security is the financial side. Our risk is spread quite widely; we don't have customers who owe us three hundred million lire, like often happens in the building industry, for example, where they work for months on credit for hundreds of millions from a single customer.
>
> (M31)

The fourth referent used in the positioning of entrepreneurship consists of the banks, and with specific regard to business expansion and the growth of investments. In this case too, the power relation is seemingly biased against the entrepreneur in that it hinges on the banks' willingness to support the latter's business initiatives.

> If turnover increases, we'll have to find the money to finance the company. We go to the bank with the customers' orders, with the letters of credit, and

on that basis they give us a percentage. Now that too will have to be discussed, because we've got to go and talk to our banks and ask them if they are willing to give us the minimum to carry on in business. So it's a risk that we're running.

(W32)

The entrepreneur's subject position is also discursively constructed through the concept of risk when reference is made to the various phases of entrepreneurial activity, and to decision-making about investment, expansion and innovation in particular.

The perception of risk seems to be particularly pronounced when the entrepreneur must decide whether to increase his/her investments in order to expand the business, or whether to settle for the existing level of turnover.

Risk becomes an issue when you say: 'what should I do, stay as I am or continue to grow?' So I may decide to take some more hundreds of millions of lire and invest the money. How should I invest it? I can take on more workers, I can innovate, I can expand the commercial network: but these are all consequences. Yet they are part of the choice, of the risk of investment. The risk is closely connected with the investment. That's when the risk arises; then it depends on the decision.

(M31)

In this excerpt, risk is associated with various stages of the decision-making process: the greatest amount of risk is assumed when the initial decision to invest is taken (and it is therefore closely bound up with an economic choice). This is followed by a series of decisions as to where investments should be made and how to diversify the company. There are numerous options available at this point, and they depend on the type of business concerned.

Innovation, too, may be a major source of risk. Innovation, in fact, may require the company to strike off in unknown directions and thereby encounter unforeseen problems: for example, the lack of a market for the company's new products.

When you launch a new product there's always a risk. [. . .] You go off and sell your new product, and you find yourself in situations that you don't really understand. There are those who gamble on buying a hundred special shirts, and then they can't sell them. There's always a risk, because even buying fabrics is risky: we buy the fabric sometimes six months beforehand, which is extremely risky because, if the order is cancelled, you've bought the fabric for shirts which you don't know if you're going to produce or sell.

(M35)

This emphasis on the pitfalls of business decision-making helps construct an entrepreneurial image connoted by two apparently contrasting dimensions:

on the one hand the 'dream' of a project to realize and the assumption of risk by gambling on the future; on the other, the 'control' required to cope with uncertainty.

> You live on future prospects, you live in hope that the political situation will improve, that the economic situation will get better. You live on illusions, because, if you lived by the day, you'd make very few investments.
>
> (M31)

Although risk is a factor intrinsic to entrepreneurial activity, there are nevertheless strategies with which to dampen its effects, in which regard our interviewees talked about 'calculated risk'. These strategies are usually the fruit of long experience, so that the greatest risks arise when a company enters an unknown market.

> You can calculate the risk to some extent; if you really know the market and your customers, then you can calculate it, otherwise not. If a new company doesn't know its market and customers well, how can it calculate the risk? It can't. Only a well-established company, one that's been in the market for at least ten years, can calculate the risk. It knows by and large what its effective risk is. But a new-born company is on a knife edge because it can't calculate the risk.
>
> (M35)

These aspects are also used in the discourses to emphasize the existence of differences within the business world based on unequal power conditions. Some interviewees, for example, said that the threat raised by external factors depends on the size of the company and its position in the market: being 'small', in fact, may exacerbate this form of risk.

> The smaller you are, the more you're exposed to risk. [. . .] The more market power you have, the less you're forced to take risks.
>
> (M40)

Risk thus seems to be a constitutive and implicit component of entrepreneurship. It is constantly present in business activity: an entrepreneur is exposed to risk not only when s/he starts up a business – incurring expenses and contracting debts which can only be redeemed over the long period – but also in all subsequent phases of day-to-day organization, product innovation and business expansion. It is ever present, therefore, and difficult to counteract because it is often determined by external factors beyond the entrepreneur's control.

Given that risk is crucial for definition of entrepreneurship, it is also a distinctive component of entrepreneurial identity. Indeed, it is used by entrepreneurs to perform the two essential actions of identity-formation:

identification and differentiation (Melucci, 1982). When our interviewees talked about themselves as entrepreneurs, they tended to emphasize their penchant for risk-taking, thereby contrasting themselves with other groups. They represented an entrepreneur as a person who assumes risk not only for him/herself but also for others. Risk was therefore connected not with chance, luck or guile but with social responsibility towards other people who do not assume risks.

Money breeds money

Whilst the subject positioning of the entrepreneur (being) is constructed around risk, his/her instrumentality (doing) is constructed around the concept of money.

> Money is life, that's all. You can't do anything here without money.

> (M35)

Interestingly, money is often described in terms of its absence, rather than its presence ('you can't do anything without money', 'you can't develop a business idea without money', and so on), and therefore as a *sine qua non*:

> Money is certainly the key, money is ever present because whenever you take a decision it's an economic decision where you've got to have an economic interest [. . .] Without money you can't even get a business idea started. It's one of the three factors: let's say, you need capital, you need human resources and you need land. Once you've got your site, people and money, you can do everything [. . .] Money is the subtle link among all the choices and decisions that are likely to arise. There's always a cost/benefit calculation involved.

> (M31)

The interviewees made frequent reference to the notion of possibility. They perceived money as the means which enables a business idea to get started and projects to be developed. We may therefore say that money belongs to the dimension of realization: only with money is it possible to realize one's goals.

> Money is of the greatest importance. Having money means that you can do what you want. The saying 'money breeds money' is true. And it's also true that if you have money you can get better terms from your suppliers, you can organize the work better, you can stock up on a product whose price you know is bound to increase.

> (W45)

The instrumental dimension of possessing ready money is represented by the fact that an entrepreneur can make planned investments, exploiting down time to reorganize stocks and to improve production efficiency, as argued in the next excerpt.

> The rotating machine industry practically comes to a halt in the months of January and February, because the building sites close down. If you've got the money, though, you can build the machines and stockpile them. So at the right moment, instead of fixing long-term delivery times, you can sell the machines immediately. But if you haven't got enough money to buy the materials, you can't do this.
>
> (W45)

A dimension of process also emerges from the interviewees' accounts and it is represented as the ability to plan strategically. It is taken for granted that, when an entrepreneur begins a business, s/he rarely enjoys an immediate return, in that all the income is re-invested and any profit accrues in the long term. It is precisely this characteristic that the interviewees use to distinguish the mental attitude of the entrepreneur from that of other workers.

> There's the worker who works from day to day, and there's the worker who says 'I work because in a year's time I'll be breaking even'. An entrepreneur, though, may not break even in a year; he may start with the hope that he'll break even in ten years' time. [. . .] It's obvious that different people have different views of the future. I start up, I invest, I take risks, but I expect to reap my reward in ten years' time [. . .] For years, whenever you buy a new machine, for example, you put up your own money, and then you have to wait to recoup it.
>
> (M31)

Thus, an entrepreneur is described as someone who reasons in the long term, who recapitalizes money, who uses it to expand the business rather than satisfy his/her immediate wants. The entrepreneurial idea requires time and far-sightedness, in contrast with the mentality of the dependent employee, who works 'only' for his/her salary and is unconcerned about the efficiency and quality of his/her work.

> You go into a supermarket and, even though you're a customer, you're treated badly, because the shop assistant couldn't care less about her work; she only does it for the money. What used to be the case of the public-sector worker is now generally true. A civil servant is someone who has paid to get his job, and so he feels entitled not to do it properly: he's paid in the form of a vote, friendship or money. Obviously, a factory can't work efficiently in a situation like this. It's like the post office: the underlying culture is so strong; there are so many people only interested in their pay cheques at the end of the month.
>
> (M40)

Note that the attitude to money is a criterion for differentiation – and therefore for the construction and positioning of identity – between the entrepreneur and other kinds of worker. The entrepreneur's greater far-sightedness marks him/her out from those who, as employees, do their work with the more contingent mind-set of the here and now. Also to be noted is that, although entrepreneurs use such discourse to define themselves with respect to a generic category of 'workers', they also use it to position themselves with specific respect to the employees in their companies.

Money also differentiates among entrepreneurs themselves. Opportunities to develop and implement a business idea differ according to the economic resources available to the aspiring entrepreneur, and thus symbolize the 'value' of the entrepreneur in a reputation-laden frame. In the following extract, the speaker reflects on the influence exerted by family background on a person's chances of starting up a business.

> If you're not a genuine entrepreneur, if you don't have an entrepreneur father who's handed on a culture and a history, you can only work as far as your economic situation lets you. [. . .] Since so much money is necessary, only the big companies are able to go into business.
>
> (M40)

Frequently, the interviewees' representations of the relationship between entrepreneurs and money highlight the presence of a further actor: the banks, which in controlling the money also control and direct the activity of the entrepreneur.

The confidence of the bank, and its willingness to grant credit, emerges as the factor that renders an entrepreneur 'prey' to external forces. This theme is touched on by all the interviewees in their discourses on money. For example, entrepreneurs are represented as victims of the inflexibility of the banks.

> It's not easy to get money from the banks. We've often asked for credit: what would seem like routine requests. But before they'd grant us anything, apart from showing them our accounts, we had to give personal guarantees, so we didn't take it any further. It makes me laugh when I hear that Mondadori [a big Italian publishing company] is in trouble because it's got losses of three hundred billion. We couldn't even get as far as ten billion, because they'd cut us off first. The problem of bank credit is a problem for many small firms.
>
> (M40)

Banks are also represented as discriminating in favour of already consolidated businesses to the detriment of those that have just started up or are expanding.

> It's an odd situation: they give you the money when you don't need it: it's always like that. It's a subtle game, but in the end these are the parameters

they use: if the company is trustworthy, if it's solid, that means they can invest one hundred million and come out with at least one hundred and fifty. A company is solid in the sense that it has years of experience; it's not one that has started up this year. So they feel more confident, but the company that gets the money probably has less need of it.

(M31)

Risk-taking – which, as we have seen, is a distinctive feature of entrepreneurship – does not emerge from the interviewees' accounts as a characteristic of banking behaviour.

Our situation with the banks is quite good, in the sense that our overdrafts aren't particularly large. Our overdrafts at four banks are five million with each of them, which is chicken feed. With a billion lire turnover we've got a five million overdraft, so our portfolio is extremely solid. The banks see that our portfolio is healthy, so they have a reasonable amount of confidence in us. Our indebtedness is ridiculous compared to our volume of business.

(M35)

The relationship with the banks, and with financial organizations more generally, links with the theme of 'virtual' money. By the latter expression is meant that money is increasingly less connected with concrete reality – raw materials or the products produced – and increasingly more with the virtual processes by which values are determined through financial speculation and manipulation. Various interviewees emphasized that rises and falls in the cost of money are by now unrelated to concrete production processes. As a consequence, construction of the figure of the entrepreneur tends to shift from the image of the *faber* to that of the financial administrator.

We had to deal with the issue of the organization and money when we used to work with copper. There was an international market for copper at that time, and prices fluctuated a great deal. You could buy copper at a low price and sell it at a high one, and make handsome profits. They were fluctuations that you could pretty well predict in advance, compared with other raw materials. Now the situation has changed completely, because the investment funds have moved into raw materials. The funds don't follow economic and productive trends; they manipulate the entire market, in the sense that they decide to sell and lower the price, and then they buy back at an even lower price.

(W45)

The most important feature to emerge from the interviewees' accounts of the relation between money and entrepreneurship is that money represents the necessary and inevitable intermediary of entrepreneurial activity. The notion of intermediary (Callon, 1991) covers diverse and heterogeneous materials

like objects, artefacts, individuals and groups, with their skills and capa-
bilities, money, texts and symbolic inscriptions. An intermediary always
constitutes the 'visible' product of the work of assembling heterogeneous
materials performed by an individual network actor as it seeks to impose
its own version of reality on others. It represents that actor in the double
sense of 'standing for' and 'acting on behalf of' it, because the actor that has
constituted the intermediary uses it to achieve an effect from a distance. In
fact, somehow inscribed in every intermediary is the relation that it institutes
among the actors which place it in circulation. For example, every artefact
distributes specific roles to humans and non-humans comprised in the
network that it institutes.

The dimension of realization – of 'doing' – is closely bound up with the
availability of money, which in turn largely depends on the attitude of the
banks. The role of money in constructing entrepreneurial subjectivity is linked
to the ability of entrepreneurs to think and act from a long-term perspective,
where money is the medium for the business's future growth.

Finally, money symbolizes the non-human intermediary with the market.
This is described as a factor external to entrepreneurship (and therefore to
concrete 'doing') which increasingly determines the value of money, and
consequently the terms on which credit is granted, business opportunities,
and the pace of the production process.

Money too, like risk, emerges from the discourses analysed as apparently
a-gendered: it is described as a neutral factor which permits or hampers the
development and management of a business.

Innovate, but not too much

Innovation is constructed discursively as a risky undertaking which also
requires the availability of economic resources.

Moreover innovation is portrayed as a feature specific to entrepreneurship,
which is distinguished from management in so far as the latter consists in
making the organizational changes required for the implementation of
entrepreneurial decisions.

> Innovation is not part of the risk; it's part of the decision. For instance, when
> you have to decide whether to expand, whether to give someone a job [. . .]
> The entrepreneur has the intuition: he decides to invest a certain amount of
> capital in a particular sector; then it's the manager's job to implement that
> decision.
>
> (M31)

When innovation is related to the product, it displays different features
according to the market sector concerned. One the one hand, innovation
corresponds to the attitude of customers towards tastes and fashion, in which
case it does not necessarily mean the creation of something entirely new, but
rather the revival of past styles in more up-to-date form.

I think that innovation is essential, especially in our field. In the fashion business, if you're not innovative and if you don't keep up with the fashions, you're likely to get squeezed out.

(M35)

Innovation is of only limited importance in our sector. Innovation for us is dusting off the old styles. It's reviving things from the past.

(M35)

Textiles firms that manufacture, for example, fashion products frequently find that the manual skills cannot be replaced by technology. Thus, in the extract that follows, the speaker tends to set greater value on human skills ('a woman's hand') than on machinery.

As far as technology is concerned, innovation may be extremely important, but in our work technology is of only limited help, because it's the woman's hand that counts. Technology can help you to the extent that one machine may work better than another, it may be cleaner, quieter, but it's still the woman's hand that does the work. Technology is essential; its important for cutting operations: with two people and a machine you can do the work of three or four. However, at our level it's not feasible because it wouldn't be utilized.

(M31)

On the other hand, however, innovation is a response to the needs and problems of customers, dealing with difficulties and improving the product, perhaps customizing it to the customer's requirements. Innovation in this case, therefore, is the ability to cope with specific problems.

We try to innovate with items manufactured on a small and large scale, ensuring that all the components can be modified, that pieces can be replaced. This is a help, because if you look after your customers they stay loyal to you.

(W45)

The third area of innovation concerns the corporate image. Conveying a new or 'fresh' image – especially in the case of companies operating in the fashion and clothing industry – is a strategic goal. In this case, innovation entails devising an effective mode of communication.

Innovation in the textiles industry is all about image. If you're good at constantly refreshing your image and conveying the idea of a lively company, that's innovation, not a new machine.

(W35)

Although innovation is considered an important component of entrepreneurial activity, the entrepreneur's task is described as a balance between innovation and economic prudence.

> Technicians are fascinated with new things, but then you have to assess their feasibility. We have different ways of looking at these things. I'm always cooler than the engineer.
>
> (W45)

> You have to be cautious [about innovation]; you can't be led by your feelings. [. . .] You have to be cautious because you can't rush into making decisions.
>
> (W32)

The innovation characteristic of the three semantic domains marked out – technology, product and image – is obviously connected with the other elements analysed previously: the cost benefit and risk. The relevance of the three themes to entrepreneurial activity is apparently taken for granted as universal, and so too is the belief that they are gender-neutral. A rhetoric of universality and neutrality is used to erase the gender sub-text.

Constructing gender through risk, money and innovation

The discourse on entrepreneurship mobilizes apparently neutral elements. The entrepreneur is depicted as a person willing to take risks and also – at least to some extent – to calculate them; able to give concrete form to business ideas; and ready to innovate in response to changes in the market. Whether these skills are attributed to a man or a woman seems unimportant. Even when questions were explicitly asked about the gender connotation of these competencies, the entrepreneurs conveyed a non-gendered image of their activities.

However, apparent indifference to gender conceals a belief that the constitutive ingredients of entrepreneurship are male and linked to the mobilization of masculinity.

But do women take risks?

The discursive strategy used in order to decouple gender from risk consists in attributing a predilection for risk-taking to personality differences, rather than to gender characteristics.

> No, no, in this business there are no differences with respect to risks, because everyone takes them, men and women to an equal extent. [. . .] More credit is given to men, but there's no difference in risk-taking.
>
> (W32)

No, risk is subjective, it doesn't have a sex. No, no, risk doesn't have a sex. No, it's a question of personality.

(M31)

On the other hand, the interviewees point out the existence of gender-determined attitudes which affect a person's attitude to entrepreneurial activity. The following excerpt is from the same interview as just cited, where the speaker denied that differences exist and attributed risk-taking behaviour to personality factors. He now propounds an explicit gender construct: women are less willing to take risks than men.

Let's say that, like here, in Italy, without exaggerating, 90 per cent, if not more, of entrepreneurs are men. So when you're talking about putting it on the line, taking a risk, those who do it are mostly men. This is only a greater acceptance of risk I'm talking about, not a capacity; I'm talking about a willingness to take a gamble. I don't see a woman quitting a steady job to open a pizzeria. I'll give you an example, something that happened here. There was a couple; both of them worked for us, and he left a well-paid job with responsibility and opened a pizzeria. The wife carried on working here, even though her husband needed her help. But here she had job security, while her husband's business, although it's now turning a profit and is sure to do well, like all new businesses was at risk during the first few years. This has been going on for years, and she's still here. The husband wanted to leave; the wife didn't. And there have been numerous situations where the husband has shown this kind of attitude.

(M31)

There is, therefore, an ambiguity in the manner in which a gender connotation is given to risk acceptance. It is evident, for example, in the account of a male entrepreneur (whose company is registered in his wife's name) who talks of the equal exposure to risk of both of them, but at the same time refers to differences 'naturally' due to the fact that he has more experience.

I have my responsibilities, but my wife has hers as well. If the work isn't finished by the evening, the risk is hers. But there are certain things that are more natural for me to do, not her, though if she were in my place nothing would change.

(M35)

From this point of view, the differences are due to structural, historical or cultural factors which impede women from taking risks. Nevertheless, there may be some women who are 'more mannish than men', as one of the (male) entrepreneurs declared. This discourse is used to ratify the anomaly of the situation: female competence in entrepreneurship is subject to the 'exception rule' (Gherardi, 1994). To speak of 'women more mannish than men' is to emphasize the exceptional nature of the situation, and thereby confirm the traditional symbolic order of gender and the attribution of masculinity to entrepreneurial activity.

There are, moreover, rhetorical strategies which point to the existence of more intrinsic differences. According to a female entrepreneur, the inability of women to take risks is so deeply rooted that it is an insurmountable obstacle. She provides the example of a woman bank official who must decide whether or not to loan money to the company.

> [Women] are unable to decide otherwise, because they never accept risks. We have dealings with the banks, where you often have to do business with another woman. And it's very difficult. They're much more inflexible; they won't take the risk. When we got the order from France, we were lucky enough to find this young man who understood our situation. If we'd had his successor, who was a woman, with a small child, it wouldn't have been possible. [. . .] That's it, women are more afraid and they're inflexible. And in fact, when there are women at a bank, we change banks.
>
> (W45)

This extract is of particular interest in the light of the previous considerations on the relationship between banks and risk. Banks, in fact, are generally described as social subjects averse to risk. According to this female entrepreneur, however, this characteristic should be set in relation to gender, so that the unwillingness of banks to accept risk is due to the presence within them of women.

Moreover, the fact that it is a female entrepreneur (and therefore a woman who by definition takes risks) who makes this claim suggests that there is some sort of representation by which, when women become entrepreneurs, their gender membership is erased – or better they become 'mannish'. In the above account, in fact, women are represented as being 'other' than the speaker. The discursive strategy that emerges from the accounts which attribute to women a sort of genetic incapacity ('women are unable' to do otherwise) and a structural inability ('with a small child') to take risks is a justificatory strategy which seeks to preserve the status quo, the reason being that women do not normally set themselves up as entrepreneurs ('they're inflexible, they're afraid, they're unable to decide otherwise').

A-sexed money

The male and female entrepreneurs describe money as a neutral object.

> Money has neither age, nor sex, nor nation.
>
> (M31)

If a gender difference does exist, it resides in the connection between money and power.

> Money is tied to power, so I believe it has a gender dimension, although its use is neutral. Money is earned by a street walker; it's earned by both men and women.
>
> (M40)

However, the fact that the example refers to an activity involving sex ('the street walker') suggests that the gender dimension is present.

Another explicit reference made to gender in the representation of money concerns the household division of roles in its management: whilst it is the man who brings the money home, it is the wife who administers it.

> Money is a-sexed, because it's a means. If we look at Lombardy, rather than at entrepreneurship, then money is female. It's earned by the man, but it's the wife who spends it or saves it. We have workers and labourers whose wives are much better educated than they are. Women try to better themselves, but men don't; they're only interested in the bar. At home, it's the women who look after the money. When men go to the supermarket, they come home with a load of junk. But women only buy the things they need.
>
> (W45)

Although money is described as a-sexed, power is gendered, the administration of money is gendered and social competence in handling money is gendered. The gender stereotypes are attributed to 'others', namely to the behaviours of banks in granting loans.

> There shouldn't be any differences [with respect to risk], but in fact there are. That's the way it is. Unfortunately, there's this mentality which tends to give greater credibility to somebody mature, possibly a man. It's a fact of life. If I go into the bank, they won't give me credit, absolutely not.
>
> (W32)

While one discursive strategy represents women as penalized in their dealings with banks, another depicts women as benefiting from their gender membership. In both cases, gender biases are mobilized in a rhetoric of devaluation of the female.

> Apart from the fact that women get better credit facilities than men . . . as well as help from agencies or associations. A woman receives more financial help than a man does. If a woman goes and talks to a bank manager, it may seem strange but she comes across better; she finds it easier to get something extra. You may think what I'm saying is baloney, but it's true. Perhaps women are more persuasive when it comes to money because the man hopes to get something out of it. Without naming names, there are some striking examples around here. From that point of view, women definitely have it easier than we do.
>
> (M35)

This explicit reference to the use of their sexuality by women to obtain benefits is a discursive tactic that treats women merely as mothers, wives, daughters or prostitutes.

Male sobriety, female excesses

Innovation too, like risk and money, is initially defined in genderless terms. However, gender overtones show up in the relation between innovation and gender, according to the interpretation given to the concept of innovation.

> There's a tie-in with gender because it's a consequence of an entrepreneur's choices, of the risks taken. But there's more to it than that, because those risks depend on the personality: both men and women are able to innovate. Some decisions are obligatory regardless of whether you're a man or a woman. Gender has lost importance in this system of impersonal rules. I believe that the issue of gender in general doesn't mean very much, and especially in this sector, where it's the laws of the market that matter.
>
> (M40)

When, as in the previous extract, innovation is considered to be a risk, the attribution is the same as in the case of risk; hence innovation assumes a male connotation.

However, when innovation concerns the fashion industry in particular, the discourse changes and attitudes are reversed: female customers are decidedly more willing to accept innovation and change, while males are more traditional in their attitudes.

> Innovation? It depends on the type of public involved in the innovation. If they're women, then even exaggerated innovation is fine; but if they're men, it may be counter-productive because men need to change more slowly, less abruptly. Women expect more radical change; they love to show off, while men are more sober, they're more conservative [. . .] a man in make-up or wearing a skirt would be over the top for me. It may be all right in show business, perhaps, but not in everyday life.
>
> (W32)

Innovation seems to comprise both a male and female core, therefore. It is the former, however, in that it is tied to risk, which carries more weight in determining the image of entrepreneurship. With regard to innovation's female core, it is interesting to note that the speaker's description immediately assumes negative overtones when it refers to female excess and exhibitionism. Thus, whereas an interviewee had earlier described women's inability to 'decide otherwise' as 'inflexibility', in this case 'changing more slowly' is given the less pejorative label of 'sobriety'.

A 'normal' woman entrepreneur?

The rhetoric of entrepreneurship describes a profession where gender 'makes no difference'. The fact that the large majority of entrepreneurs are men is regarded as a hangover from the past which will sooner or later disappear.

> I know a lot of women entrepreneurs with great responsibilities. To be sure, the majority are still men, but it's only a matter of time. How many women entrepreneurs have set up in business recently? The trouble is, you only know about those who appear in the newspapers, but even locally around here I know lots. [. . .] I tell you, in textiles, in the garments industry, there are more women entrepreneurs than men.
>
> (W35)

In reality, however, matters are not so straightforward when the difficulty of balancing family commitments and work arises.

> My wife spends a great deal of time in the company, but she's never neglected the family, absolutely not. Because of her efforts, we've never lacked for anything. But there are only twenty-four hours in a day, and it's obvious that the time she spends in the company she doesn't spend at home [. . .] My mother devoted much more time to the company compared with other working mothers, and that's because she was much better at dealing with the situation and never had problems in that respect. And, in any case, she wasn't faced with the problem because she joined the company when we children were already quite big [. . .] But imagine a woman with two small children, only a few months old, if she has to devote eight, ten hours a day to her work; that's not easy.
>
> (M31)

But the difficulty is beginning to affect not just women but men as well.

> The pressure of work very soon forces you to choose between work and your family; I can cope because I don't have to answer to anyone. But I realize that, although I've got this freedom, some of my colleagues, those I worked with as a team until a couple of years ago, when they got home in the evening they had problems with their wives, with their children; anyway, these are responsibilities that you can't evade.
>
> (M31)

Gender specificity is instead mobilized when differences among industrial sectors are discussed.

> In general, though, if I think about a building firm I think of a man as the entrepreneur. That's because I've only met male entrepreneurs in the construction

industry. I have a female friend who took over her father's building firm; she's the only one I know and she's having quite a few problems.

(W32)

There is greater social legitimation for women entrepreneurs in sectors where the workforce is mainly female, while women with leadership roles are less easily accepted in traditionally male industries. However, some of the accounts bring out the idea of a difference that may become a resource. In many areas, and irrespective of sex and the ownership of the company, a group of mixed gender with a synergy of differences constitutes a strength – or even, as the following extract illustrates, the vital core of a company.

I tend to think that a person on his own, even when he has lots of ideas, must be backed by other people, and, according to me, among these other people, there are certainly women who give you strength. I can't see an entrepreneur as a single person; I always see a group; I have this vision of a group, and therefore of a mixed group.

(W32)

As entrepreneurship is discursively constructed through the three topics considered, the importance of gender is at first denied and then asserted. And this happens, albeit with different nuances, in the discourses of both men and women.

The images that emerge from the cases analysed are (with one exception) four snapshots of families still evidently influenced by a traditional patriarchal culture. The feminine figure is not necessarily demeaned; rather, it is protected and preserved in the conventional archetypes of mother, wife and daughter. Regardless of whether the speaker is a man or a woman, the discursive construction of entrepreneurial activity tends to reproduce the stereotype of the male *qua* entrepreneur and breadwinner.

The conversational identity constructed by the women entrepreneurs through their accounts frequently tends to be residual, or at least subordinate to that of a dominant male.

Being a woman and an entrepreneur is still somewhat unusual. And the attitudes of the women themselves to their gender identity are ambiguous – as evidenced by the following two remarks made by the same interviewee.

Dealing with men is simpler, much simpler. It's difficult to find a normal woman.

(W45)

We're not seen as particularly different, especially if they already know us. We think we're absolutely normal people.

(W45)

Women occupying positions of responsibility in organizations – whether as entrepreneurs or managers – find themselves in particularly ambiguous and contradictory circumstances as regards construction of their professional and gender identities (Gherardi and Poggio, 2003; Poggio, 1999, 2000). Being neither like other women nor like men they must constantly seek out strategies with which to construct their professional and organizational identities. The above two remarks encapsulate the ambiguity implicit in the experience of a female entrepreneur, and the importance as she constructs her image of positioning herself with respect to others and to the context. On the one hand, therefore, she encounters the traditional aversion of male settings to the female presence; on the other, she asserts a presence legitimated by the recognition afforded by others.

Narrating entrepreneurship and gender

Gender and entrepreneurship are two social phenomena which discursive practices seek to allocate to different spheres. In this section we shall analyse various modes of narrating, or how the interviewees constructed subjectivity and objectivity.

We shall describe the specific characteristics of seven ways to narrate the story of a business, thereby showing how the subjectivity of the male or female entrepreneur is discursively constructed.

As they narrate, individuals organize their experience by means of a scheme that assumes the intentionality of human action (Bruner, 1986; Czarniawska, 1997b): they use, that is to say, a plot to arrange events into a meaningful sequence. The plot of a story is constantly revised (Polkinghorne, 1987) and may vary according to the occasion, the audience and the purpose for which the story is being recounted. Each of the narratives that we collected, therefore, is only one of many possible variations.

The narrated explanations of how the companies began and developed can be treated as texts which set out implicit and personal theories about managerial action (Pitt, 1998). They are used by the subjects – in our case male and female entrepreneurs – both to give meaning to their world in narrative terms (Weick, 1995) and proactively to produce narratives coherent with their values and expectations (Czarniawska, 1997b). Therefore, the stories not only reflect processes but also help shape them. Moreover, narrating may also be a strategic practice with which to contest dominant meanings and power relations (Langellier and Peterson, 1993).

In what follows we shall examine seven stories. In one case, the story is told jointly by two people, while in two other cases the story of the same business is recounted by different narrators. It will thus be possible to observe how different subjectivities give rise to different interpretations of events and place them in relation by imposing a sequential order upon them.

The stories were analysed in a series of readings which singled out their main narrative components, as follows:

- *Narrator*: the person who tells the story.
- *Characters*: the subjects cited by the narrative.
- *Plot*: the order in which the reader or listener is made aware of what happened, that is, the order in which the events are presented by the narrator, an order which does not necessarily replicate the actual sequence of the occurrence (Linde, 1993).
- *Agency*: to whom is the action attributed? Indicated here are the subjectivities that determine the course of events in the narrative.

We shall identify a set of narrative units for each story, our purpose being to conduct detailed analysis of the rhetorics used to recount – and therefore narratively to construct – the subjectivity of an entrepreneur. We shall show that each account comprises three overlapping and interweaving stories (that of the individual, that of the family and that of the company) which assume differing significances. Finally, our narrative analysis will pay particularly close attention to the type of positioning performed: that is, the process by which individuals position themselves discursively with respect to others and construct their identities in relational terms.

The heiresses

Narrators: The story is recounted by the two voices of the Somma sisters (the owners of the company). The voices interweave to form a single text.

Characters (in order of appearance): The grandfather, the father, the two narrators, the customers, the husbands, the children, the personnel, the engineer, the daughters and wives of customers, the engineer's son, the daughter's boyfriend.

Plot: The company was founded by the grandfather, run by the father and then, in the absence of male heirs, inherited by the two sisters. The Somma sisters found themselves having to run an engineering business at a time of profound change in the market and the industry. They consequently restructured the company, laying off staff and concentrating on the design and construction of sophisticated machines. Today, their lack of technical expertise makes the engineer a figure of especial importance in the company. The sisters are planning to reduce their personal involvement in the business and hand responsibility over to the engineer, to his son or to some other young person, for example the fiancé of the daughter of one of the sisters, or to the still young son of the other.

Agency: This is mainly denoted by 'us', namely the sisters, although there are passages in which it is their two identities that are highlighted, or that of the engineer.

The entrepreneurial history of the Somma sisters belongs to the tragic genre: it seems that the two women have been forced by fate into a profession which they never chose, and one which their predecessors had never wished upon them.

The preamble to the story rapidly summarizes the transmission of the company across three generations. The central elements of this abstract[4] are the deaths of the two male characters and the inevitable and 'residual' entrance of the two female narrators.

> It was started by my grandfather and he carried on the business. Then there was my father, together with my grandfather, and then us: at the beginning with my grandfather, but he died shortly afterwards, when I took over. We've been on our own since last year, because my father died last year.

The image of the grandfather close to death as he summons his young granddaughter and entrusts her with the destiny of the business gives a fatefulness to the story reminiscent of the beginnings to numerous folk tales.

The reference – repeated on several occasions – to the sick grandfather forced to hand the business over to his granddaughter also serves to emphasize her function as a care-giver, thus mitigating the exceptional nature of her inheritance of the company.

> My grandfather's problem was falling so sick when he was still relatively young. He was forced to make a quick decision. I was quite close to him during his illness; he had an operation and stayed at home. I was studying and so I could keep him company. It was then, unfortunately, that he grabbed hold of me and said: 'this is your legacy and you must carry it forward!'

The phrase with which the younger sister intervenes in the narrative reiterates the obligatory nature of the duty inherited and the ethical (and psychological) imperative of its fulfilment.

> A few years ago I felt I had a moral obligation because there was my father, who would have taken it badly.

The dramatic tone that accompanies the story does not concern family relations and events alone; it also connotes the historical and social context in which the company operates. When the two women took over the company, they found it in the throes of a crisis that forced them to take the difficult decision that their grandfather had avoided.

> It was a time of severe crisis when mass-produced machines were not selling. The problem was that we had to concentrate on quality. We were very important at the beginning, but we had to invest heavily in standard machines to beat off the competition.

The sisters took drastic but effective action. They cut back on personnel (helped by the retirement of several workers) and geared production to higher product quality. At the time of the interview, this difficult process seemed to have concluded, and the company was about to be relaunched. However, the two female entrepreneurs emphasized their fatigue after the labours required of them. One notes that their accounts depict their experience as being at odds with the 'normality' of entrepreneurial stories.

> We went through a process different from the one normally associated with a business career. We took over the company and we were forced to restructure, because it was in trouble. It's now that our period as entrepreneurs should begin; that is, twenty years on, and with the money that we instead had to invest to plug the leaks in the company, and which we could now invest as entrepreneurs.

It is against this background that the topic of succession is introduced. Now that restructuring has restored the business to health, the sisters are ready to make way for the engineer, or for his son, or even for the boyfriend of the daughter of one them.

> The company is now ready to be relaunched; we should leave more space for the engineer, who's never been able to do what he wanted in all these years [. . .] We expect the engineer to take charge. He has a son doing business studies at university, so he could look after the administration. The only problem is that this might not work. So we hope that they'll be really good; we'll help them as much as we can; obviously there'll be a period of transition. I've a daughter whose boyfriend is studying engineering, so perhaps . . .

As the sisters tell their story – marked by complex twists and turns and with emphasis on their ability to assume risks and take difficult decisions – they stress their discreetness: they have worked behind the scenes, so to speak, giving the engineer broad leeway for manoeuvre and high visibility. The extracts in which they describe their relationship with the engineer shed interesting light on the type of positioning performed by the two narrators: the engineer is portrayed as the expert, as the person who knows. His character provides reassurance: he is the guarantee that the work has been done competently, and above all not by a woman. The following extract shows how the two women deal with this situation.

> You sense whether the other person wants to talk to us or to the engineer. Even on the telephone they behave differently. If we take the phone call, they behave in a certain way; if the engineer answers, the technical talk starts immediately.

Of particular interest in this regard is the way in which the sisters describe business negotiations, seeking to justify the fact that they delegate them to the engineer.

> For instance, the policy in purchasing offices is always to ask for a discount, because the person concerned has to assert himself. When this happens, we know how to behave. There are well-defined rules, even if they're unwritten. You go to a company, they beat around the bush for two hours and then get to the point exactly as we predicted, and it could have taken them just five minutes. I get bored in these situations. One says 'a hundred' and the other says 'fifty'. But you could have said 'seventy-five' straight away. For us it's all a waste of time because we don't have to answer to anybody. But for them it's very important, because they have to be able to show that they got seventy-five. Instead, the engineer is very good at these things. He sits there; he haggles; he pretends to close his briefcase and leave. It's worse than at the market.

What is described is not a simple bargaining process but a more complex social process where the actors involved must assert their presence, and where there are rules and a ceremonial (beating about the bush). Saying that one is bored is to declare one's extraneousness to the game and to stress one's diversity: the drawing of a contrast between 'us' and 'them' underlines this difference. At the same time, the manner in which the engineer's prowess is emphasized, though ambivalently, confirms his high status in the company.

The tragic tone of much of the narrative attenuates as the finale approaches, and in the part where the sisters discuss the future. They now express confidence, as well as the hope that their children will continue to run the business, albeit in more comfortable circumstances.

> For example, her daughter finished high school and took the entrance test for all the university faculties, even engineering, but then she decided to study medicine. I would have preferred her to go in for engineering. Because we thought she might want to take over the business. [. . .] We came into the company out of necessity. But we'll let our children decide for themselves.

Although their company makes welding machines, the Somma sisters bring to mind the image of two weavers called upon to repair the damage caused by the lack of a male heir, to resolve the company's crisis by excising an outmoded organizational pattern and to weave the corporate fabric back together again. The purpose of the metaphor is to emphasize the fact that, although the product belongs – in a gender classification of industrial output – to a typically male sector, in reality the gender culture underlying the two sisters' narratives is a male one. Despite their proven managerial ability (notwithstanding a lack of specific training and of explicit recognition by their predecessors), the sisters constantly understate their importance and emphasize their extraneousness to the world in which they have worked for so many years. While this suggests disenchantment and a rejection of the traditionally male model of total dedication to work, one surmises from their statements – which reveal close commitment to the fortunes of the company – that this is in fact a strategy to repair the damage caused by the presence of two women in a male role.

This presence – justified by the need to 'care' for the company and for their sick grandfather – is no longer necessary when the company is restored to health. It may now return to safer male hands.

Entrepreneur or wife?

Narrator: Mrs Erba, registered owner of the company

Characters (in order of appearance): The narrator, the husband, the aunt, the cousin, the investor, the workers, the daughter, the sister, the daughter's fiancé.

Plot: The story began ten years ago when the narrator and her husband – mainly on the initiative of the latter – set up a shirt-manufacturing company in partnership with an aunt. The company soon turned a profit but the couple left following a series of conflicts with the cousin. Thanks to a private loan, they started up another company, which they registered in the wife's name in order to qualify for grants to promote female entrepreneurship. Years of great sacrifice ensued, with the couple's time entirely taken up by the company. Today this hard work is bearing its fruits. The company produces shirts of recognized quality, and the couple are highly satisfied with their achievement. However, they now need someone to take some of the responsibility off their shoulders. Since their daughter does not want to join the company, at the moment Mrs Erba is instructing her sister in the business.

Agency: The protagonists are the couple (us) and the husband; the narrator plays a secondary role.

The history of the company began with the start-up of a previous business jointly with an aunt, although the idea was the husband's.

> I and my husband started ten years ago in partnership with my aunt. She used to work for a big shirt-making company and my husband was a clothes salesman. While he was doing his rounds, he realized that there was a good market for shirts. So we got together and made some samples, and started to sell.

However, although the family may be a resource it may also cause problems, as when the cousin joined the company and very soon clashed with the narrator's husband over how the business should be run.

> When the company reached sales of three billion a year, the children, especially this aunt's daughter, came to work for us. Because this aunt owned 51 per cent of the company, she brought in this daughter of hers, who wanted to do everything. She'd only been there a short while but it was as if she'd been making shirts for twenty years. She took it out on my husband, and then the aunt; in short, there were problems and we made up our minds: my husband came here in '95 and I followed in '96.

When the husband left his former company, he found a job with a large textiles group, where his work was so appreciated that a partner in the group urged him to start his own business, offering him the capital to do so. The narrative places particular emphasis on the importance of this investor, who is described as the crucial factor in the start-up of the new company.

> [My husband] made the samples, like he's doing now; he chose the fabrics; he chose the patterns. People liked the samples very much and he sold lots of them. And then one of the partners in the group said to him: seeing you're so young, why don't you start up your own company? Why don't I start up my own company? Because I haven't got the cash. And so he got us all the machinery [. . .] he practically gave us 150 million-worth of machines and he told us: get started, and you can pay me back as and when you earn. [. . .] Without a helping hand we could never have done it.

It is evident from these first extracts, and likewise from the ones that follow, that the protagonist of the story is the husband: it was he who had the idea of the first company; it was he who clashed with the cousin; it was his abilities that caught the attention of the investor in the new company.

> It was my husband who had the idea of making shirts, because he was obsessed with men's shirts and had lots of good ideas. He knows what is going to sell next season, he knows all about fabrics and he also knows how to advise people. [. . .] He's got a gift for it.

The narrator instead depicts her role as more routine, although in fact she supervises all the phases of production.

> I monitor the entire process, from when the cutting starts, that's where I come in, and then the customers, how customers are sorted into more urgent and less urgent ones, those to be cultivated, the less important ones . . . everything . . . from checking to ironing . . . from A to Z.

The work is represented as a source of both great satisfaction and great sacrifice. Mrs Erba is extremely proud of the quality of the company's products and of its excellent reputation, but she also emphasizes the sacrifices that this kind of business demands – which is the reason why her daughter has decided not to join the company.

> She always says that she would never do this kind of work, because you have to like it, because she sees the sacrifices that I and her father have made, in the sense that we're here twenty-four hours a day, and when we're at home we still talk about work. On Saturdays, we're here all day, and often on Sundays as well. We go away on holiday but then come back after a week because there's this to do, there's that to do. I mean we're really tied down.

The unwillingness of the daughter to continue her parents' work raises the problem of finding someone to relieve them of at least some of their responsibilities. Consequently, Mrs Erba is trying to instruct her sister in the business, but this she finds difficult.

> I'm training my sister because she's someone I can trust, but I can see that she's not suited to management: she always needs to be pushed; she can't take the initiative.

Mrs Erba's account of the history of her company therefore centres on the importance of the family. Besides the fact that the business is run by herself and her husband, her story also features the aunt, the cousins, the daughter, the sister and the daughter's fiancé (who also works for the company). Family membership is seen as guaranteeing trustworthiness, as in the case of the sister; but at the same time it may give rise to abuse, as in the case of the aunt, 'who exploited us; she had my husband start the company and then was completely ungrateful'.

While the husband is viewed as the creator of the company, the joint effort of the couple is not under-valued. But nor is the existence of distinct responsibilities. The allocation of organizational tasks that emerges from Mrs Erba's account replicates the classic gendered division of labour: the husband works 'outside' the company/home, obtaining orders, taking decisions, planning activities; the narrator occupies herself with 'reproduction activity', supervising in-company/home processes and caring for the personnel.

The entrepreneur wife

Narrator: Mrs Primo, wife of the owner.

Characters (in order of appearance): The narrator, the husband, the children, the accountant, the grandparents.

Plot: Mrs Primo's first job was in a public office, while her husband worked as a joiner. Although the craftsmen in the area preferred dependent employment, Mr Primo (because he could rely on his wife's steady income) decided to set up a small factory and manufacture fitted kitchens. His wife at first helped out with the business while she juggled her work with caring for their three children. She then quit her job so that she could devote herself full time to administering the company's accounts. After great sacrifices, the business has now expanded to the point that it produces three complete fitted kitchens a day.

Agency: Both the narrator and her husband are the protagonists of the company's story. The husband performs the leading role, but the narrator plays a key part as well.

The characters in this story are almost all the members of the family, and one is struck by how closely family and work interweave.

The story starts with the work situation of the narrator and her husband, immediately introducing a distinctive feature of the couple: their determination to do 'something more'.

> Well, I'm a trained nursery school teacher, but I've never done anything with my qualification. I used to work for the local health authority . . . my husband has always been a joiner and he used to have a workshop where he made window frames. We got by, but we always tried to do something more; but not pure crafts work, because competition was fierce and there wasn't much work around.

Carpentry was a common trade in the area, until the situation changed dramatically with the opening of a large factory, which hired numerous local carpenters. However, the husband chose a different option from the other craftsmen because he decided to continue on his own, being enabled to do so by his wife's salary.

> My husband has never wanted to work for someone else, even though he's had several opportunities to do so. And in any case, he could rely on the fact that I had a steady income. Because if there was a customer who didn't pay,

or in more difficult situations, there was always my income to keep the family going. He continued with window frames for a while, and then he started to make money with fitted kitchen units. A couple gets married; they buy a mass-produced kitchen. He started going to trade fairs and learning about the materials, so that he could move into the sector and do more diversified work with better prospects.

The narrative highlights the distinctive character of the couple: the husband's business acumen in opting for independence and the crucial importance of the wife's steady income. The importance of conjugal collaboration is constantly emphasized, perhaps most notably in the following extract, where the narrator explains her use of 'we'.

At the beginning we used to . . . I say 'we' used to because I've always helped him out. When the accounts needed doing, I'd work two or three hours in the evening after the children had gone to bed.

The success of the company is presented as being entirely due to the collaboration and shared sacrifices of the two spouses.

After we'd put the children to bed, we'd come downstairs and do these things; after supper, we'd get back to work. We managed to break into the fitted kitchen market, but the sacrifices were almost excessive.

When the business began to expand, it became necessary to have someone trustworthy in charge of the administration. Mr Primo asked his wife to leave her job and work alongside him full time in running the company.

In '85 my husband had an unfortunate experience with the bookkeeper; and he had to replace him in any case because we had to endorse drafts, the books had to be in order for the tax inspectors. A craftsman can't handle tax matters because he knows how to work with wood and he knows how to write . . . So he asked me to leave my job; I wanted at least to qualify for the minimum pension and then retire; I only had five years left, but I lost my pension.

To be noted is the reason adduced by the husband to persuade Mrs Primo to quit her job and give up her pension so that she could devote herself to the company's accounts.

My husband's reply to this argument was: 'But I don't want a pensioner as a wife!', and so I decided to quit.

The wife's full-time involvement in the husband's business was therefore taken for granted. The mingling of family and work is a constant theme in the narrative, although Mrs Primo stresses that the two spheres should be kept separate.

> The family, thank God, we've taken good care of them as well. We had a fundamental rule that, after we'd shut up the business in the evening, we wouldn't talk about it at home. The children grew up quite trouble-free. Of course, they missed out on some things, but the grandparents helped; they made up for our absence.

What is important – 'the fundamental rule' – is striking a balance between the two spheres of work and the family, but with priority nevertheless given to the well-being of the children.

> We have a saying around here: 'fry the fish and watch the cat' . . . We made sure that we never lost sight of the two things. We'd neglect the business to look after the children if there were problems. If everything was going well at home, we had more time to devote to work. It's not easy but you can do it. [. . .] The company, the business is a monster, if you give it ten hours it wants twenty, and the more you give the more you get back, so you have to say: this is as far as it goes, but no further.

In Mrs Primo's account the children are the future of the company. Having always been part of the family business, they now want to be actively involved in it.

> Their ambition is to come and work for the company, of which they've always been an integral part. They've always worked here during the holidays.

Mrs Primo's narrative foregrounds her family history, beginning with the joint efforts of the couple when they started the company, and concluding with the future prospects of their children. Although she stresses the need to keep business and family separate, the two spheres in fact constantly mix and merge.

The narrator depicts her role as that of partner and supporter to her husband, who could afford to take the risk of setting up on his own because he had his wife's income to rely upon, and could count on her when he needed a reliable bookkeeper. Evident in Mrs Primo's account is her pride at achieving a difficult balance between her own work, that of her husband, and her family responsibilities. She regards her renunciation of personal time and space as an acceptable price to pay for fulfilling her role as a wife and mother.

The second generation: the manager son

Narrator: Mr Mario Primo, son and partner of the company's owner.

Characters (in order of appearance): The company, the father, one of his father's assistants, the market, 'us', the business consultant, the narrator, the customers, the sales staff.

Plot: Frau Kitchens was created as a single-ownership crafts firm in the early 1970s by Mr Primo (the father) at a time when starting a business of this kind was still relatively straightforward. As the market grew, after fifteen years or so the firm became a limited company. Its work organization was overhauled at the same time. Since then the company has constantly increased its turnover, and it is now about to complete a five-year development and reorganization plan. Its future prospects are growth and consolidation, and perhaps development of a new business idea.

Agency: The account is highly impersonal; a large part of the narrative is delivered in the third person or the first person plural. Only towards its conclusion does the narrator talk about himself.

Although the story recounted by Mr Primo concerns the same company as before, it is very different as regards both narrative structure and content.

The story begins with a description of the social and historical context in which the company began. It is in this first phase that the sole reference is made to a member of the family (the father) – and then regarding only his role in the company, not within the family.

> It was founded in 1974. A strictly crafts-based company, two workmen, my father and an assistant, and in 1974 the first fitted kitchen was produced.

Unlike in the other stories, the creation of the firm is described not in epic terms, but in unpretentious ones which evidence how setting up a business of this kind used to be simpler than nowadays.

> We're talking about a time when fitted kitchens . . . we're talking about the heyday of kitchens, when they were very easy to make, and you could gear production to a couple of models. And that was our good fortune, because starting from this kind of set-up, beginning at the right time when the market was undemanding, we could mature together with the market. [. . .] Starting up the production of fitted kitchens today means that you immediately have to deliver what the market wants; and that's not at all easy. The company stayed in its old premises, around 400 square metres, until 1988, and in 1988 we moved here and then the business went public.

From this point onwards, the narrative becomes detailed and carefully phrased: on the one hand because it is now that the narrator assumes a more active role; on the other, because with the corporate changeover the story grows richer and more complex, and is therefore regarded as more interesting by the narrator. Mr Primo dwells on the difficulties caused by the productive and organizational changeover, but also on the specific features of the company's product.

> Ours is a product made to measure, it's highly personalized, a high level of . . . a wide choice, but the difficulty is that as you grow you've got to stick to your type of business, which for us is design, service, customer care.

The account now highlights the company's constant growth, despite various setbacks, which, however, did not comprise its success. The consolidation of the company then continued with a five-year plan which today is bearing its first fruits.

> In 1996 we introduced a five-year plan which instead envisaged the development of customized lines. The project started with creation of the commercial network, sales outlets, training the new salesmen, with training for all the company's personnel.

The narrative now gives more detailed description of the contents and aims of the plan, which is presented as a necessary choice.

> Something had to give because the company's crafts-based structure was decidedly inadequate; even if we didn't have today's level of output, we couldn't produce two kitchens a day with that structure. We had to act quickly to get production in sync with sales, the commercial network with the productive structure; otherwise we'd have found ourselves with a large production capacity and very few orders. So once we'd invested in the machinery, we immediately set about investing on the commercial side.

It is now that a number of difficulties emerge from the description. The metaphor of 'rebuffs' used in the following extract attenuates the linearity of the story.

> Our first initiative was the retail outlet: poor results, and afterwards three years of rebuffs because it required constant investment, even though this was limited in extent because we didn't put up the fixed capital, we didn't buy machinery, we didn't take on new personnel, but we had major management costs.

The account also singles out a number of critical junctures – events which signal that one phase has been completed and the next one can begin.

> The first sales outlet that we opened was a test for the company. We went into the furniture district and figured out what the situation was. If we passed this test it meant that we could get into the market, that there was room for us as well. And there was.

The narrator only introduces himself into the account when prompted to do so by the interviewer. But he makes only very brief reference to himself and then concentrates on most recent developments, emphasizing that the commercial side of the business is now crucial. In the following extract, the narrator uses the example of the table to demonstrate the central importance of sales in the present corporate set-up.

> It may seem trivial, but there are customers who complain because, for example, they say: 'a salesman gave me a table that's too small; he gave me a four-place table, but there are six of us in my family, and every day I've got this problem with the table'. Which shows that you only have to overlook a minor detail and you've got a dissatisfied customer. We try to put things right by replacing the table when possible; I mean, we say it's our fault and the customer is happy. After all, it was the customer who decided: he saw the table and chose it. But the salesman was to blame because he didn't make sure that it was the right table. So this is our story, the business of our company.

As in the past, so the company's future seems to be one of constant growth, a future where its development – and the problems connected with it – have already been carefully planned.

> We expect no more than 50 per cent growth over the next five years. It'll be difficult to achieve more because our product, organization and customers mean that the company inevitably grows in fits and starts. Ours isn't the straightforward kind of business which receives an order and simply doubles its output. [. . .] To do that you've got to have the right sort of sales network, skilled assemblers, an efficient customer service; which means growth in all areas. [. . .] So I'm sure that we'll grow, but it won't be spectacular growth, only slow. Because we have a structure where problems are proportional to turnover. Doubling sales also means doubling our problems. So it's a kind of set-up where we can grow in customized production, grow even more, but I already know more or less to what extent.

It is only in the final sentences of the account that the narrator uses the first person singular ('I'm beginning to realize', 'I'm going to concentrate', 'I know'), as if to emphasize his presence and responsibility in the future management of the company, marking out a more decisive role for himself than transpires in previous passages from the account. The narrator hints that an important decision will soon have to be taken, and that he will play an important, if not crucial, part in it.

We've got to decide. I'm not just talking about expansion. Further investment is needed for a new business idea, one with a structure similar to the present one but nevertheless different. Something more specialized; it could even be an exclusively commercial sector; but not services, because providing only services would be excessive. Concentrating either on production or marketing.

Mario Primo's narrative is apparently the most neutral of the stories collected. Indeed, it is almost a 'textbook' account in which family and personal histories are less intrusive than in the others. However, there are some features that enable us to penetrate its apparent neutrality. The narrative development *in crescendo*, where all events are organized in relation to the present, serves to depict the young entrepreneur as already standing at the helm of the company and determined to steer it safely through troubled waters. The emphasis on the commercial side, on which the narrator is an expert and an enthusiast, and whose complexity is contrasted with the relative ease of setting up a production company, serves this purpose. The absence of other important characters in the narrative consolidates the traditional entrepreneurial image of the heroic lone explorer.

The second generation: the reliable daughter

Narrator: Mrs Creta, co-owner of the company.

Characters (in order of appearance): 'Us', the father, the mother, a friendly consultant, the brothers, the sister-in-law, the customers, other companies, the narrator.

Plot: LeCò was created out of the company founded by the narrator's parents. A government enterprise grant was used for the purpose. After approval of the project submitted for the grant, the fur business (on which the project centred) collapsed, and it was decided to change type of production. The changeover caused numerous difficulties, but once these had been overcome the company began to grow. It is now thriving and the problem is to plan efficiently: Mrs Creta would like to set up her own business in a different sector.

Agency: Mrs Creta's story has three principal actors: while agency is initially attributed to the parents, the main part of the story refers to a generic 'us'; only towards the end does the focus shift to the narrator.

Mrs Creta's family history, that of the company and that of herself are closely interconnected in her account. The narrative begins with the entrepreneurial experience of her parents, of which the current company is the continuation. The birth of LeCò is depicted as resulting from a decision taken by the parents to provide a better future for their children.

> At a certain point in their lives they decided to expand; also because they had four children and they thought they could give us a better future. They had a friend who was a lecturer in business studies, and he suggested that they should do this . . . that they should apply for an enterprise grant. So they submitted a project, and after a while it was approved. Various things happened, but they managed to set up the company which now exists.

The complicating factor in the story – which appears in the narrative on several occasions – is the difficulties that arose once the parents had received the enterprise grant. As soon as they started up the company, in fact, changes in the market forced them to change their type of product. They abandoned the manufacture of fur coats and switched to leather goods, but this brought considerable problems.

> If they had given us a chance to change while the work was in progress . . . because we started off by making fur coats, so we had high turnover, the machines and equipment to work with furs. But then the market slumped, and we tried to modify the project, and therefore to modify the machinery, and even the structure itself. When we realized from a market survey that even so there was no future for us, we submitted a variant on the project, but it was rejected. So we had to keep the machinery, which is now completely useless. [. . .] We had liquidity problems in getting the company started, because at a certain point all the money allocated to the initiative dried up.

When describing this crisis, the narrative highlights the commitment and synergy of the group in tackling and overcoming it.

> This was a very serious matter, and for a while we were at a loss. An unskilled workforce, a slump in the market and then a severe economic crisis: no wonder we had problems. But then, with our strength, tenacity, stubbornness and determination we managed it . . . the fact that we worked all together as a group . . .

After dwelling on these initial difficulties, Mrs Creta describes a company in constant growth. She acknowledges the importance of the basis laid by her parents, from whom the company inherited not only its business idea but also a large number of customers. In fact, LeCò is described as a continuation of the parents' firm.

> According to me, the business idea started with them. The fact that they were factory workers employed by the brother-in-law; the fact that they had

children and wanted to do better for them; their ambition to succeed because they had the ability to do so: that's what drove them . . . And they were right, because they ran their own business for twenty-five years, with excellent results, gaining great satisfaction, and built themselves a reputation throughout the world even though they were a small company.

On returning to the problems caused by the rigidity of the law that should have awarded them the enterprise grant, the narrator on the one hand envisages a different outcome, and on the other compares her company with others for which that inflexibility had even more dramatic consequences.

The only minor fault was exaggerated because we started with one idea and then they wouldn't let us change it. [. . .] The problem with that law was that it was too inflexible, really too inflexible. We managed to survive, but there were other businesses that suffered terribly; they went bust before they'd even got started.

Overall, however, Mrs Creta describes the company's present situation as decidedly healthy. She expresses evident satisfaction over the company's prospects for growth, although she emphasizes the need for careful planning, with the customers' needs constantly in mind.

We can't complain. The company is growing rapidly, and we can't help feeling pleased at that. But one thing we should worry about is . . . I mean, we have to plan carefully because, well, we have to respect delivery times, which are extremely important, because if customers are satisfied with deliveries and with the quality, then you've got security for the future.

Only now does the narrator start talking about herself and her aspirations. Once the company has consolidated, Mrs Creta would like to fulfil her own ambitions.

We had to devote all our energies to coping with a crisis. Now that the critical period is behind us, we have to devote all our energies to dealing with the work we've got. But, of course, if you organize yourself well, I think you can find your own freedom, your own space. I'd like to find mine, because then I'd have a chance to get around more. I'd like to travel, have closer contacts with people, which is something I really miss. I'd like to do something different. I mean, the company would still be my base, I wouldn't want to leave it, but I think you can do several things if you coordinate them properly, if you have people you can rely on, because there's nobody who can do everything on their own. But now that the company's bigger, I'd like to do something just for myself to feel really fulfilled.

Here too, in a passage where the narrator gives space to her personal identity, the collective dimension, the importance of the group, is emphasized as a key resource in entrepreneurial activity. The narrative depicts the group – the Creta family but more in general the business team – as the mainstay of the company. The narrator places herself at the centre of these relations by describing herself as the '*trait d'union*', the element that links all the actors together.

Like other women in other stories, Mrs Creta subordinates her aspirations to the family business, towards which she feels beholden. The type of identity thus discursively constructed is closely bound up with family membership, although an endeavour to carve out a personal space emerges at the end of the account. And yet this option, too, depends on the future of the family business: only when the company has consolidated will Mrs Creta be able to strike off on her own.

The great mother

Narrator: Mrs Creta's mother.

Characters (in order of appearance): The narrator, the husband, the children (the sons), the brother-in-law, the workers, the banks.

Plot: Mrs Creta's mother and her husband at first worked for her brother-in-law. Then, thanks to their enthusiasm and desire to get ahead, they set up their own business. However, this decision, intended to ensure a better future for their children, led to a year of great hardship. In order to keep the company going, and to avoid laying off workers, they accepted less profitable and more laborious work orders. They also had to put up with exploitation by the banks. They persevered nevertheless and managed to achieve good product quality.

Agency: Predominant in the account is a generic 'we' denoting the family, although the narrator sometimes refers to herself, to her children and to her husband.

The narrative of Mrs Creta (the mother) acts as counterpoint to her daughter's account: it was collected during the interview with the daughter, in fact, but because it constitutes a free-standing story it is discussed separately here.

Collaboration with the husband immediately emerges as a leitmotif.

> A great desire to work, to do well, to be efficient, to be of constant assistance to my husband. Something that we still do with great pleasure, even though there have been great difficulties.

The pleasure to be gained from work is a distinctive feature of this account. The narrator repeatedly emphasizes her enthusiasm and satisfaction with regard to her work.

> What we've done we've done for the children, but also because we wanted to. It was we who decided, we were only kids and we were working for my brother-in-law. But the enthusiasm, I liked learning, I like working, I liked . . . and of course I became a 'master of the form' because it was something that I liked doing.

Just as much satisfaction and enthusiasm are apparent in the words used by Mrs Creta's mother to recount the growth of the company and the success of its products. Quality, she says, is the benchmark for every aspect of the business.

> We've always been appreciated, not financially because we've always had problems, less difficult times and more difficult ones, but there's always been the enthusiasm. We've always worked really well; that's not a boast; it's been a necessity.

The mother's narrative posits beauty and quality as the distinctive feature of the owners' relationship with the workforce.

> What's really nice is our relationship with the workers, who aren't treated as workers but as a team to create a beautiful product. So they, too, have learnt this sensitivity.

Times of crisis and adversity are seen as essential for the company's growth and development. In the following passage, Mrs Creta's mother describes the emergency that arose when it was decided to increase the workforce. She presents the company in its present form as the result of those travails.

> The changeover had an enormous impact because I found myself with a handful of male workers – the thirteen or fourteen who'd worked for us previously – and these thirty-five women who had to be taught everything because they knew nothing at all. I was available to teach them everything while they regularly received their wages. So one crisis combined with another created this company.

A further difficulty highlighted by the narrator is the behaviour of the banks. This she describes in distinctly critical terms. However, she depicts the difficulties caused by the banks as only a transitional phase, her purpose being to stress how the members of the family were able to cope by 'tightening their belts'.

> We were determined to carry on, slowly and surely, by tightening our belts, because there was a period of great hardship but we were able to cope with it. Also because we'd made our plans and it was only a transitional period. And then the banks around here have always been shylocks, in the sense that they don't care if you're in trouble, they demand their pound of flesh; the ten million they lend you today become fifty a month later.

Careful planning, confidence in one's abilities, and determination are therefore the key factors in the corporate success story narrated by Mrs Creta's mother.

> We had a clear idea of what we were doing; the work required the maximum amount of planning; we were all ready, raring to go; we had the skills because of our previous experience and, I repeat, a real desire to work. [. . .] We never despaired. We believed in our abilities.

The current managerial set-up, which centres on the children, is the result of long-term planning. The children, in fact, have always worked in the sector, where they have accumulated experience which they are now able to put into the organization.

> All the children have worked in the fashion business. They weren't part of the previous company, that's true, but they were all in Milan working in the fashion business, all of them in specialized areas, and they learnt a lot from it.

Like her daughter, Mrs Creta (the mother) emphasizes the importance of cooperation and synergy among the members of the family (in particular between husband and wife), and within the organization. However, compared with the previous account, greater salience is given to the narrator's personal identity. There are several passages, in fact, in which the speaker comments on her own role and her own work. However, she concludes her narrative by attributing principal credit for the company's success to her husband.

> All this didn't come about by chance: there was my husband, who's very good at these things. He's always been the most decisive of us, perhaps even when we've been critical. He's been determined, strong-minded. They've all been excellent helpers, but it's my husband who's set his stamp on the company.

Mrs Creta senior's account of the company's history alternates between the pleasure of being involved in the business and the hardships overcome in carrying it forward. Although the final extract gives especial emphasis to the husband's role, the rest of Mrs Creta's account constantly stresses the importance of collaboration between the husband and wife, and the support provided by the children. Her final crediting of the company's success to her husband's efforts can be interpreted as an attempt to shift the limelight back to her husband, thereby repairing the breach of the gender order caused by her previous focusing of it upon herself.

The realist

Narrator: Mr Air editor of the magazine.

Characters (in order of appearance): Various members of the gay movement, the founders of the magazine, the editorial staff, the publisher, the partners.

Plot: The idea of publishing the magazine Atlantis first arose within the Italian gay movement, following other publishing ventures and the success of a similar magazine in France. The project started with a makeshift editorial staff who turned out a somewhat rudimentary product, and for some time the magazine was beset by difficulties. After a period of changes and staff turnover, it was decided to form a company. The magazine continued to grow. However, the problems of high costs and constant improvisation exacerbated conflict among the partners, prompting Mr Air to resign his editorship. After a change of partners and a revision of policy in order to increase circulation – it now being decided to abandon the magazine's political militancy and its association with the gay movement – Mr Air returned to the editor's chair.

Agency: The discourse is conducted in largely impersonal terms, although there are some situations in which the narrator refers to himself in the first person.

The story of Atlantis began in the early 1980s, in concomitance with the burgeoning gay movement in Italy. The success of other gay publishing ventures in Italy and abroad suggested that there was a market for a magazine of a similar kind.

> Talk about starting up the magazine began in 1982. It was led by the editor of 'Landa', a small magazine which came out sporadically and had previously split off from 'Fuori', a magazine linked with the radical party, and in the 1970s the only periodical catering to the gay movement. It seemed that the time was right to try out a magazine to be sold in newsagents. A similar magazine had been started in France some years before, and it had been successful. As we talked we began to realize that a magazine of this kind was feasible.

The first contributors were from a variety of backgrounds, but they had a common interest in the success of the undertaking. At the time the narrator had a different job.

> The members of the group were available to varying extents and they had different expectations. At that time I was the least involved. I was working for a company, and I had a steady job, so I made a leap in the dark.

At first, the magazine was put together on an improvised and unprofessional basis, without offices or a proper organizational structure. The magazine had an ideological affinity with the gay movement, although it also had to adjust to market demand. The latter aspect soon proved to be crucial.

> It started as a private initiative, but in fact the magazine largely reflected the ideology of the movement. And so it was identified (with the movement). Mainly because there was nothing else, no association. That was all right as far as it went, but it also created problems, because the magazine wasn't intended to be a club newsletter. Substantially, although the movement was a source of subscriptions, in effect the magazine was bound by the laws of the market.

Mr Air's account now describes the break-up of the original group and the arrival of new members, until a stable group of eight partners formed.

> At the beginning there were three of us, plus some others who came in from time to time. But there were personal frictions; [. . .] also because four or five years had passed and earnings were still low. There was no gratification apart from saying 'I work at Atlantis'. Only myself and Igor were left. But the magazine still continued. And then Igor got fed up because he wanted to be a writer. So he left as well. There were some other people who hung around the office, and then some new guys joined us to form a company. Perhaps that was the only option. In the end there was this limited company with seven, eight persons who because they were partners had a guaranteed job and therefore also a salary.

The economic situation, however, continued to be precarious. Indeed, only one employee was taken on, while the only other workers were the partners. Motivation was therefore of central importance.

> In fact, with a company like ours, if we had to hire or pay according to trade union standards, we'd have already closed. In a situation like ours you can't stick to the rules that apply elsewhere. So the fact of the matter is, either you have a motivation that goes beyond . . . or it doesn't work.

As in other stories, the narrator underlines the exceptional nature of the experience, in this case in order to reiterate that it was impossible in their situation to obey general rules. Uncertainty – which is the recurrent theme in Mr Air's account – eventually gave rise to a situation of irremediable conflict. At a tense meeting, he was out-voted and forced to resign.

> The situation of uncertainty ended up by creating personal problems. I resigned from the administrative board because there were eight of us all earning the same amount, so I couldn't understand why I had more responsibilities than the others. So someone else took over as editor. We started arguing about decisions I'd taken about the magazine, which some people didn't like, and so I resigned. I told them: this is a company; everyone has the right to vote; so if the company doesn't like the way I run the magazine, it can appoint another editor. So there was this split between a majority and a minority, and the problem was that they couldn't get along with each other.

The difficulty was resolved, however, when a redistribution of shares in the company enabled Mr Air to regain control. He now imposed a radical change of policy on the magazine.

> In the end we said: if we find someone interested in a new project, then we can buy the other ten shareholders out. We found two people, who bought some of the shares; the rest we bought ourselves, and we formed this new company, with a new business plan.

The novelty of the plan was that the magazine would abandon its original ideological commitment and adopt a more overtly commercial approach, aimed at a broader and more diversified readership.

> It was a new business plan because we wanted to sever our ties with the movement, with politics, with the left. We wanted to leave that stuff behind, get more people writing for us, find better and different contributors, and make a product that would sell and give us some financial stability, like in other countries. This didn't mean getting rich, only solving our problems of day-to-day management. If it went well, fine; if not, tough. We said we'd try it for a year.

In this final extract, too, with the setting of a deadline for the project, the speaker again emphasizes the precariousness that traverses his entire narrative. As he recounts his entrepreneurial experience, Mr Air repeatedly emphasizes this constant uncertainty, which he contrasts with his previous situation (the security of dependent employment). This is the only narrative in which no reference is made to the family, although the narrator's individual story and the corporate story closely intertwine: all the actors in the company change, in fact; so too does the reference setting, and the only stable component is the narrator himself.

The subjectivity that Mr Air constructs through his account is marked by the 'evolutionary stages' of the company. While the start-up of the company was driven more by political-ideological idealism than by economic considerations (the phrase 'a leap in the dark' is significant), Mr Air gradually introduces elements of 'realism' into his account as he talks about the need to adjust to the laws of the market, to economic constraints and factors, and describes how he steered the magazine away from the gay movement and towards a more businesslike set-up. A distinctive feature of the first part of the story is the explicit and recurrent presence of conflict and instability. But when describing the current situation, the account instead conveys a more typically corporate and market-oriented image of the magazine.

By analysing the entrepreneurial stories by a narrative approach we have seen that the narratives with which the interviewees recounted the stories of their companies differed even when they concerned the same company. And different, too, were the images that they evoked, compared with those that emerged during the ethnographic fieldwork. This diversity is due to the fact that the stories originated from different subjectivities and from different discursive practices. As we have seen, each narrative followed a different plot or, in other words, a different system used by the speaker to organize events into unitary patterns that gives them meaningfulness, but above all to define the role of the narrator and his/her positioning with respect to the others in the story. Striking in these narratives, despite their diversity, are two features shared by all of them. The first is the close interweaving of individual, familial and entrepreneurial destinies, where the subjectivity of the female entrepreneurs – more than that of the male ones – rotates around the dual concept of family/business, with a sort of contiguity or continuity between the private and public spheres. In some cases we have seen that entrepreneurial subjectivity is closely connected to the type of gender dynamics characterizing the couple relationship. The second is the persistence of discursive practices intended to safeguard traditional gender models in which any account of entrepreneurship is seemingly unable to dispense with reference to a male agency: so that the narratives of the female entrepreneurs emphasize their role as the wives, mothers, daughters and granddaughters of the company's men.

Analysis of the gender sub-text (Benshop and Doorewaard, 1998) underlying the narrative construction of entrepreneurial identity has therefore shown that gender stereotypes devalue the female and construct masculinity as a positional rent. In the stories recounted, even when responsibility is formally attributed to a woman, the 'true' entrepreneur is a man, while the woman occupies an ancillary position, however significant her role in the company may be.

Conclusions

This chapter has presented narratives of various kinds: on the one hand, it has discussed narratives collected in the field where male and female entrepreneurs talk about entrepreneurship and the stories of their companies; on the other, the presentation of the results of an analysis is also a story, in which the various elements and events yielded by the research are pieced together to produce a new set of meanings (Van Maanen, 1998). Like the interviewees in their stories, the present writer has sought to produce a story that will interest the reader in how male and female entrepreneurs discursively and narratively construct their identities, and in how gender interacts with this process. The moral of the story is that recounting is primarily an act of identity construction in which individuals 'cut and paste' their experiences in order to construct meaningful discourses and plots within a limited range of culturally accessible stories, and also on the basis of gender membership. By means of discursive practices, individuals (in our case the male and female entrepreneurs interviewed) construct their subjectivity and objectify the histories of their companies: the meaning of entrepreneurship (and of its gender connotation) is constructed by being recounted, but this construction is mediated by the meanings that the organizational culture and experience make available.

This part of our work has concentrated on examination of how discursive practices on entrepreneurship were mobilized to produce and reproduce specific gender configurations. Analysis moved through two main stages. The first concerned exposition of the theory or, in other words, the conceptual ingredients with which the entrepreneurs defined, articulated and thematized the subject position of the entrepreneur and the relative knowledge field. We sought to show how entrepreneurship is constructed around a set of distinctive discourse figures – the 'ingredients' – in apparently gender-neutral fashion. We then examined how these elements are used in discursive practices which systematically devalue the female by deploying gender stereotypes in an operation of second-sexing which supports the idea of entrepreneurship as a male construct. The erasure of gender by means of discursive practices thus permits maintenance of the dominant model, namely the patriarchate.

The second stage of analysis instead considered the 'theory in use', that is, the way in which the ingredients of entrepreneurship acquire meaning not in abstract but by being framed within the entrepreneurial stories, and thus by being situated in a specific spatial and temporal setting. Highlighted by the narrative analysis of the stories collected was the interweaving between the business and the family in its dimensions of gender and generation. This was particularly evident when we considered discourses on projectuality for oneself and the family (the couple or the parents) which, contrary to the standard literature on entrepreneurship, is not distinct from projectuality for the business. Nor did we find the existence of a sharp separation between public and private; rather, the narratives were laden with interpenetrations between the two domains.

The archetype of the entrepreneur conveyed by the discursive practices analysed was gendered: what was said, but also and especially what was not said, legitimated and celebrated an entrepreneurial figure in the form of a heroic male bent on risk-taking, conquest, domination and control, while it reiterated the conventional female stereotype of subordination, support and dependence. The hegemonic discourse that thus emerges replicates the traditional dichotomous view of gender where male experience is the reference standard.

Our analysis of the textual representation of entrepreneurship calls to mind a term used by Foucault, that of 'governmentality' (Foucault, 1991), to denote 'the conduct of conduct' (Gordon, 1991: 2) or the emergence of

> a way or system of thinking about the nature of the practice of government (who can govern; what governing is; what or who is governed), capable of making some form of that activity thinkable and practicable both to its practitioners and to those upon whom it was practised.
>
> (Gordon, 1991: 2)

As proposed in Chapter 1, we may transpose to our field of analysis the neologism 'entrepreneur-mentality' to signal the existence of a discourse on the art of being an entrepreneur and the nature of entrepreneurial practice (who can be an entrepreneur, what kind of activity s/he undertakes, who or what s/he manages). The texts analysed show that this entrepreneur-mentality is constructed though the discursive practices of the entrepreneurs and in its turn becomes the plot and constraint for entrepreneurial action and discourse. Like Foucault's governmentality, this concept is tied to economy, in its original meaning of the correct manner to organize individuals, goods and wealth in a family and enable them to prosper, within a cultural tradition that associates this competence and responsibility with the paternal role and therefore assumes a profoundly gendered connotation. The interweaving between the family and the business, or more precisely between the running of a family and a business, is perhaps the most striking aspect to emerge from the foregoing analysis of entrepreneurial discourses. The subject position of entrepreneur seems to require a performative practice which replicates the relations typical of the patriarchal family system in a social setting where, however, this familial model is disappearing. The deconstructive approach used by our analysis has enabled us to show that the discourses analysed present the traditional model of roles division as implicitly natural, rendering their potential for conflict invisible and conveying a harmonious and unitary image of them.

6 'Doing family' while doing gender and business

Concluding remarks

Those who have had the patience to read these pages from the introduction as far as these concluding reflections may have been surprised to see an unexpected protagonist – the family – slowly emerge from the wings to occupy centre stage. That the family business is of major importance in the Italian system of small and medium-sized firms, and that it is a distinctive feature of Italian industry, we knew from the literature (Boldizzoni and Serio, 1996) and from colleagues who had analysed female entrepreneurship statistically (Barbieri, 1999). Bearing this in mind, we deliberately included a family-run business in our five ethnographic cases, yet we were surprised to find that the family has such an important role in relation to gender and entrepreneurship. These concluding reflections on gender and entrepreneurship as cultural practices start from the family's influence in shaping both entrepreneurship practices and gender practices in the family and in society.

The family characterizes small and medium-sized firms in Italy, compared with other European and industrialized countries, not only as an economic fact but as a distinctive cultural feature, and as a gender practice which anchors other practices. As Gagliardi and Turner (1993: 151) point out, the family is important as reality, structure and metaphor. As reality it is manifest in the law, in habitative patterns and in socialization processes; as structure it is reproduced mimetically in the ramifications of industrial development; and as metaphor it extends the expectations and obligations of the domestic sphere to the productive one, to the point that those who do not belong to the family clan are treated with suspicion. We may therefore say that, at the cultural level, the family is a metaphor for the enterprise, but also that the enterprise is a metaphor of social relations for the family.

The relation between how gender is 'done' in the family and how it is 'done' in entrepreneurial activity is a complex one, because the family acts as the intermediary for it. As a consequence, we find it opportune first to reflect on how the family affects 'doing business', then how it affects 'doing the entrepreneur' and only afterwards examine how it affects 'doing gender'.

The economic role of the family is amply discussed in the literature. Mere mention of that role will suffice to direct the reader's attention to how it both offers opportunities and imposes constraints on the members of a family, or more generally on the members of a kinship network. The family – as viewed in the light of our five ethnographic field studies – exerts significant influence on doing business by contributing three assets: financial capital, a set of trust relations, and a stock of entrepreneurial knowledge and skills learnt at home.

The Asie company, the one with the longest corporate history and presently owned by two sisters, provides a paradigm example of the intergenerational transmission of capital, trust relations and expertise. In cases like this one, what the literature calls 'barriers to entry' against female entrepreneurship (capital, network and knowledge) are overcome by membership of a family. Conversely, the only case among those studied in which the economic role of the family did not have a direct bearing on doing business was the editorial office of the magazine. In this case, solidarity was forthcoming from the gay and lesbian community.

The case deliberately chosen as typifying the family business – Frau Kitchens – prompts further reflection on the relationship between family and enterprise. Here, intergenerational transfer also involved a shift towards greater formalization of the undertaking, and towards a managerial business culture.

The economic role of the family was also evident at the LeCò firm, owned by three brothers and a sister but which had been set up following closure of the firm run by their parents and the transfer of their capital, knowledge and trust relations.

A younger couple – belonging to the same generational cohort as the LeCò entrepreneurs – had started up the youngest of the businesses studied: Erba Shirts, which has been in operation for only three years. Behind a single-proprietor business, registered in the name of a woman, we found the business 'dream' of a couple, the same dream that we discerned among two other entrepreneur couples (at Frau Kitchens and LeCò) belonging to an older generation. The Erba Shirts couple brought expertise accumulated in previous work as dependent employees to the business, as well as access to public funds for the promotion of female entrepreneurship (in the case of LeCò to promote young entrepreneurship). The couple's previous jobs were with a company owned by a relative, so that one now finds that the economic role of the family is not restricted to asset transfer alone, but creates employment by privileging the kinship network, thus yielding reciprocal benefits which range from trust to flexibility to protection against market forces. The family also displays its Janus-faced nature in economic relations: on the one hand, it provides solidarity and financial stability; on the other, it gives rise to constriction and economic exploitation.

The family is not solely an economic resource for a business, although its economic role is the one that is most apparent and most easily described in objective terms. It is also an identity resource and a source of social roles founded on family roles and made socially legitimate. Put in other words, the family stands in a close relation with 'doing' the female entrepreneurial subjectivity. Identity is acknowledged externally to the individual through recognition of the enactment of its relations: being 'wife of', 'mother of', 'daughter of', 'granddaughter of'. Given the pervasiveness of familial relations within firms, familial and social roles become inseparable. How roles are ordered within the person would be an interesting topic of inquiry, but it is one beyond our disciplinary competence; what we propose for reflection here is the process by which the entrepreneurial function ramifies through the family, and how the family role interweaves with social and work roles.

If we inspect the various forms of social representation, we find a core of shared beliefs which unhesitatingly concur on exactly who the entrepreneur is: the person who came up with the original business idea. On this definition, none of the women that we met during our fieldwork enjoyed this social recognition, even when in her role as wife she was part of the couple who set up the business. It is the ideative element that distinguishes 'the entrepreneur' as a social and professional identity; the others – even if they comprise an entrepreneurial component – are allocated to a space where they are socially defined in relational and familial terms. Alongside the creator of the firm – who in our cases was invariably male – there are a set of social roles attributed to persons who, although they engage in entrepreneurial activities, are socially identified (or identify themselves) on the basis of their familial roles as 'granddaughter of', 'daughter of', 'wife of' an entrepreneur. The second generation that inherits the business also inherits a semantic space for signification of an entrepreneurial identity in minor key. Once again, in the intergenerational transmission of a business, gender interweaves with generation to form a single practice of 'gen(d)eration'. The male heir may participate vicariously in the pride of the firm's creator by positioning his entrepreneurial identity as managerialism and the rationalization of a traditional organization; the female heir joins the management as someone who can be relied upon to continue a tradition and renew it.

However, examination of work practices shows that, as the family celebrates and mythicizes the creator of the firm, at the same time it exemplifies the function of diffused entrepreneurship. In this case, the discursive practice that mobilizes the 'entrepreneurial discourse' sustains the celebratory ritual that renews faith in 'textbook' entrepreneurial values, while social practices mobilize participation by family members in the activities that require trustworthy people.

Not only is the functional differentiation of entrepreneurial tasks performed within the family, but authority in the firm replicates authority within the family. Setting aside the asymmetrical relationships between parents and children, or those among the children by virtue of gender and age, it is the process of distribution of the entrepreneurial function within the couple that raises the most interesting questions. We could observe the existence of a relation between more or less egalitarian relationships within the couple and its division of entrepreneurial roles: corresponding to traditional couple relationships are patterns of authority distribution and management modelled on management of authority within the family, while corresponding to more egalitarian couples is the more equal sharing of the entrepreneurial function. Moreover, gender cultures – traditional or egalitarian – within couples do not correspond to age cohorts which have experienced similar social or generational vicissitudes.

On the other hand, also, quantitative studies in the literature confirm the extent to which so-called 'female' work is based on the management of vicarious authority, and also the extent to which women in the four broad categories of predominantly female work – clerical work, sales work in contact with the public, service work with 'difficult' categories, and medium- to low-level managerial work – perform what Grant and Tancred (1992) call an 'adjunct control of the labour process'. Within the entrepreneurial function, gender performs a control function deputed by an authority either in the first person or on its behalf if the person who exercises it is a woman. It is reasonable to assume, therefore, that within the entrepreneurial function – when this is distributed among the members of the family – vicarious authority is wielded in the same way as authority within the family. In this case too, the family may be a positive identity resource in that it acts as a 'training ground' for certain authority roles, and a negative one in that it obstructs personal development because it stereotypes the family role and extends it to the work role as well.

We may now turn to the way in which the family influences 'doing gender' – and reflect on how the small firm and the social environment in which it operates help to reproduce the patriarchate.

The term 'patriarchate' seems somewhat outmoded in these times of postmodern discourses. Yet it still proves valid as an interpretative category; and it is perhaps even more valid, the more the traditional family continues to flourish alongside new familial arrangements. The patriarchate is not just a system of domination; it is also a cultural system which celebrates femaleness (Goffman, 1977) and ratifies its subordinate role. The patriarchate honours and protects women when they act as 'wife of', 'daughter of' or 'sister of'. Women belonging to a patriarchal culture find it easier to manage gender relations by formally obeying the rules of the game and by seeking to subvert them from within, or by exploiting their margins of advantages, or by distancing themselves from it through irony.

We found this type of interaction on several occasions during our fieldwork. It was particularly evident at Asie, a business in which the female owners ironically called themselves 'dis-entrepreneurs' and deliberately utilized a female positioning to exploit the 'resource of the female' to their advantage. Less clear cut was the case of the youngest female entrepreneur – at LeCò – who wavered between tradition and innovation as she sought to assert her authority outside the patriarchal culture.

Support for the culture and values system that indirectly buttress the subordinate position of women within the family springs from 'naturalization' of their relationship with work. We have seen how widespread are the social representations that attribute to women and the female a priority role in reproduction and care. Justification for this representation system is couched in terms of a female 'nature' which determines a social destiny. Work for the market is consequently considered to be subordinate to other responsibilities. Mobilization of this female-naturalizing discourse is apparent just as much in the discursive practices of women as in those of men; but the fact that it is targeted on dependent female employment, rather than on self-employment (and the identity of the woman entrepreneur), indicates a discursive strategy which positions the working woman in relation to her social reliability/ unreliability. On this social conviction rest the organizational practices of gender-based segregation and typification of job tasks. There are two arguments adduced to naturalize gender in relation to dependent employment: maternity and working hours. Both are mobilized to position women as unreliable with respect to work.

Instead, in order to show how entrepreneurship – in small and medium-sized businesses – weaves public and private relations together in a gendered organizational model, we shall reflect on two dimensions that were pervasively present in our research: the continuity between home and the business, and that between the informal and the formal. To gain thorough understanding of the dichotomous categories of public/private and formal/informal one should consider the conditions attendant on the birth of the bureaucratic model as a consequence of the process of rationalization.

When at the beginning of the last century Weber (1922) described the process of societal rationalization and framed it within an ideal-typical bureaucratic-rational model, one of the features that he thought distinctive of it was the separation between the office and the relative means of production. A second distinctive feature was the depersonalization of the employment relationship, and the latter's consequent formalization by means of norms with universal validity. Thus, if rationalization is to be considered the process by which the formal organization was born, then the small firms studied during our ethnographic fieldwork are to be considered pre-modern and pre-rational. Let us now see how all this carries a gender connotation which sustains and reproduces a patriarchal culture.

To begin with, in some situations (Asie and LeCò) the home/business continuity was established directly by physical contiguity, given that the family's dwelling and firm were situated next to each other. But apart from these extreme cases, we have seen how the home extended into the business domain through the presence of children, domestic preoccupations, and the alternation between work for the market and work for the family. Other researchers (Magatti, Monaci and Ruggerone, 2000) have documented the way in which female entrepreneurs tend to import an entrepreneurial mentality into the domestic sphere. They substitute domestic work with services purchased in the market, imposing a long-period time horizon on activity and identity projects, subjecting family life to the rhythms of business schedules, and merging the family's life-phases with those of the firm.

Physical contiguity is inextricably bound up with temporal continuity. It is the scant distinction between home and business that enables female entrepreneurs to reconcile their work roles and their family roles. Conflicting needs in terms of space, time and female identity are harmonized in a manner which also marks out the difference between the female entrepreneur and 'the other women', those in dependent employment.

The continuity between home and the business is also apparent in the relational patterns that emanate from the domestic sphere to pervade the organization. Informality in hierarchical relationships, flexibility in the distribution of tasks and responsibilities, and the particularism of work relations expand to the point that employees become general factotums who may be asked to work as much for the family as for the firm. The continuity between informality and formality, which the literature regards as one of the strengths of the small firm because it ensures flexibility, also springs from the extension of relational patterns typical of the home to the sphere of organized activity.

The dichotomy between public and private sustains a symbolic gender order in which the public sphere is assigned to the male, and the private sphere to the female. When this distinction is relaxed and antithesis and separation are replaced by continuity, the economic, cultural and relational modes of the domestic economy spill over into that of the market. This process has a close bearing on one of the central issues of the debate on women and entrepreneurship: the business culture of female entrepreneurs.

There is a body of research which endeavours to single out the specifically female component of the organizational and managerial behaviour of female entrepreneurs. Admitting that this may consist in a managerial style intended to foster trust relations and the sharing of power and information, the question still remains of its origin. Offered on the one hand are existentialist explanations to the effect that women tend by their nature towards co-operation and communication; on the other, there are explanations which are equally deterministic but couched in social terms: primary socialization inculcates women with an orientation to care and listening work.

Although we do not wish to take up a position in this debate, we would nevertheless emphasize a point that emerges from our analysis of business culture and of how gender is produced in everyday practices: namely, that our ethnographic case studies did not yield evidence for the existence of a specifically female business culture. Indeed, we would go even further and argue that, in the absence of a politically oriented 'feminine thought', there are no organizational practices that are imprinted with difference. It is not sufficient to be a woman – by nature or by socialization – to do business in the feminine. Analogously to what we found in the editorial office of the gay and lesbian magazine, there are no leadership styles or alternative organizational methods in pre-intentional or non-intentional form. A business culture that questions the normative assumptions of heterosexuality or male dominance is a political project to be consciously pursued. One cannot say that this project is assuming a distinct identity at the present time in Italy. And without a cultural movement inspired by it, and which shapes its form, it is bound to fail. Put otherwise, a female business culture is more a political project than a social phenomenon describable by empirical research which investigates the managerial methods of female entrepreneurs. To confuse these two analytical levels – that of research and that of political action – is to commit a methodological error, to lapse into ideology.

A final point concerns one of the principal assumptions that guided our research: the crisis of hegemonic masculinity. Examination of how gender is constructed by the social practices that organize an enterprise obliges us to conclude that still predominant in business are forms of interaction which reproduce traditional gender relationships – relationships in which the male receives greater social consideration than the female, and in which the female is subordinate to the male. Discursive practices confirm these representations by both 'naturalizing' the social destiny of women and by 'socializing' the practices that construct them as less reliable. We should therefore conclude that entrepreneurial activity in small and medium-sized firms sustains hegemonic masculinity because it sustains the patriarchal culture. Yet this assertion is excessive, because it fails to consider the enterprise within its external environment of interaction and within the broader social context. The greater social legitimacy of women's work, changes in their motivational attitudes towards entrepreneurship, structural changes in the family as an institution, public policies to redress gender inequalities, and a social culture that punishes overt discrimination are all factors which shape the external environment of small firms, and by combating hegemonic masculinity they also induce change in the gender sub-text of entrepreneurship.

We may consequently conclude by saying that gender is a routine activity, inscribed in bodies, habits, discourses, spaces, artefacts, dress, food, music, sports. It is an individual routine and an organizational one. Moreover, it is a cultural practice that – in Ann Swidler's words – anchors other practices. Not all practices have the same weight in organizing, shaping or directing activities; there are some that are more central, more enduring and more influential than others. For example, as Swidler writes, the structure of capitalism and its associated practices, such as paying to buy a house which one then owns, is more enduring and pervasive than this year's fad in kitchen countertops. Swidler (2001: 87) defines as anchoring practices 'those that enact constitutive rules [. . .] anchoring larger domains of practice and discourse'. And anchoring practices 'may be more firmly anchored when they are at the center of antagonistic social relations' (ibid.). A constitutive rule states that something will count as something in a particular context, and practices play a crucial role as repeated ritual confirmation that something is indeed what it is (Swidler, 2001: 89). Following Swidler, we may state that gender practices are enacted in a context of both compliance and antagonism, and they are rooted in a dichotomous meaning system which is highly institutionalized and pervasive. The constitutive rule of gender relation, repeated in interactional patterns and discursive mobilizations, is that male and female are mutually exclusive symbolic universes: the male constitutes the prime gender, while the female is defined as the second sex. The effect of this cultural practice is that other practices – entrepreneurship, for example – are anchored in a symbolic order of gender which expresses a firmly institutionalized understanding of what it is to be an entrepreneur, and of how to become an entrepreneur whom others recognize as being one: what we named entrepreneur-mentality. The practice of behaving in an appropriate, gendered entrepreneurial manner is accomplished in conformity with a set of ritual practices that celebrate the constitutive rule, while at the same time crossing gender boundaries and transgressing that rule. Gender acts as an anchor for entrepreneurial practices when the following processes are enacted for the purpose of performing as an entrepreneur:

- Handling the dual presence in a dichotomous symbolic field. The dualisms of Male/Female, Heterosexual/Homosexual, Private/Public, Formal/Informal keep symbolically apart what is in practice entwined, and ceremonial acknowledgement of difference and separation allows activities to be kept separate from discourses.
- Performing remedial work to restore the alignment between symbolic universes and to repair the cultural order in crosswise situations.
- Keeping the boundaries of a Male/Female symbolic domain in order to enjoy its positional rent.
- Footing, as the alignment of the gender of the person engaged in an activity and the gender connotations of the symbolic order of which that practice is part.
- Gender commodification, as the inscription of gender in artefacts and their mobilization within practices and as intermediaries for gender relations.

While it is relatively easy to view entrepreneurship as a practice that organizes other practices performed in a system of discourse and action, the notion of gender as a practice which in turn anchors entrepreneurship is less readily understandable, precisely because it more intimately pervades the habits and routine activities which reproduce cultural practices.

In our research, therefore, we set out to examine patterns of entrepreneurship and gender on the assumption that both can be interpreted as symbolic forms which subtend interactive and discursive practices. We sought the meanings of both in the interpretations given to them by entrepreneurs in what they do and what they say. The result is this book or, in other words, this text sustained by a rhetoric which seeks to convince its readers, not by using the canonical principles of science founded on objectivity and detachment, but by inviting them to draw on their imaginations to enter the world presupposed by the text.

In our exploration of the indeterminacy of reality and in soliciting such exploration in our readers, we have relied on narrative knowledge. A narrative is effective (and the reader may assess whether ours is) inasmuch as it turns reality in the subjunctive:

> the reader of a well told story grasps the situation from the points of view of the diverse actors of the drama, experiencing their actions and the story as indeterminate and open, even though the text or the story has a fixed structure and ending.
>
> (Good, 1994: 153)

Hence, our reason for conducting ethnographic analysis of gender in entrepreneurial contexts was to press the reader's empathic knowledge and imagination into the service of various scenarios. It is now up to the reader to decide whether our book has stimulated her or him to enter a world where reality is thought in the subjunctive.

Appendix: ethnography of practices and ethnographic practice

Self-interrogation on the research method adopted and its implications for future research is by now customary among qualitative analysts (Alvesson and Skoldberg, 2000). In our case, we shall organize our treatment on the basis of the three questions that Garfinkel (1996: 9) suggested that researchers should ask themselves on concluding their inquiry:

- 'What did we do?'
- 'What did we learn, but only in and as lived doings, that we can teach?'
- 'How can we teach it?'

'What did we do?' Negotiating access, doing fieldwork and analysing the data

We start with a schematic reconstruction of the stages through which our research moved. However, we would immediately stress the a posteriori nature of this schematization, given that we were not entirely aware of 'where' some of our methodological choices would lead us. In this sense, we implicitly shared the idea that following casualities can be a research rationale (Becker, 1994) which enables the method to 'situate' itself in a particular research field and thus characterize itself as emerging (at least in part) from the situations contingent on the data collection.

Our 'theoretical sampling' (Glaser and Strauss, 1967) consisted in a search for situations in which:

- entrepreneurship was not concentrated in a single individual, so that we could observe how the joint action of people constructed their everyday organizational and enterpreneurial relations;
- the gender of the entrepreneurs mingled with the gender inscribed in the product, so that we could observe how 'doing gender' and 'doing business' were two mutually influential activities in our subjects' practical experience;
- firms belonged to the industrial cultures of both the north and south of Italy, so that we could wonder whether different contexts activated

different practices and/or whether the same practice was declined differently according to the context.

On this basis, we began to negotiate access to the different organizational context.

Negotiating access

Negotiating access to the field took a long time. This was because of the amount of intrusion in their lives that subjects felt that shadowing entailed. Sociology has developed an array of techniques to 'protect' the subjects of its field research: guaranteed anonymity, respect for privacy, and minimum intrusiveness by the researcher, to cite the most common ones. But what does this mean in practice? Imagine being contacted by someone unknown to you, a social researcher who asks if s/he can follow you for five consecutive days during your work. It may be that the researcher reassures you that s/he will do nothing but observe and make notes, and that when necessary you need only ask to be left on your own. The researcher also promises that, when the observation is concluded, there will be nothing in the text to disclose the identities of people or of the organization, and that the ethnographic notes will be immediately available should you wish to read them. Would you accept?

In our experience, these three forms of 'protection' (or of 'reassurance') are not enough for people to accept the idea of acquiring a 'reflexive shadow', even for a short period of time. It was therefore necessary to contact the companies repeatedly. We sometimes went to them to introduce ourselves in person, or got other researchers already known to the organization to introduce us. It is interesting to reconsider the various ways in which we gained access to the organizations that we studied:

- In the case of Asie Welders, a meeting (entirely informal) by Silvia Gherardi with one of the two female entrepreneurs set up the contact. Only a few telephone calls were required to agree on the shadowing schedule, and it was not necessary to produce any kind of formal written communication.
- We contacted Erba Shirts through colleagues who had previously done consultancy work for the firm. The initial contact was handled formally: we sent a fax describing the research to the owner, who replied (again by fax) that she was willing to collaborate.
- In the case of Frau Kitchens we tried to contact the company management for months but got no further than the person who answered the telephone. We only managed to speak to the owner when we introduced ourselves as 'friends of . . .', someone whom we had reached by activating a wide network of friends.
- Mrs Creta of LeCò was a guest on a television programme as an 'outstanding example' of young female enterpreneurship. As chance

would have it, Silvia Gherardi was also a guest on the programme (as an expert on gender and organization), and at precisely the time when we were selecting the firms for our fieldwork. The mutual liking between them enabled us to agree on the terms of our observation immediately.

- We gained access to Atlantis by being introduced to the editor by a mutual friend who has previously been a member of a gay cultural club. We were also helped by the enthusiasm of the entire editorial board for research which problematized the assumptions of heterosexual masculinity and of business and the market as 'natural' factors. Nevertheless, one of us (the researcher, because it was he who was to do the fieldwork) had to present our research in detail before the board gave its final consent.

Doing the fieldwork

Fieldwork in the five companies lasted an entire working week in each organization, during which time the researcher 'shadowed' the male or female entrepreneur. The researcher went into the firm at the same time in the morning as the male/female entrepreneur, and for the rest of the day (sometimes until well after office hours) constantly took notes on the actions and interactions witnessed and in which he found himself involved. He often shared 'breaks' (lunch, for example) with the subjects, but equally frequently he detached himself from the actors to follow the path of interactions.

Although shadowing is mentioned in numerous ethnographic-qualitative studies, it is almost never defined, and, when it is, the definitions provided are often contradictory.

Marianella Sclavi (1989, 2000), for example, presents shadowing as a 'methodology in its own right', rooted in feminist anthropology (Bohannan, 1954; Golde, 1970; Briggs, 1970) and in opposition to participant observation. According to Sclavi, participant observation suffers from a positivist matrix which privileges verbal communication and analytical categories; whereas shadowing privileges non-verbal communication, the analogic code, the language of the emotions, and thus characterizes itself as dynamic, circular, impressionistic and self-reflexive. In particular, it is a methodology by which the researcher intrudes into an alien setting and uses the various difficulties and incidents provoked by this intrusion to study the setting itself. Stephen Reder (1993), on the contrary, links shadowing to the cognitive ecology work of Barker (1968) and structures it around the observation of different levels of action ('tasks', 'events' and 'episodes'). Sachs (1993) claims that shadowing was first used in a research (unpublished) conducted in 1986 by herself and Sylvia Scribner. In Sachs's view, shadowing is a set of methods used to gather data about 'on-the-ground' phenomena within predetermined periods of time. At whatever level of observation, it yields a combination of documentary data on how people engage in their everyday activities, individual and collective. Finally, Joyce Fletcher (1999) relates shadowing to the 'structured observation' theorized by Mintzberg (1971, 1973), describing it as an observation technique which focuses on the micro-level actions and interactions which construct the various elements (sometimes contradictory and not always interrelated) of what at a more general level we recognize as 'behaviour'. In describing how she moved 'like a shadow' during her fieldwork, Fletcher (1999) writes that she sought to make herself invisible and concentrated on taking notes on the interactive actions of the people observed, asking questions only when she was alone with them.

Borrowing different aspects from the various authors' conceptions, the researcher preferred to behave as an 'intruder' rather than as an 'outsider', adjusting his level of intrusiveness from time to time. He interpreted his role as 'shadow', not in the static sense of a reflecting surface, but rather in processual terms as an opaque body interposed between the light and the object (or the zone) illuminated; as an indistinct or vaguely defined figure who generated misunderstanding, curiosity or suspicion. In fact, though the researcher was the 'shadow' of one person in particular, he maintained an attitude of what one might call 'diffuse attention': settings, members of the organization, aesthetic aspects, technologies, ritual and/or simply random events were all investigated to gain understanding of how/when the 'shadow' of the entrepreneur was projected on to them or obscured by them. Where the enterpreneurial function was distributed, the researcher focused his observation on the joint action of the subjects, or on how 'disjoint' action was carried out coherently. In order to find his bearings, the researcher often adopted the behaviour of Garfinkel's (1967) 'secret apprentice':

- He noted situations in which he felt that the other assumed that they shared particular assumptions.
- He learnt these assumptions during the interaction (without realizing that he was doing so).
- He took part in situations in which the others presumed that the principles being learnt were already shared.

Each day's fieldwork concluded with an (audio) recording of an interview on the following topics:

- the history of the firm;
- entrepreneurial risk;
- innovation;
- the money factor;
- future prospects.

These topics were selected in order to open an interpretative window on the construction that the male and female entrepreneurs placed on their activities (and on themselves) as institutional action (and subjects). 'Risk/innovation/ money' is the triptych which, since Schumpeter, has articulated discourse on entrepreneurial activity itself through logical, temporal and environmental linkages. In recounting their experiences of risk-taking with regard to innovation and capital investment, therefore, people 'narrate entrepreneurship' and situate the construction of their subjectivity (as entrepreneurs and gender actors) in their narrative. The purpose of asking about the firm's history and future prospects was to create a moment devoted to the imagination, so that observation could be made of the time horizon within which the subjects reconstructed and 'activated' past and future action in relation to other issues (whether gender-related or otherwise).

The duration of the interviews varied between forty-five and ninety minutes according to:

- *Contingent events*: on some days the entrepreneurs were too busy to find time for the interview. On other occasions, interviews were interrupted by an unexpected event which required the entrepreneur's presence, or they were constantly interrupted by telephone calls and other persons. In one case the researcher had to ask the subject to repeat the interview (because the one conducted previously had been continuously interrupted) but in another the last ten minutes were lost because of a technical error (the researcher pressed 'play' instead of 'rec' while rapidly changing the tape) and 'repeating' them would not have replicated the conversation.
- *The topic and the person interviewed*: some topics (money in particular) were too 'taken for granted' and 'banal' for the entrepreneurs to talk about. Others only had sense in relation to each other (typically money and risk), and yet others (usually the history of the firm and future prospects) were thought to be disagreeable and inappropriate. Moreover, not all the interviewees found it equally easy and pleasant to talk about themselves. In one case in particular, the entrepreneur told the researcher that he no longer wanted to be interviewed, so that the five interviews scheduled had to be condensed into two long ones: the first on the topoi of entrepreneurship, the second on the company's past and its future prospects.

Analysing the data

When interpreting the data, we decided that the ethnographer should not carry out the discourse analysis of the texts. This was because we wanted to exploit the distance between the interpreter of an interview and the person who had conducted it and therefore knew the relational context. We also wanted to shift the focus of attention to the text, considering the relationship between gender and entrepreneurship as a discursive practice and treating the narratives collected to be 'impersonal' texts. As a consequence, the requirement that the person who collects the text in the field should coincide with the interpreter of that text does not arise, because the field becomes the text itself.

Conducting discourse analysis of the accounts and narratives produced by people belonging to an organization requires the researcher to single out the discursive and textual strategies with which they give meaning to their actions, to their interactions and to the context in which they operate. We followed two different approaches which jointly yield insight into the meanings and explanations that people attribute to their own actions and those of others:

1 *Discourses as artefacts*: what narratives are recounted in organizations (paradigmatic analysis). This approach views narratives as objects, products and indicators – amongst other things – of a particular organizational culture. Through them the researcher seeks to identify the social discourses available to the individuals in a given organizational and social culture at some particular time.
2 *Discourses as processes*: how narratives are recounted in organizations (narrative analysis). When this type of approach is used, attention shifts from narratives as objects to the actual process of narrating, so as to identify the plot and the rhetorical devices that act retrospectively to combine the elements of a story and give them meaningfulness, producing nexuses of sequentiality and causality as parts of a temporal development which culminates in the finale of the story.

Paradigmatic analysis endeavours to identify categories and taxonomies. It seeks to uncover themes and concepts shared by the stories collected by the researcher and to develop general knowledge from particular stories. If we use the example of a data matrix, we may say that the researcher moves vertically, extrapolating nuclei of meaning which traverse the various narratives and discourses collected. In order to analyse the discursive construction of an entrepreneurial subjectivity, our conversations with the interviewees centred on certain '*topoi*' recurrent in the literature on entrepreneurship (risk, money and innovation). The texts that we collected were analysed with a view to revealing the manner in which the accounts relative to these three topics construct the subjectivity of the entrepreneur discursively. We first showed how the various themes are developed in the discourses of the male and female entrepreneurs interviewed. Analysing the texts, we endeavoured to go beyond the meanings intentionally expressed by the interviews, on the assumption that discourses are practices characterized not by linearity but rather by ambiguities and contradictions, and that every discourse is framed by a specific power relation. We then concentrated on the accounts in which the three themes helped define gender attributions and competences. Finally, we discussed the way in which – crosswise to the three themes analysed – the interviewees set gender and entrepreneurship in relation to each other.

In narrative analysis the main purpose is to reveal the uniqueness and complexity of individual narratives and cases. We carried out narrative analysis of the texts relative to the first and the last interviews, when the interviewees were prompted to perform their actual identities from the past and future perspective. We analysed various modes of narrating and how the interviewees construct subjectivity and objectivity, thereby showing how the subjectivity of the male or female entrepreneur is discursively constructed. The stories were analysed in a series of readings which singled out their main narrative components, as follows:

- *Characters*: or the subjects cited by the narrative.
- *Plot*: the order in which the reader or listener was made aware of what happened, that is, the order in which the events were presented by the narrator, an order which did not necessarily replicate the actual sequence of the occurrence (Linde, 1993).
- *Agency*: to whom was the action attributed? Indicated here were the subjectivities that determined the course of events in the narrative.

Finally, our narrative analysis paid particularly close attention to the type of positioning performed: that is, the process by which individuals position themselves discursively with respect to others and construct their identities in relational terms.

We used an entirely different approach when analysing the ethnographic accounts.

Firstly, we thought it important that these should be analysed by the same person who collected them, because of the importance of his contextual knowledge of material which was essentially descriptive in character. Assigning the analysis to someone else would have precluded exploitation of what, from our point of view, is the value added of ethnography: knowing through direct participation, being able to give a 'correct' interpretation in the terms that the actors deem it to be.

Secondly, we decided that each ethnography should be followed by a day of collective work in which the research group listened to the accounts ('hot from the press', so to speak) from the person who had collected them in the field. This served to activate the process of distancing from the field so useful at the state of theoretical sense-making, and to bring out any discrepancies and grey areas, to identify the most significant episodes and details, and to restore the experience just concluded to the researcher in critical terms. The observations were then re-elaborated and given a narrative structure, not just as an expedient with which to evade the pure temporal sequentiality of events, but as a deliberate strategy to construct units of action/interaction for scrutiny during the sense-making phase. In fact, we thought it important that the data should be first presented in the 'raw' state, shorn of interpretation, in order to prompt conjectures and intuitions. Moreover, we wanted to construct polyphonous texts in which different positions could be expressed, and in which the figure of the researcher was always recognizable. Our prioritizing of the narrative dimension in the ethnographic accounts, too, was driven by the same logic that guided our analysis of the interviews: constructing a text which foregrounded the actors' practices rather than their intentionality. Accordingly, rather than pointing up similarities and differences, we wanted first to concentrate on the specificities of the realities observed, endeavouring to highlight the variety of ways in which gender is embedded and enacted in organizational and relational practices. We then moved inductively from the particularity of episodes, singling out and discussing the concepts and assumptions that arose from them and were subsumed by them.

The interpretation of the ethnographic observations thus emerged from a series of readings and re-readings of various episodes which eschewed the particular and highlighted practices of action and reasoning. We first concentrated on each individual story in order to grasp its distinctive features. Having extrapolated the processes, we borrowed from Grounded Theory (Glaser and Strauss, 1967) the idea of 'investigating' them: that is, abstracting them from the specific context to verify their interpretative utility in other situations. It was thus possible to avoid comparison among the stories as such (which would have flattened their differences) and concentrate instead on the relations that now appeared among practices of action.

'What did we learn that we can teach?' Negotiating access, doing fieldwork and analysing the data in practice

Having described our research process, we shall conclude with final reflection on the methodological significance of the elements that, with hindsight, we believe characterize our inquiry; that means, from our point of view, extrapolating the practical and 'emerging' dimension of the methodology that we (more or less consciously) used and in which we were (more or less knowingly) involved. What follows is therefore what we think we have learnt. It will, we hope, serve as a stimulus and suggestion for other researchers interested in the practical dimension of everyday action.

Negotiating access in practice

How can one negotiate the involvement of subjects in a research technique which they regard as intrusive?

It is ideological, we submit, to believe that a request to observe and participate in everyday action can be based on 'analytical distance', on a claim that one is entirely extraneous and disinterested. In our cases, the crux of the negotiation lay in our ability to present ourselves as participants just like the actors, and therefore in 'passing' (Garfinkel, 1967) as participants, as privileging (probably) elements arising from the researcher's empathy with the context.

Seen from a broader perspective, one can argue that the processes that led to acceptance of our presence in the firms studied did not relate to a logic extraneous to the one we saw applied in everyday organizational practices. The way in which we 'passed' further characterized every individual case,

and in some of them it was a useful benchmark for observation and interpretation (cf. Asie Welders). For the sake of expository simplicity, we
preferred not to encumber our treatment with detailed description of how
we negotiated access (so that every story starts at the moment when the
researcher made his official appearance on the scene), although from a
methodological point of view much useful information lies in that experience:
negotiating access to the field (where the focus is on courses of action) is
a significant moment of interaction at which to begin observing and noting
the practical action of the actors. It is an activity that takes place in a
dimension which relates both to the subjects' patterns of everyday action and
to the assumptions which inform the research.

Doing fieldwork in practice

The above description of our fieldwork highlights a point of discussion quite
common in the methodological debate: the researcher's behaviour.

Qualitative sociology has often emphasized the distance that separates
(or should separate) the situation observed and the observer (Burgess, 1988),
as well as a certain 'neutrality' in the latter's behaviour (Hammersley and
Atkinson, 1995). However, the fact that in our case the researcher's
appearance and subjectivity triggered small incidents and to some extent
upset organizational routine made the observation substantially different
from that of 'a fly on the wall'. The researcher was able not only to observe
a series of events but to activate others, constructing his shadowing as a
situation negotiated by the people involved on the basis of diverse practices,
and thereby providing the various actors involved (the researcher included)
with opportunities to 'perform' their quotidianity. An ethnographer, in a
reflexive conception of his/her role, participates and observes just as much
as s/he is observed and made a participant by the people whom s/he meets.
S/he helps to bring about, make visible and collaboratively interpret the 'small
events' or incidents caused by his/her presence, and his/her identity is derived
and fabricated from the practices, discourses and relations produced in the
action space of the fieldwork (Navarini, 2001). As emphasized by Garfinkel
(1967), the researcher's identity may be interpreted in various ways until it
becomes an ambiguous and precarious synthesis of diverse identities which
do not necessarily correspond to the one which the researcher attributes to
him/herself, claims or is convinced that s/he expresses.

Analysing data in practice

Our analysis of the data proceeded along two tracks: analysis of practices of
action, and analysis of discursive practices. We decided to work on these two
dimensions in order to find out how talking and doing interweave in practical
action and common-sense reasoning. The interactive and discursive practices

that constitute organizational action at the same time construct organized action, both because 'the essential reflexivity of accounts' (Garfinkel, 1967) is used to create a sense of order in action, and because it reflexively creates the context of action. We accordingly concur with the idea that any social situation can be studied as self-organizing with respect to its manifestations (Heritage, 1984), whether these latter are considered to be representations or 'proofs-of-social-order' (Garfinkel, 1974). When following another person as his/her shadow, the meanings and interpretations that the researcher may give to that person's actions are 'emerging', and they do not necessarily have to be related to a broader cultural context. Because of the way in which the researcher has interpreted his role, the shadowing has constituted 'in and of itself' a situation in which the persons concerned have negotiated on the basis of different practices. At the write-up stage, this kind of fieldwork behaviour gave rise to ethnographic accounts which not only situated the researcher within the action contexts observed, but constituted units of action/interaction on which to focus during analysis and theoretical sense-making. Accordingly, we sought to construct accounts in which reflexivity was a means to control the assumptions of the research and the researcher but also occasioned reflection of a meta-ethnographic nature. Convinced as we are of the 'mundane' (Pollner, 1987) character of common-sense reasoning – or of the circular and reflexive relationship that arises between practices and discourses in every space of action, and therefore including scientific research and fieldwork – we tried to ensure that the accounts followed courses of action, rather than actors, as closely as possible, interpreting personages (researcher and participating subjects) and events (since these involve the actors or the researcher) as 'accomplishments' (Schutz, 1932) or as dynamic and reconstructible social facts which constitute the practices and discourses subject to investigation.

Language was of absolutely crucial importance for analysis, because of the emphasis that we placed on the actors' words and discourses, because of the attention that we devoted to their use and because of the various rhetorical devices that we selected in order to convey our interpretations to the reader. Writing is not formal description but an activity both analytical and creative (Morgan, 1986; Strati, 2000); when 'recounting' a study, a researcher employs a style, a vocabulary and a set of metaphors which further modify the data and theory, so that the act of writing itself becomes a 'form of inquiry' (Richardson, 1994). Thus, interpretation took the form of scientific inquiry that explored ambivalent possibilities and problematized 'facts that are not necessarily true or which are not true in so necessary a sense' (Eco, 1981: 1050).

'How can we teach it?' A question of practice

We have organized this methodological appendix around 'what we did' and 'what we learnt' and 'how we can teach it' with the (modest) aim of furnishing the reader with a synopsis of our research design and with the (immodest) aim of highlighting its peculiarities.

To Garfinkel's third question (1996: 9) we can only provide the blunt reply that it is a question of doing it in practice.

Notes

Introduction: gender and entrepreneurship as entwined practices

1 The quotation refers to the title of the article by S. Gherardi, 'The Gender We Think, The Gender We Do in Our Everyday Organizational Lives' (1994), which has been taken up several times in the debate.
2 Patricia Martin (2003) states that practising gender is more than a person and the activities this person engages in: 'it is a moving phenomenon, done quickly, (often) non-reflexively, in concert or interaction with others'. It is difficult to study because it is permeated with tacit knowledge that cannot be verbally expressed; practising gender is more readily experienced and observed than narratively described or pinned down. She makes a difference between the gender which is 'said and done' and the actual saying and doing: 'While past or "said and done" gendering practices can be captured in narratives or texts, the literal dynamics of practicing gender – the "saying and doing" – are less amenable to this effort'.

1 How a gender approach to entrepreneurship differs from the study of women entrepreneurs

1 There are a number of systematic strategies under the label 'deconstruction' for analysing the silences and the absences in a text. Here we are not using a proper deconstructionist methodology, but we refer to a deconstructionist gaze to point to the basic idea that a text says as much by what it does not say as by what it says. For an introduction to deconstruction see Joanne Martin (1990).
2 Foucault's term 'governmentality' denotes the emergence of a mode or a system of thought about the practice of government, i.e. who can govern, what is governing, what or who is governed?
3 Massimiliano Monaci has written a review of the literature – Italian and international – which he has circulated among the various research groups working at ISTUD. We are grateful to him for allowing us to deconstruct and supplement his text. Obviously, responsibility for the outcome is ours alone.
4 Helene Ahl (2002) uses a partially overlapping distinction in the following thematic areas: personal background and firm characteristics, attitude towards and interest in starting a business, psychology, the start-up process, management practice and strategy, networking, the role of family, access to capital, performance, other questions.
5 Recent research in Europe and the United States reports that around half of female-run enterprises do not have employees, and that predominant among those that do employ personnel are ones with fewer than ten employees.
6 The alleged economic underperformance of women entrepreneurs has recently been questioned on the ground that the 'classic' studies on the matter under-

estimate the impact of important variables like the differing concentration of men and women in sectors with very diverse average values of size/profitability. On the point see Durietz and Henrekson (2000).

2 Gender as a social practice, entrepreneurship as a form of masculinity: a theoretical framework

1 Martin uses the term 'conflation' for the dynamic of fusing masculinities with working processes, and she conducts an empirical analysis from the women's standpoint of men's masculinities mobilizing practices. She identifies two substantive categories of masculinity ('contesting' and 'affiliating'), the audiences for men's mobilizing work (for women, for men or for both) and the dynamic of conflation (work occasions masculinity/ies).

2 Curiously, in the article by Carrigan, Connell and Lee (1985) the concept of hegemonic masculinity is constantly mentioned, but without being defined; it was Connell who finally came up with a definition of it in 1995 (pp. 75–6) as 'configuration of practices. [. . .] The masculinity that occupies the hegemonic position in a given pattern of gender relations, a position always contestable'.

3 The rhetorics identified by Collinson and Hearn roughly correspond to the areas investigated by authors interested in the male component of/in organizations. They are therefore presented here with the twofold purpose of their illustration and to provide the reader with a means to find his/her way through the organizational studies literature on the formation of masculinity. These authors do not adopt a single frame, since this would impede treatment of the processual nature of masculinity; however, for explanatory purposes they are grouped here by thematic area.

3 Doing and saying gender: a methodological framework

1 Far from wishing to reduce anthropology to its methodology alone, we nevertheless agree with the anthropologist Paul Stoller (1989: 13) that 'anthropology has one strength: ethnography, the original, albeit imperfect product of our discipline. Despite its taken for granted status, ethnography [. . .] has been and will continue to be our core contribution'.

2 Manning (1992, 1995) repeatedly stresses that the figure of the researcher as a *bricoleur* is no different from Lévi-Strauss's (1966) idea of him or her as a 'modest collector of fragments'.

3 Clifford and Marcus (1986) emphasize the distance of their work from realist ethnography by talking of 'ethnographic surrealism' and drawing a direct parallel with the linguistic experiments of the French literary avant-garde during the early 1900s.

4 The names of the firms and the names of the people are fictitious, in order to ensure the anonymity of the persons concerned.

5 On 'shadowing' and its (contradictory) definitions see the Appendix.

6 These interviews provided the material for the discourse analysis conducted in Chapter 5.

4 Company ethnographies: the gendering of entrepreneurship and the enterprising of gender

1 Mrs X is in charge of the bank's business services department, and has never got on with the Somma sisters.

2 In this regard, Fiore explains me that: *It's always him they want; they regard him as the mainstay of the company.*

3 They are Simone's paintings, which he sometimes stores in the showroom.

4 I get the impression that the women's clothes are easy to remove, the men's clothes much less so, as if there were a tendency to see women as much more 'undressed' than men.

5 To be precise, Goffman (1974, 1980) applies the notion of footing mainly to discourse dynamics. However, he does not provide a thorough definition of the notion, which authorizes us to use it for analysis of practical activity, not just of discourse.

6 Marginal note: How did it work out? It worked out well, fortunately. After the embarrassment of the first fifteen seconds, I continued to talk as if nothing strange had happened (did something strange happen?) and my 'research subject' (a term which, after what had just happened, seemed to me no better than any other 'politically correct' expression) was more surprised at his error than at my gaffe. Which raises the question of whether one should pay more attention to errors or to gaffes in ethnographic research.

5 Gender and entrepreneurship as discursive practices

1 As anticipated in Chapter 3, the text analysis will not be performed by the same person who conducted the ethnographic fieldwork and the interviews. This decision was taken in order to introduce distance between the text and its interpreter, since the person who collected the field data would have contextual knowledge of the discourse analysed.

2 The discourses analysed have been drawn from interviews with the male and female entrepreneurs responsible for running the businesses covered by the survey. In some cases, because the role of entrepreneur was performed by more than one individual, several interviews were conducted so that a plurality of voices could be heard. The interviews – which accompanied the ethnographic observation on a day-to-day basis – were organized as follows: on the first day of observation the interviewees were invited to recount the story of their company; during the next three days the interviews instead concentrated on aspects – risk, innovation and money – traditionally considered to be crucial ingredients of entrepreneurship, while the fifth and final interview concentrated on future prospects. In the sections that follow we shall conduct paradigmatic analysis of the texts collected during the thematic interviews (which focused on specific themes decided beforehand by the researcher). We shall instead carry out narrative analysis of the texts relative to the first and the last interviews, when the interviewees were prompted to perform their actual identity with respect to the past and the future.

3 The codes assigned to the interview extracts indicate the sex (W = woman, M = man) and the age of the interviewees.

4 'Abstract' is the term used by Labov (1972) for the introductory part of an account which briefly anticipates the content of the narrative.

References

Aaltio-Marjosola, I. and Mills, A.J. (2002) *Gender, Identities and the Culture of Organizations*, London: Routledge.

Acker, J. (1990) 'Hierarchies, Jobs, Bodies: A Theory of Gendered Organizations', *Gender and Society*, 4: 139–58.

Acker, J. (1995) 'Feminist Goals and Organizing Processes', in M. Ferree and P.Y. Martin (eds), *Feminist Organizations: Harvest of the New Women Movement*, Philadelphia: Temple University Press.

Adler, N.J. and Izraeli, D.N. (1988) 'Women in Management Worldwide', in N.J. Adler and D.N. Izraeli (eds), *Women in Management Worldwide*, New York: M.E. Sharpe.

Adler, N.J. and Izraeli, D.N. (1994) *Competitive Frontiers: Women Managers in a Global Economy*, Oxford: Blackwell.

Agar, M. (1980) *The Professional Stranger*, New York: Academic Press.

Ahl, H. (2002) *The Making of the Female Entrepreneur: A Discourse Analysis of Research Texts on Women's Entrepreneurship*, Jönköping International Business School, Dissertation series, n. 015.

Aldrich, H., Reese, P. and Dubini, P. (1989) 'Women on the Verge of a Break-through: Networking among Entrepreneurs in the United States and in Italy', *Entrepreneurship and Regional Development*, 1: 339–56.

Alvesson, M. (1993) *Cultural Perspectives on Organizations*, Cambridge: Cambridge University Press.

Alvesson, M. (1998) 'Gender Relations and Identity at Work: A Case Study of Masculinities and Femininities in an Advertising Agency', *Human Relations*, 51: 969–1005.

Alvesson, M. and Willmott, H. (1996) *Making Sense of Management*, London: Sage.

Alvesson, M. and Skoldberg, K. (2000) *Reflexive Methodology*, London; Thousand Oaks, CA; New Delhi: Sage.

Amit, R., Glosten, L. and Muller, E. (1993) 'Challenges to Theory Development in Entrepreneurship Research', *Journal of Management Studies*, 30: 815–34.

Anna, A., Chandler, G., Jansen, E. and Mero, N. (2000) 'Women Business Owners in Traditional and Non-traditional Industries', *Journal of Business Venturing*, 15: 279–303.

Atkinson, P. (1990) *The Ethnographic Imagination: Textual Construction of Reality*, London: Routledge.

Auster, P. (1986) *The New York Trilogy: City of Glass, Ghosts, The Locked Room*, Los Angeles: Sun & Moon Press.

Baker, T., Aldrich, H. and Liou, N. (1997) 'Invisible Entrepreneurs: The Neglect of Women Business Owners by Mass-media and Scholarly Journals in the USA', *Entrepreneurship and Regional Development*, 9: 221–38.

Balbo, L. (1979) 'La doppia presenza', *Inchiesta*, 32: 3–6.

Barbieri, P. (1999) 'Caratteristiche ed evoluzione del lavoro indipendente femminile negli anni Novanta in Italia', in S. Negrelli (ed.), *Istituzioni e imprenditorialità femminile*, Milan: Guerini e Associati.

Barker, R.G. (1968) *Ecological Psychology: Concepts and Methods for Studying the Environment of Human Behavior*, Stanford, CA: Stanford University Press.

Barley, N. (1983) *Adventures in a Mud Hut: An Innocent Anthropologist Abroad*, New York: Vanguard Press.

Barrett, F.J. (1996) 'The Organizational Construction of Hegemonic Masculinity: The Case of the U.S. Navy', *Gender, Work and Organization*, 3: 129–42.

Barthes, R. (1964) *Elements of Semiology*, New York: Hill & Wang.

Barthes, R. (1977) *Fragments d'un discours amoureux*, Paris: Editions du Seuil (transl. *Fragments of a Lover's Discourse*, New York: Hill & Wang, 1978).

Baudrillard, J. (1988) *Selected Writings*, Stanford, CA: Stanford University Press.

Baumol, W.J. (1993) 'Formal Entrepreneurship Theory in Economics: The Existence and Bounds', *Journal of Business Venturing*, 8: 197–210.

Beccalli, B. (1991) 'Per una analisi di genere nella sociologia economica', in G. Bonazzi, C. Saraceno and B. Beccalli (eds), *Donne e uomini nella divisione del lavoro*, Milan: Angeli.

Beck, U., Giddens, A. and Lash, S. (1994) *Reflexive Modernization: Politics, Tradition and Aesthetics in the Modern Social Order*, Stanford, CA: Stanford University Press.

Becker, H.S. (1982) *Art Worlds*, Berkeley, CA: University of California Press.

Becker, H.S. (1994) '"Foi Por Acaso": Conceptualizing Coincidence', *Sociological Quarterly*, 5: 183–94.

Beer, C. and Munyard, J.T. (1983) *Gay Workers: Trade Unions and the Law*, London: NCCL.

Bellu, R. (1993) 'Task Role Motivation and Attributional Styles as Predictors of Entrepreneurial Performance: Female Sample Findings', *Entrepreneurial and Regional Development*, 5: 331–44.

Benschop, Y. and Doorewaard, H. (1998) 'Covered by Equality: The Gender Subtext of Organizations', *Organization Studies*, 19: 787–805.

Benschop, Y. and Meihuizen, H.E. (2002) 'Reporting Gender: Representations of Gender in Financial and Social Annual Reports', in A.J. Mills and I. Aaltio-Marjosola (eds), *Gender, Identities and the Culture of Organizations*, London: Blackwell.

Berger, P.L. and Luckmann, T. (1967) *The Social Construction of Reality: A Treatise in the Sociology of Knowledge*, New York: Doubleday.

Bergvall, V., Bing, J.M. and Freed, A.F. (eds) (1996) *Rethinking Language and Gender Research: Theory and Practice*, Harlow: Addison Wesley Longman.

Bernhardt, E. (1985) *Mitobiografia*, Milan: Adelphi.

Bhabba, H. (1994) *The Location of Culture*, London: Routledge.

Bigoness, W. (1988) 'Sex Differences in Job Attribute Preferences', *Journal of Organizational Behavior*, 9: 139–47.

Bly, R. (1990) *Iron John*, New York: Addison Wesley.

Bohannan, L. (1954) *Return to Laughter*, New York: Harper & Row.

Boldizzoni, D. and Serio, L. (1996) *Il fenomeno piccola impresa*, Milan: Guerini e Associati.

Bolen, J.S. (1989) *Gods in Every Man*, New York: Harper & Row.

Bourlot, A. (1999) 'L'imprenditoria femminile e il mutamento culturale', Milan: Dipartimento di Sociologia, Università Cattolica di Milano.

Braidotti, R. (1994) *Nomadic Subjects: Embodiment and Sexual Difference in Contemporary Feminist Theory*, New York: Columbia University Press.

Bray, A. (1982) *Homosexuality in Renaissance England*, London: Gay Men's Press.

Brewis, J. and Linstead, S. (2000) *Sex, Work and Sex Work: Eroticizing Organization*, London and New York: Routledge.

Briggs, J. (1970) *Never in Anger: Portrait of an Eskimo Family*, Cambridge, MA: Harvard University Press.

Brown, R.H. (1993) *Women Organizing*, London: Routledge.

Bruner, J. (1986) *Actual Minds, Possible Worlds*, Cambridge, MA: Harvard University Press.

Bruni, A. and Gherardi, S. (2001) 'Omega's Story: The Heterogeneous Engineering of a Gendered Professional Self', in M. Dent and S. Whitehead (eds), *Managing Professional Identities: Knowledge, Performativity and the New Professional*, London: Routledge.

Bruni, A. and Gherardi, S. (2002) 'En-gendering Differences, Transgressing the Boundaries, Coping with the Dual Presence', in L. Aaltio-Marjosola and A.J. Mills (eds), *Gender, Identity and the Culture of Organizations*, London: Blackwell.

Brush, C.G. (1992) 'Research on Women Business Owners: Past Trends, a New Perspective and Future Directions', *Entrepreneurship Theory and Practice*, 16: 5–30.

Bryman, A. (1992) *Charisma and Leadership in Organizations*, London: Sage.

Bryman, A. and Burgess, R.G. (eds) (1999) *Handbook of Qualitative Research*, London, Thousand Oaks, CA, New Delhi: Sage.

Bull, I. and Willard, G.E. (1993) 'Towards a Theory of Entrepreneurship', *Journal of Business Venturing*, 8: 183–95.

Burgess, R.G. (1988) *Studies in Qualitative Methodology*, Greenwich, CT: JAI Press.

Burrell, G. and Hearn, J. (1989) 'The Sexuality of Organization', in J. Hearn, D.L. Sheppard, P. Tancred-Sheriff and G. Burrell (eds), *The Sexuality of Organization*, London: Sage.

Butler, J. (1990) *Gender Trouble: Feminism and the Subversion of Identity*, London: Routledge.

Butler, J. (1993) *Bodies that Matter*, New York: Routledge.

Butler, J. (1994) 'Gender as Performance: An Interview with Judith Butler', *Radical Philosophy*, 67: 32–9 (reprinted in P. Osborne (ed.), *A Critical Sense: Interviews with Intellectuals*, London and New York: Routledge, 1996).

Butler, J. (1997) 'Against Proper Objects', in E. Weed and N. Schor (eds), *Feminism Meets Queer Theory*, Bloomington, IN: Indiana University Press.

Butler, J. (1999) 'Revisiting Bodies and Pleasures', *Theory, Culture and Society*, 16: 11–20.

Butler, J.S. (1991) *Entrepreneurship and Self-help among Black Americans*, New York: State University of New York Press.

Buttner, E. (2001) 'Examining Female Entrepreneurs' Management Styles: An Application of a Relational Frame', *Journal of Business Ethics*, 29: 253–69.

Buttner, H. and Moore, D. (1997) 'Women's Organizational Exodus to

Entrepreneurship: Self-reported Motivations and Correlates with Success', *Journal of Small Business Management*, 35: 34–46.

Calàs, M. and Smircich, L. (1991) 'Voicing Seduction to Silence Leadership', *Organization Studies*, 12: 567–602.

Calàs, M. and Smircich, L. (1993) 'Dangerous Liaisons: The "Feminine-in-Management" Meets Globalization', *Business Horizons*, March–April: 73–83.

Calàs, M. and Smircich, L. (1996) 'From the Woman's Point of View: Feminist Approaches to Organization Studies', in R.S. Clegg, C. Hardy and W.R. Nord (eds), *Handbook of Organization Studies*, London: Sage.

Callon, M. (1986a) 'Some Elements of Sociology of Translation: Domestication of the Scallops and the Fishermen of St. Brieuc Bay', in J. Law (ed.), *Power, Action and Belief: A New Sociology of Knowledge?*, London: Routledge & Kegan Paul.

Callon, M. (1986b) 'The Sociology of an Actor-network', in M. Callon, J. Law and A. Rip (eds), *Mapping the Dynamic of Science and Technology*, London: Macmillan.

Callon, M. (1991) 'Techno-economic Networks and Irreversibility', in J. Law (ed.), *A Sociology of Monster: Essays on Power, Technology and Domination*, London: Routledge.

Calvert, L.M. and Ramsey, V.J. (1992) 'Bringing Women's Voice to Research on Women Management: A Feminist Perspective', *Journal of Management Inquiry*, 1: 79–88.

Campaign for Homosexual Equality (1981) *What about the Gay Workers?*, London: CHE.

Carrigan T., Connell, R.W. and Lee, J. (1985) 'Toward a New Sociology of Masculinity', *Theory and Society*, 14: 551–603.

Carter N., Williams, M. and Reynolds, P. (1997) 'Discontinuance among New Firms in Retail: The Influence of Initial Resources, Strategy and Gender', *Journal of Business Venturing*, 12: 125–45.

Casagrande, J.B. (1960) *In the Company of Man: Twenty Portraits by Anthropologists*, New York: Harper & Co.

Cavarero, A. (1990) *Nonostante Platone*, Rome: Editori Riuniti.

Chaganti, R. (1986) 'Management in Women-owned Enterprise', *Journal of Small Business Management*, 24: 18–29.

Chodorow, N. (1978) *The Reproduction of Mothering*, Berkeley, CA: University of California.

Chotigeat, T., Balsmeier, P.W. and Stanley, T.O. (1991) 'Fueling Asian Immigrants' Entrepreneurship: A Source of Capital', *Journal of Small Business Management*, 29 (3): 50–61.

Cixous, H. and Clément, C. (1986) *The Newly Born Woman*, Minneapolis, MN: University of Minnesota Press.

Clarke, J. and Newman, J. (1997) *The Management State*, London: Sage.

Clatterbaugh, K. (1990) *Contemporary Perspectives on Masculinity*, Boulder, CO: Westview Press.

Clegg, C. and Hardy, C. (1997) 'Representations', in C. Clegg, C. Hardy and W. Nord (eds), *Handbook of Organization Studies*, London: Sage.

Clifford, J. (1983) 'On Ethnographic Authority', *Representations*, 1: 118–46 (repr. in A. Bryman and R.G. Burgess (eds), *Qualitative Research*, London: Sage, 1999).

Clifford, J. (1988) *The Predicament of Culture: Twentieth-Century Ethnography, Literature and Art*, Cambridge, MA: Harvard University Press.

Clifford, J. and Marcus, G.E. (1986) *Writing Culture: Poetics and Politics in Ethnography*, Berkeley, CA: University of California Press.

Cockburn, C. (1983) *Brothers: Male Dominance and Technological Change*, London: Pluto Press.

Codara, L. (1999) 'Imprenditorialità femminile: ruolo delle istituzioni e credenze individuali', in S. Negrelli (ed.), *Istituzioni e imprenditorialità femminile*, Milan: Guerini e Associati.

Cole, A.H. (1959) *Business Enterprise in its Social Setting*, Cambridge, MA: Harvard University Press.

Collins, O.F. and Moore, D.G. (1964) *The Enterprising Man*, East Lansing, MI: Michigan State University Press.

Collinson, D.L. (1988) 'Engineering Humour: Masculinity, Joking and Conflict in Shop-floor Relations', *Organization Studies*, 9: 181–99.

Collinson, D.L. (1992) *Managing the Shopfloor: Subjectivity, Masculinity and Workplace Culture*, Berlin: de Gruyter.

Collinson, D.L. and Hearn, J. (1994) 'Naming Men as Men: Implications for Work, Organization and Management', *Gender, Work and Organization*, 1: 2–22.

Collinson, D.L. and Hearn, J. (1996) *Men as Managers, Managers as Men: Critical Perspectives on Masculinity*, London: Sage.

Colombo, E. (1998) 'De-scrivere il sociale. Stili di scrittura e ricerca empirica', in A. Melucci (ed.), *Verso una sociologia riflessiva*, Bologna: Il Mulino.

Connell, R.W. (1987) *Gender and Power*, Cambridge: Polity Press.

Connell, R.W. (1995) *Masculinities*, London: University of California Press.

Connell, R.W. (2000) *The Men and the Boys*, Cambridge: Polity Press.

Cooper, R.J. (1989) 'Modernism, Postmodernism and Organizational Analysis: The Contribution of Jacques Derrida', *Organization Studies*, 10: 479–502.

Crapanzano, V. (1986) 'Hermes' Dilemma: The Masking of Subversion in Ethnographic Description', in J. Clifford and G.E. Marcus, (eds), *Writing Culture: Poetics and Politics in Ethnography*, Berkeley, CA: University of California Press.

Cromie, S. and Hayes, J. (1988) 'Toward a Typology of Female Entrepreneurs', *The Sociological Review*, 36: 87–113.

Czarniawska, B. (1997a) *A Narrative Approach to Organization Studies*, Thousand Oaks, CA: Sage.

Czarniawska, B. (1997b) *Narrating the Organization*, Chicago: University of Chicago Press.

Czarniawska, B. and Joerges, B. (1995) 'Winds of Change', in S. Bacharach, S. and P. Gagliardi (eds), *Research in the Sociology of Organizations*, Greenwich, CT: JAI Press.

Czarniawska-Joerges, B. and Wolff, R. (1991) 'Leaders, Managers, Entrepreneurs On and Off the Organizational Stage', *Organization Studies*, 12: 529–46.

Dalton, M. (1959) *Men Who Manage*, New York: John Wiley & Sons.

David, P. and Vicarelli, G. (eds) (1994) *Donne nelle professioni degli uomini*, Milan: Angeli.

Davies, B. and Harré, R. (1990) 'Positioning: The Discursive Production of Selves', *Journal of the Theory of Social Behaviour*, 1: 43–63.

de Beauvoir, S. (1949) *Le deuxieme sexe*, Paris: Gallimard.

De Lauretis, T. (1987) *Technologies of Gender: Essays in Theory, Film and Fiction*, Bloomington, IN: Indiana University Press.

De Lauretis, T. (1999) *Soggetti Eccentrici*, Milan: Feltrinelli (a first version in English: 'Eccentric Subjects', *Feminist Studies*, 1990, 16: 115–50).

Dent, M. and Whitehead, S. (eds) (2001) *Managing Professional Identities: Knowledge, Performativity and the 'New' Professional*, London: Routledge.

Derrida, J. (1971) *L'écriture et la difference*, Paris: de Seuil.

Di Tomaso, N. (1989) 'Sexuality in the Workplace: Discrimination and Harassment', in J. Hearn, D.L. Sheppard, P. Tancred-Sheriff and G. Burrell (eds), *The Sexuality of Organization*, London: Sage.

Du Gay, P. (1996) *Consumption and Identity at Work*, London: Sage.

Du Gay, P. and Salaman, G. (1992) 'The Cult(ure) of the Customer', *Journal of Management Studies*, 29: 616–33.

Duchéneaut, B. (1997) 'Women Entrepreneurs in SMEs', report presented at the OCSE Conference 'Women Entrepreneurs in Small and Medium Enterprises: A Major Force for Innovation and Job Creation', Paris.

Dundas Todd, A. and Fisher, S. (eds) (1988) *Gender and Discourse: The Power of Talk*, Norwood, NJ: Ablex.

Durietz, A. and Henrekson, M. (2000) 'Testing the Female Underperformance Hypothesis', *Small Business Economics*, 14: 41–55.

Dwyer, T. (1992) 'Humour, Power and Change in Organizations', *Human Relations*, 44: 1–19.

Eco, U. (1981) *Metafora*, Voce dell'Enciclopedia Einaudi, vol. 9.

Eco, U. (1986) *Travels in Hyperreality*, New York: Harcourt Brace Jovanovich.

Eisenstein, Z. (1981) *The Radical Future of Liberal Feminism*, New York: Longman.

Fanon, F. (1961) *Les damnés de la terre*, Paris: François Maspéro éditeur/La Découverte & Syros.

Farrell, W. (1974) *The Liberated Man, Beyond Masculinity: Freeing Men and Their Relationships with Women*, New York: Random House.

Farrell, W. (1986) *Why Men Are the Way They Are: The Male–Female Dynamic*, New York: McGraw-Hill.

Fay, M. and Williams, L. (1993) 'Gender Bias and the Availability of Business Loans', *Journal of Business Venturing*, 8: 363–74.

Feagin, F. (1987) 'Changing Black Americans to Fit a Racist System?', *Journal of Social Issues*, 43: 85–9.

Fein, S.B. and Nuehring, E.M. (1981) 'Intrapsychic Effects of Stigma: A Process of Breakdown and Reconstruction of Social Reality', *Journal of Homosexuality*, 7: 3–13.

Ferber, M. and Nelson, J. (eds) (1993) *Beyond Economic Man: Feminist Theory and Economics*, Chicago: University of Chicago Press.

Fernbach, D. (1981) *The Spiral Path*, Boston, MA: Alyson Publications.

Ferree, M. and Martin, P.Y. (eds) (1995) *Feminist Organizations: Harvest of the New Women Movement*, Philadelphia, PA: Temple University Press.

Festinger, L. (1954) 'A Theory of Social Comparison Processes', *Human Relations*, 7: 117–40.

Fine, M. (1994) 'Working with Hypens: Reinventing Self and Other in Qualitative Research', in N. Denzin and Y. Lincoln (eds), *Handbook of Qualitative Research*, Thousand Oaks, CA: Sage.

Fisher, E., Reuber, R. and Dyke, L. (1993) 'A Theoretical Overview and Extension of Research on Sex, Gender and Entrepreneurship', *Journal of Business Venturing*, 8: 151–68.

Fletcher, J.K. (1998) 'Relational Practice: A Feminist Reconstruction of Work', *Journal of Management Inquiry*, 7: 163–86.

Fletcher, J.K. (1999) *Disappearing Acts: Gender, Power and Relational Practice at Work*, Cambridge, MA and London: MIT Press.

Foucault, M. (1972) *The Archaeology of Knowledge*, New York: Harper & Row.

Foucault, M. (1973) *The Order of Things*, New York: Vintage.

Foucault, M. (1978) *Les Mémoires d'Herculine Barbin, dit Alexine B., Hermafrodite du XIX siècle*, Paris: Gallimard.

Foucault, M. (1980) *Power/Knowledge*, New York: Pantheon.

Foucault, M. (1982) 'Afterword: The Subject and Power', in H.F. Dreyfus and P. Rainbow (eds), *Michel Foucault: Beyond Structuralism and Hermeneutics*, Brighton: Harvester Press.

Foucault, M. (1984) 'Sex, Power and the Politics of Identity', *The Advocate*, 400: 26–30.

Foucault, M. (1986) *The History of Sexuality, iii*, New York: Pantheon.

Foucault, M. (1991) 'Governmentality', in G. Burchell, C. Gordon and P. Miller (eds), *The Foucault Effect: Studies in Governmentality*, London: Harvester.

Fournier, V. and Grey, C. (1999) 'Too Much, Too Little and Too Often: A Critique of du Gay's Analysis of Enterprise', *Organization*, 6: 107–28.

Franchi, M. (1992) *Donne Imprenditrici. Le regole del gioco*, Milan: Franco Angeli.

Franchi, M. (1994) 'Api o tartarughe?', in P. David and G. Vicarelli (eds), *Donne nelle professioni di uomini*, Milan: Angeli.

Franklyn, S., Lury, C. and Stacey, J. (2000) *Global Nature, Global Culture*, London: Sage.

Gagliardi, P. and Turner, B. (1993) 'Aspects of Italian Management', in D. Hickson (ed.), *Management in Western Europe*, Berlin: de Gruyter.

Garfinkel, H. (1967) *Studies in Ethnomethodology*, Englewood Cliffs, NJ: Prentice Hall.

Garfinkel, H. (1974) 'The Origins of the Term Ethnomethodology', in R. Turner (ed.), *Ethnomethodology*, Harmondsworth: Penguin.

Garfinkel, H. (1996) 'Ethnomethodology's Program', *Social Psychology Quarterly*, 59: 5–21.

Gartner, W.B. (1993) 'Words Lead to Deeds: Towards an Organizational Emergence Vocabulary', *Journal of Business Venturing*, 8: 231–9.

Gavey, N. (1997) 'Feminist Poststructuralism and Discourse Analysis', in M.M. Gergen and S.N. Davis (eds), *Toward a New Psychology of Gender*, New York: Routledge.

Geertz, C. (1973) *The Interpretation of Cultures*, New York: Basic Books.

Gergen, K. (1982) *Toward Transformation in Social Knowledge*, New York: Springer-Verlag.

Gherardi, S. (1994) 'The Gender We Think, The Gender We Do in Our Everyday Organizational Lives', *Human Relations*, 47: 591–610.

Gherardi, S. (1995) *Gender, Symbolism and Organizational Cultures*, London: Sage.

Gherardi, S. (2003a) 'Feminist Theory and Organization Theory: A Dialogue on New Bases', in C. Knudsen and H. Tsoukas (eds), *Organizational Theory as Science: Prospects and Limitations*, Oxford: Oxford University Press.

Gherardi, S. (2003b) 'Gender Citizenship in Organizations', in P. Jeffcut (ed.), *The Foundations of Management Knowledge*, London: Routledge.

Gherardi, S. and Poggio, B. (2001) 'Creating and Recreating Gender Order in Organizations', *Journal of World Business*, 36 (3): 245–59.

Gherardi, S. and Poggio, B. (2003) *Donna per fortuna, uomo per destino*, Milan: Etas.

Giddens, A. (1979) *Central Problems in Social Theory: Action, Structure and Contradiction in Social Analysis*, London: Macmillan.

Gilligan, C. (1982) *In a Different Voice*, Cambridge, MA: Harvard University Press.

Glaser, B.G. and Strauss, A.L. (1967) *The Discovery of Grounded Theory: Strategies for Qualitative Research*, Chicago: Aldine.

Gobo, G. (1993) 'Le forme della riflessività: da costrutto epistemologico a practical issue', *Studi di Sociologia*, 31: 299–317.

Goffee, R. and Scase, R. (1985) *Women in Charge: The Experience of Women Entrepreneurs*, London: Allen & Unwin.

Goffman, E. (1959) *The Presentation of Self in Everyday Life*, Garden City, NY: Doubleday.

Goffman, E. (1963) *Stigma*, Englewood Cliffs, NJ: Prentice Hall.

Goffman, E. (1974) *Frame Analysis: An Essay on the Organization of Experience*, New York: Harper & Row.

Goffman, E. (1976) 'Gender Display', *Studies in the Anthropology of Visual Communication*, 3: 69–77.

Goffman, E. (1977) 'The Arrangement between the Sexes', *Theory and Society*, 4: 301–31.

Goffman, E. (1980) *Forms of Talk*, Oxford: Basil Blackwell.

Goldberg, H. (1976) *The Hazards of Being Male: Surviving the Myth of Masculine Privilege*, New York: Nash.

Goldberg, H. (1988) *The Inner Male: Overcoming Roadblocks to Intimacy*, New York: Signet.

Goldberg, S. (1993) *Why Men Rule: A Theory of Male Dominance*, Chicago: Open Court.

Golde, P. (1970) *Women in the Field*, Chicago: Aldine.

Gomart, E. and Hennion, A. (1999) 'A Sociology of Attachment: Music Amateurs, Drug Users', in J. Law and J. Hassard (eds), *Actor Network Theory and After*, Oxford: Blackwell.

Gonsoriek, J.C. and Weinrich, J.D. (1991) *Homosexuality*, Newbury Park, CA: Sage.

Good, B. (1994) *Medicine, Rationality and Experience: An Anthropological Perspective*, Cambridge: Cambridge University Press.

Gordon, C. (1991) 'Governmental Rationality: An Introduction', in G. Burchell, C. Gordon and P. Miller (eds), *The Foucault Effect: Studies in Governmentality*, London: Harvester.

Grant, J. and Tancred, P. (1992) 'A Feminist Perspective on State Bureaucracy', in A.J. Mills and P. Tancred (eds), *Gendering Organizational Analysis*, London: Sage.

Grint, K. (1997) *The Fuzzy Management*, Oxford: Oxford University Press.

Guerrier, Y. and Adib, A. (1999) 'The Interlocking of Gender with Nationality, Race, Ethnicity and Class: The Narratives of Women in Hotel Work', *Gender, Work and Organization*, 10: 413–32.

Gutek, B. and Larwood, L. (1987) *Women's Career Development*, Newbury Park, CA: Sage.

Hammersley, M. and Atkinson, P. (1995) *Ethnography*, London and New York: Routledge.

Haraway, D. (1991) *A Manifest for Cyborg*, New York: Routledge.

Harding, S. (1987) 'Introduction: Is There a Feminist Method?', in S. Harding (ed.), *Feminism and Methodology*, Milton Keynes: Open University Press.

Harlow, E., Hearn, J. and Parkin, W. (1995) 'Gendered Noise: Organizations and the Silence and Din of Domination', in C. Itzin and J. Newman (eds), *Gender, Culture and Organizational Change*, London: Routledge.

Hassard, J. (1990) 'Ethnomethodology and Organizational Research: An Introduction', in J. Hassard and D. Pym (eds), *The Theory and Philosophy of Organization: Critical Issue and Perspectives*, London and New York: Routledge.

Hassard, J. and Parker, M. (eds) (1993) *Postmodernism and Organizations*, London: Sage.

Hatch, M.J. (1997) *Organization Theory: Modern, Symbolic and Postmodern Perspectives*, Oxford: Oxford University Press.

Hearn, J. (1987) *The Gender of Oppression*, Brighton: Harvester Press.

Hearn, J. (1992) *Men in the Public Eye*, London: Routledge.

Heidegger, M. (1927) *Sein und Zeit* (transl. *Being and Time*, New York: Harper & Row, 1962).

Herdt, G. (1981) *Guardians of the Flutes*, vol. I, *Idioms of Masculinity*, Chicago and London: University of Chicago Press.

Heritage, J. (1984) Garfinkel and Ethnomethodology, Cambridge: Polity Press.

Hernes, H.M. (1987) *Welfare State and Woman Power*, Oslo: Norwegian University Press.

Hoch, P. (1979) *White Hero, Black Beast: Racism, Sexism and the Mask of Masculinity*, London: Pluto Press.

Hocquenghem, G. (1972) *Le desire homosexuel*, Paris: PUF.

Hocquenghem, G. (1978) *Homosexual Desire*, London: Allison and Busby.

Hollway, W. (1996) 'Recognition and Heterosexual Desire', in D. Richardson (ed.), *Theorizing Heterosexuality: Telling It Straight*, Buckingham: Open University Press.

Holmes, J. and Meyerhoff, M. (eds) (2003) *The Handbook of Language and Gender*, Oxford: Blackwell.

Holter, H. (1984) *Patriarchy in a Welfare State*, Oslo: Universitetsforlaget.

Horrocks, R. (1994) *Masculinity in Crisis*, New York: St Martin's Press.

Hughes, E.C. (1958) *Men and Their Work*, Glencoe, IL: Free Press.

Iannello, K. (1992) *Decisions without Hierarchy: Feminist Interventions in Organization Theory and Practice*, London: Routledge.

Illich, I. (1982) *Gender*, London: Marion Boyars Publishers.

Irigaray, L. (1974) *Speculum. De l'autre femme*, Paris: Minuit.

Irigaray, L. (1982) *Passions élémentaires*, Paris: Minuit (English trans. *Elemental Passions*, New York: Routledge, 1992).

Jacques, R. (1996) *Manufacturing the Employee: Management Knowledge from the 19th to 21st Centuries*, London: Sage.

Jacques, R. (1997) 'The Unbearable Whiteness of Being', in P. Prasad, A. Mills, M. Elmes and A. Prasad (eds), *Managing the Organizational Melting Pot: Dilemmas of Workplace Diversity*, Thousand Oaks, CA; London; New Delhi: Sage.

Jagose, A. (1997) *Queer Theory: An Introduction*, New York: New York University Press.

Jung, C.G. (1964) *Man and His Symbols*, London: Aldus Books.

Kanter, R.M. (1977) *Men and Women of the Corporation*, New York: Basic Books.

Katila, S. (2002) 'Emotions and the Moral Order of Farm Business Families in Finland', in D. Fletcher (ed.), *Understanding the Small Family Business*, London: Routledge.

Keenoy, T., Oswick, C. and Grant, D. (1997) 'Organizational Discourse: Text and Context', *Organization*, 4: 147–57.

Kerfoot, D. and Knights, D. (1993) 'Management, Masculinity and Manipulation: From Paternalism to Corporate Strategy in Financial Services in Britain', *Journal of Management Studies*, 30: 659–79.

Kerfoot, D. and Knights, D. (1996) '"The Best is Yet to Come?": The Quest for Embodiment in Managerial Work', in D. Collinson and J. Hearn (eds), *Men as Managers, Managers as Men*, London: Sage.

Kerfoot, D. and Whitehead, S. (1998) '"Boys Own" Stuff: Masculinity and the Management of Further Education', *The Sociological Review*, 46: 437–57.

Kessler, S.J. and McKenna, W. (1978) *Gender: An Ethnomethodological Approach*, New York: Wiley.

Kimmel, M. (1987) *Changing Men: New Directions in Research on Men and Masculinity*, Beverly Hills, CA: Sage.

Kimmel, N.S. (1996) *Manhood in America: A Cultural History*, New York: Free Press.

Knight, F. (1921) *Risk, Uncertainty and Profit*, Boston, MA: Houghton, Mifflin.

Koen, S. (1984) 'Feminist Workplaces: Alternative Models for the Organization of Work', PhD dissertation, Union for Experimenting Colleges, University of Michigan Dissertation Information Service.

Kondo, D. (1990) *Rafting Selves: Power, Gender and Discourses of Identity in a Japanese Workplace*, Chicago: University of Chicago Press.

Kristeva, J. (1977) *Pouvoirs de l'horreur*, Paris: Seuil.

Kunda, G. (1992) *Engineering Culture: Control and Commitment in a High-Tech Corporation*, Philadelphia: Temple University Press.

La Cecla, F. (1999) *Saperci fare*, Milan: Mondadori.

La Cecla, F. (2000) *Modi bruschi. Antropologia del maschio*, Milan: Mondadori.

Labov, W. (1972) *Sociolinguistic Patterns*, Philadelphia, PA: University of Pennsylvania Press.

Langellier, K.M. and Peterson, E.E. (1993) 'Family Storytelling as a Strategy of Social Control', in D.K. Mumby (ed.), *Narrative and Social Control: Critical Perspectives*, Newbury Park, CA: Sage.

Laqueur, T. (1990) *Making Sex: Body and Gender from the Greeks to Freud*, Cambridge, MA: Harvard University Press.

Latour, B. (1999) 'On Recalling ANT', in J. Law and J. Hassard (eds), *Actor Network and After*, Oxford: Blackwell.

Laville, J.-L. (1992) *Les services de proximité en Europe*, Paris: Syros/Alternatives.

Law, J. (1994) *Organizing Modernity*, Oxford: Blackwell.

Law, J. (1999) 'After ANT: Complexity, Naming and Topology', in J. Law and J. Hassard (eds), *Actor Network Theory and After*, Oxford: Blackwell.

Levine, M.P. (1979) 'Employment Discrimination against Gay Men', *International Review of Modern Sociology*, 9: 151–63.

Lévi-Strauss, C. (1966) *The Savage Mind*, Chicago: University of Chicago Press.

Linde, C. (1993) *Life Stories: The Creation of Coherence*, Oxford: Oxford University Press.

Linde, C. (1998) 'Narrative in Institutions', in D. Schiffrin, D. Tannen and H. Hamilton (eds), *Handbook of Discourse Analysis*, Oxford: Blackwell.

Linstead, S. (1985) 'Jokers Wild: The Importance of Humour in the Maintenance of Organizational Culture', *Sociological Review*, 4: 741–67.

Linstead, S. (1993) 'From Postmodern Anthropology to Deconstructive Ethnography', *Human Relations*, 46: 97–120.

Linton, R. (1936) *The Study of Man: An Introduction*, New York: Appleton Century Crofts.

Litosseliti, L. and Sunderland, J. (eds) (2002) *Gender Identity and Discourse Analysis*, Amsterdam: John Benjamins.

Lorber, J. (1994) *Paradoxes of Gender*, New Haven, CT: Yale University Press.

Low, M.B. and MacMillan, I.C. (1988) 'Entrepreneurship: Past Research and Future Challenges', *Journal of Management*, 14: 139–61.

Lugones, M.C. and Spelman, E.V. (1986) 'Have We Got a Theory for You! Feminist Theory, Cultural Imperialism and the Demand for "The Woman's Voice"', in M. Pearsall (ed.), *Women and Values: Readings in Recent Feminist Philosophy*, Belmont, CA: Wadsworth Publishing Company.

Lynch, M. (2000) 'Against Reflexivity as an Academic Virtue and Source of Privileged Knowledge', *Theory, Culture and Society*, 17: 26–54.

Lyotard, J.F. (1979) *La condition postmoderne*, Paris: Minuit (*The Postmodern Condition: A Report on Knowledge*, Manchester: Manchester University Press, 1984).

Mac an Gahill, M. (1994) 'The Making of Black English Masculinities', in H. Brod and M. Kaufman (eds), *Theorizing Masculinities*, Thousand Oaks, CA: Sage.

Macfarlane, R. and Laville, J.-L. (1992) *Developing Community Partnerships in Europe: New Ways of Meeting Social Needs in Europe*, London: Directory of Social Change and Calouste Gulbenkian Foundation.

McKay, J. (1997) *Managing Gender*, New York: State University of New York Press.

Maddock, S. and Parkin, D. (1993) 'Gender Cultures: How They Affect Men and Women at Work', in M.J. Davidson and R.J. Burke (eds), *Women in Management: Current Research Issues*, London: Paul Chapman.

Magatti, M., Monaci, M. and Ruggerone, L. (2000) *Donne esploratrici*, Milan: Guerini e Associati.

Malinowski, B. (1922) *Argonauts of the Western Pacific*, London: Routledge.

Manning, P.K. (1992) *Organizational Communication*, New York: Aldine de Gruyter.

Manning, P.K. (1995) 'The Challenges of Postmodernism', in J. Van Maanen (ed.), *Representation in Ethnography*, Thousand Oaks, CA: Sage (repr. in A. Bryman and R.G. Burgess (eds), *Qualitative Research*, London: Sage, 1999).

Marcus, G.E. and Cushman, D. (1982) 'Ethnographies as Texts', *Annual Review of Anthropology*, 11: 25–69.

Marcus, G.E. and Fischer, M.M.J. (1986) *Anthropology as Cultural Critique: An Experimental Moment in the Human Sciences*, Chicago: University of Chicago Press.

Martin, J. (1990) 'Deconstructing Organizational Taboos: The Suppression of Gender Conflict in Organizations', *Organization Science*, 1: 339–59.

Martin, J. (1992) *Cultures in Organizations: Three Perspectives*, London: Oxford University Press.

Martin, P.Y. (1993) 'Feminism and Management', in E. Fagenson (ed.), *Women in Management: Trends, Perspective and Challenges*, Newbury Park, CA: Sage.

Martin, P.Y. (1996) 'Men, Masculinities and Managements: Gendering and Evaluating Dynamics', in D.L. Collinson and J. Hearn (eds), *Men as Managers, Managers as Men: Critical Perspectives on Masculinity*, London: Sage.

Martin, P.Y. (2001) '"Mobilizing Masculinities": Women's Experience of Men at Work', *Organization*, 8: 587–618.

Martin, P.Y. (2003) '"Said & Done" Vs. "Saying & Doing". Gendered Practices/Practicing Gender at Work', *Gender & Society*, 17: 342–66.

Marzano, M. (1999) 'Decostruire l'etnografia? Tra limiti della tradizione e rischi della sperimentazione', *Rassegna Italiana di Sociologia*, 4: 567–603.

Masters, R. and Meier, R. (1988) 'Sex Differences and Risk-taking Propensity of Entrepreneurs', *Journal of Small Business Management*, 26: 31–5.

Mauss, M. (1936) 'Les techniques du corps', *Journal de Psychologie*, XXXII: 784–97.

Melucci, A. (1982) *L'invenzione del presente*, Bologna: Il Mulino.

Melucci, A. (1989) *Sistema politico, partiti e movimenti sociali*, Milan: Feltrinelli.

Melucci, A. (1998) *Verso una sociologia riflessiva*, Bologna: Il Mulino.

Mendelssohn, K. (1976) *Science and Western Domination*, London: Thames and Hudson.

Messner, M. (1992) *Power at Play: Sports and the Problem of Masculinity*, Boston, MA: Beacon Press.

Messner, M. and Sabo, D. (1990) *Sport, Men and the Gender Order*, Champaign, IL: Human Kinetics Books.

Mieli, M. (1980) *Homosexuality and Liberation: Elements of a Gay Critique*, London: Gay Men's Press.

Mintzberg, H. (1971) 'Managerial Work: Analysis from Observation', *Management Science*, 18: 97–110.

Mintzberg, H. (1973) *The Nature of Managerial Work*, New York: Harper & Row.

Mirchandani, K. (1999) 'Feminist Insight on Gendered Work: New Directions in Research on Women and Entrepreneurship', *Gender, Work and Organization*, 6: 224–35.

Monaci, M. (1998) 'L'imprenditorialità femminile: tendenze, teorie, interventi', Internal working paper, ISTUD, April.

Moore, D. and Buttner, H. (1997) *Women Entrepreneurs: Moving Beyond the Glass Ceiling*, Thousand Oaks, CA: Sage.

Morgan, D.H.J. (1992) *Discovering Men*, London and New York: Routledge.

Morgan, G. (1986) *Images of Organization*, London: Sage.

Morris, D. (1969) *The Naked Ape*, St Albans: Panther.

Mosse, G.L. (1996) *The Image of Man*, New York: Oxford University Press.

Mulholland, K. (1996) 'Entrepreneurialism, Masculinities and the Self-made Man', in D. Collinson and J. Hearn (eds), *Men as Managers, Managers as Men*, London: Sage.

Mumby, D.K. and Putnam, L.L. (1992) 'The Politics of Emotion: A Feminist Reading of Bounded Rationality', *Academy of Management Review*, 17: 465–86.

Muraro, L. (1991) *L'ordine simbolico della madre*, Rome: Editori Riuniti.

Muraro, L. (2000) 'Donne dell'altro mondo', *Via Dogana*, 50/51: 3–5.

Navarini, G. (2001) 'Etnografia dei confini: dilemma clinico e polisemia', *Rassegna Italiana di Sociologia*, 2: 283–308.

Neuberger, O. (1990) *Fuhren und gefuhrt werden*, Stuttgart: Enke.

NFWBO (National Foundation for Women Business Owners) (1995) *Women-owned Business: Breaking the Boundaries. Progress and Achievement of Women-owned Enterprises*, Silver Spring, MD.

Nicholson, L. (1994) 'Interpreting Gender', *Signs*, 20: 79–105.

Nkomo, S.M. (1992) 'The Emperor Has No Clothes: Rewriting Race in Organizations', *Academy of Management Review*, 17: 489–513.

Ogbor, J.O. (2000) 'Mythicizing and Reification in Entrepreneurial Discourse: Ideology-Critique of Entrepreneurial Studies', *Journal of Management Studies*, 37: 605–35.

Parker, M. (2001) 'Fucking Management: Queer, Theory and Reflexivity', *Ephemera*, 1: 36–53.

Parkin, W. (1993) 'The Public and the Private: Gender, Sexuality and Emotion', in S. Fineman (ed.), *Emotions in Organizations*, London: Sage.

Parsons, T. and Bales, R.F. (1956) *Family Socialization and Interaction Process*, London: Routledge & Kegan Paul.

Paton, R., Duhm, R., Gherardi, S. and Laville, J.-L. (1989) *Reluctant Entrepreneurs*, Milton Keynes: Open University Press.

Piccardo, C., Varchetta, G. and Zanarini, G. (1990) 'Car Makers and Marathon Runners: In Pursuit of Culture through the Language of Leadership', in P. Gagliardi (ed.), *Symbols and Artifacts: Views of the Corporate Landscape*, Berlin: de Gruyter.

Pitt, M. (1998) 'A Tale of Two Gladiators: "Reading" Entrepreneurs as Texts', *Organization Studies*, 19: 387–414.

Plummer, K. (1981) *The Making of the Modern Homosexual*, London: Hutchinson.

Poggio, B. (1999) 'Narrating Challenges in Organizational Cultures', paper presented at the 15th Egos Colloquium, 'Organizations in a Challenging World: Theories' Practices and Societies', Warwick, 4–6 July.

Poggio, B. (2000) 'Between Bytes and Bricks: Gender Cultures in Work Contexts', *Economic and Industrial Democracy*, 21: 381–402.

Polkinghorne, D.E. (1987) *Narrative, Knowing and the Human Sciences*, Albany, NY: State University of New York Press.

Polkinghorne, D.E. (1995) 'Narrative Configuration in Qualitative Analysis', in J.A. Hatch and R. Wisniewski (eds), *Life, History and Narrative*, London: Falmer.

Pollner, M. (1987) *Mundane Reason: Reality in Everyday and Sociological Discourse*, Cambridge: Cambridge University Press.

Potter, J. and Wetherell, M. (1987) *Discourse and Social Psychology*, London: Sage.

Potter, J. and Wetherell, M. (1993) *Analyzing Discourse*, Thousand Oaks, CA: Sage.

Powell, G.N. (1993) *Women and Men in Management* (2nd edn), Newbury Park, CA: Sage.

Powell, W.W. and Di Maggio, P.J. (1991) *The New Institutionalism in Organizational Analysis*, Chicago: University of Chicago Press.

Prasad, A. and Prasad, P. (2002) 'Otherness at Large: Identity and Difference in a New Globalized Organizational Landscape', in I. Aaltio-Marjosola and A.J. Mills (eds), *Gender, Identities and the Culture of Organizations*, London: Routledge.

Prasad, P. (1998) 'When the Ethnographic Subject Speaks Back', *Journal of Management Inquiry*, 7: 31–6.

Queneau, R. (1947) *Exercises de style*, Paris: Editions Gallimard.

Quine, W.V.O. (1960) *Word and Object*, New York: John Wiley and Sons.

Rabinow, P. (1977) *Reflections on Fieldwork in Morocco*, Berkeley, CA: University of California Press.

Radin, P. (1927) *The Story of the American Indian*, New York: Boni & Liveright.

Red Collective (1978) *The Politics of Sexuality in Capitalism*, London: Red Collective/PDC.

Reder, S. (1993) 'Watching Flowers Grow: Polycontextuality and Heterochronity at Work', *Quarterly Newsletter of the Laboratory of Comparative Human Cognition*, 15: 116–23.

Reed, R. (1996) 'Entrepreneurialism and Paternalism in Australian Management: A Gender Critique of the "Self-Made" Man', in D. Collinson and J. Hearn (eds), *Men as Managers, Managers as Men*, London: Sage.

Reskin, B. (1988) 'Bringing the Men Back In: Sex Differentiation and the Devaluation of Women's Work', *Gender and Society*, 2: 58–81.

Richardson, L. (1994) 'Writing: A Method of Inquiry', in K. Denzin and Y.S. Lincoln (eds), *Handbook of Qualitative Research*, Thousand Oaks, CA: Sage.

Ricoeur, P. (1973) *Phenomenology, Language and the Social Sciences*, London: Routledge & Kegan Paul.

Ricoeur, P. (1990) *Soi-même comme un autre*, Paris: de Seuil.

Riding, A. and Swift, C. (1990) 'Women Business Owners and Terms of Credit: Some Empirical Findings of the Canadian Experience', *Journal of Business Venturing*, 5: 327–40.

Rorty, R. (1982) *Consequences of Pragmatism*, Minneapolis, MN: University of Minnesota Press.

Rosa, P., Hamilton, D., Carter, S. and Burns, H. (1994) 'The Impact of Gender on Small Business Management: Preliminary Findings of a British Study', *International Small Business Journal*, 12: 25–32.

Rosaldo, R. (1986) 'From the Door of His Tent: The Fieldworker and the Inquisitor', in J. Clifford and G.E. Marcus (eds), *Writing Culture: Poetics and Politics in Ethnography*, Berkeley, CA: University of California Press.

Rosen, M. (1984) 'Myth and Reproduction: The Contextualization of Management Theory, Method, and Practice', *Journal of Management Studies*, 21: 303–22.

Rosen, M. (1991) 'Coming to Terms with the Field: Understanding and Doing Organizational Ethnography', *Journal of Management Studies*, 28: 1–28.

Rosener, J.B. (1990) 'Ways Women Lead', *Harvard Business Review*, 68: 119–20.

Rothschild, J. (1990) 'Feminist Values and the Democratic Management of Work Organization', paper presented at the XIIth World Congress of Sociology, Madrid, July.

Rothschild, J. (1992) 'Principles of Feminist Trade Union Organizations', paper presented at the Workshop on Feminist Organizations, Washington, DC.

Roy, D. (1959) 'Banana Time: Job Satisfaction and Informal Interaction', *Human Organization*, 18: 158–68.

Rubin, G. (1975) 'The Traffic in Women: Notes on the "Political Economy" of Sex', in R. Reiter (ed.), *Towards an Anthropology of Women*, New York: Monthly Review Press.

Sachs, P. (1993) 'Shadows in the Soup: Conceptions of Work and Nature of Evidence', *Quarterly Newsletter of the Laboratory of Human Cognition*, 15: 125–32.

Saraceno, C. (1993) 'Elementi per un'analisi delle trasformazioni di genere nella società contemporanea', *Rassegna Italiana di Sociologia*, 34: 19–57.

Schatzki, T.R., Knorr Cetina, K. and von Savigny, E. (eds) (2001) *The Practice Turn in Contemporary Theory*, London and New York: Routledge.

Schumpeter, J.A. (1934) *The Theory of Economic Development: An Inquiry into Profits, Capital, Credit, Interest, and the Business Cycle*, Cambridge, MA: Harvard University Press.

Schumpeter, J.A. (1939) *Business Cycles: A Theoretical, Historical and Statistical Analysis of the Capitalist Process*, New York: McGraw-Hill.

Schutz, A. (1932) *Der Sinhafte Aufbau der Sozialen Welt* (transl. *The Phenomenology of the Social World*, Chicago: Northwestern University Press, 1967).

Schwalbe, M., Godwin, S., Holden, D., Shrock, D., Thompson, S. and Wolkomir, M. (2000) 'Generic Processes in the Reproduction of Inequality', *Social Forces*, 79: 419–52.

Sclavi, M. (1989) *A una spanna da terra*, Milan: Feltrinelli.

Sclavi, M. (2000) *Arte di ascoltare e mondi possibili*, Pescara, Milan: Le Vespe.

Sedgwick, E.K. (1990) *Epistemology of the Closet*, London: Penguin.

Segal, L. (1993) 'Changing Men: Masculinities in Context', *Theory and Society*, 22: 625–42.

Shallenberger, D. (1994) 'Professional and Openly Gay: A Narrative Study of the Experience', *Journal of Management Inquiry*, 3: 119–43.

Silverman, D. (1972) 'Philosophy and Meaning', in P. Filmer, M. Philipson, D. Silverman and D. Walsh (eds), *New Directions in Sociological Theory*, London: Collier-Macmillan.

Sinha, M. (1987) 'Gender and Imperialism', in M. Kimmel (eds), *Changing Men: New Directions in Research on Men and Masculinity*, Beverly Hills: Sage.

Smith, D.E. (1990) *The Conceptual Practices of Power, A Feminist Sociology of Knowledge*, Boston, MA: Northeastern University Press.

Spivak, G. (1987) *In Other Worlds*, New York: Routledge.

Stacey, M. and Davies, C. (1983) *Division of Labour in Child Health Care*, Coventry: University of Warwick.

Steyner, J. (1998) 'Charisma and the Archetypes of Leadership', *Organization Studies*, 19: 807–28.

Stoller, P. (1989) *Fusion of the Worlds: An Ethnography of Possession among the Songhay of Niger*, Chicago: University of Chicago Press.

Stone, A.S. (1995) *The War of Desire and Technology at the Close of the Mechanical Age*, Cambridge, MA: MIT Press.

Strati, A. (2000) *Theory and Method in Organization Studies*, London: Sage.

Swidler, A. (2001) 'What Anchors Cultural Practices', in T.R. Schatzki, K. Knorr Cetina and E. von Savigny (eds), *The Practice Turn in Contemporary Theory*, London and New York: Routledge.

Tajfel, H. (1981) *Human Groups and Social Categories: Studies in Social Psychology*, Cambridge: Cambrige University Press.

Tedlock, B. (1991) 'From Participant Observation to Observation of Participation: The Emergence of Narrative Ethnography', *Journal of Anthropological Research*, 47: 69–74.

Theberge, N. (1991) 'Reflections on the Body in the Sociology of Sport', *Quest*, 43: 123–34.

Thompson, R.H. (1989) *Theories of Ethnicity: A Critical Appraisal*, New York: Greenwood Press.

Thornborrow, Joanna (2002) *Power Talk: Language and Interaction in Institutional Discourse*, Harlow: Longman.

Tiger, L. (1969) *Men in Groups*, London: Nelson.

Tiger, L. and Fox, R. (1971) *The Imperial Animal*, New York: Holt, Rinehart and Winston.

Tolson, A. (1977) *The Limits of Masculinity*, London: Tavistock.

Turner, B.A. (1992) 'The Symbolic Understanding of Organizations', in M. Reed and M. Hughes (eds), *Rethinking Organization*, London: Sage.

Tyler, S.A. (1986) 'Post-Modern Ethnography: From Document of the Occult, to Occult Document', in J. Clifford and G.E. Marcus (eds), *Writing Culture: Poetics and Politics in Ethnography*, Berkeley, CA: University of California Press.

Van Dijk, T.A. (1985) *Handbook of Discourse Analysis*, London: Academic.

Van Maanen, J. (1979) 'The Fact of Fiction in Organizational Ethnography', *Administrative Science Quarterly*, 24: 539–50.

Van Maanen, J. (1988) *Tales of the Field: On Writing Ethnography*, Chicago: University of Chicago Press.

Van Maanen, J. (1995) *Representation in Ethnography*, London: Sage.

Van Maanen, J. (1998) 'Different Strokes', in J. Van Maanen (ed.), *Qualitative Studies of Organizations*, Thousand Oaks, CA: Sage.

Van Maanen, J. and Kolb, D. (1985) 'The Professional Apprentice: Observations on Fieldwork Roles in Two Organizational Settings', *Research in the Sociology of Organizations*, 4: 1–33.

Walby, S. (1986) *Patriarchy at Work*, Cambridge: Polity Press.

Walby, S. (1989) 'Theorizing Patriarchy', *Sociology*, 23: 213–34.

Walby, S. (1990) *Theorizing Patriarchy*, Oxford: Blackwell.

Walsh, C. (2001) *Gender and Discourse: Language and Power in Politics, the Church and Organizations*, London: Longman.

Ward, J. and Winstanley, D. (2003) 'The Absent Presence: Negative Space within Discourse and the Construction of Minority Sexual Identity in the Workplace', *Human Relations*, 56: 1255–80.

Weatherall, A. (2002) *Gender, Language and Discourse*, London: Routledge.

Weber, M. (1922) *Wirtschaft und Gesellschaft*, Tübingen: Mohr.

Weed, E. and Schor, N. (1997) *Feminism Meets Queer Theory*, Bloomington, IN: Indiana University Press.

Weedon, C. (1987) *Feminist Practice and Poststructuralist Theory*, Oxford and New York: Blackwell.

Weick, K.E. (1995) *Sensemaking in Organizations*, Thousand Oaks, CA: Sage.

West, C. and Zimmerman, D. (1987) 'Doing Gender', *Gender and Society*, 1: 125–51.

Westwood, S. (1990) 'Racism, Black Masculinity and the Politics of Space', in J. Hearn and D.H.J. Morgan (eds), *Men, Masculinities and Social Theory*, London and Boston, MA: Unwin Hyman.

Wilson, E.O. (1978) *On Human Nature*, Cambridge, MA: Harvard University Press.

Wittig, M. (1992) *The Straight Mind*, Hemel Hempstead: Harvester Wheatsheaf.

Wodak, R. (1997) *Gender and Discourse*, London: Sage.

Woolgar, S. (1988) *Knowledge and Reflexivity: New Frontiers in the Sociology of Knowledge*, London; Newbury Park, CA; Beverly Hills, CA; New Delhi: Sage.

Zanfrini, L. (1999) *Immigrati, mercati del lavoro e programmazione dei flussi d'ingresso*, Milan: Fondazione Cariplo.

Zanuso, L. (1987) 'Gli studi sulla doppia presenza: dal conflitto alla norma', in M.C. Marcuzzo and A.R. Doria (eds), *La ricerca delle donne. Studi femministi in Italia*, Turin: Rosemberg & Sellier.

Index